FIAT 124 Owners Workshop Manual

by J H Haynes
Member of the Guild of Motoring Writers
and D H Stead

Models covered

UK: FIAT 124 Saloon, 1197 cc
         FIAT 124 Estate, 1197 cc
         FIAT 124 Special, 1438 cc
         FIAT 124 Special T, 1438 & 1592 cc

USA: FIAT 124 Sedan, 73 cu in (1197 cc)
         FIAT 124 Wagon, 73 cu in and 87.8 cu in (1197 & 1438 cc)
         FIAT 124 Special, 87.8 cu in (1438 cc)
         FIAT 124 Special TC, 97.2 cu in (1592 cc)

Does not cover 124 Sport Coupe or 124 Sport Spider

ISBN   0 85696 508 1

Printed in England *(080 — 4E2)*

HAYNES PUBLISHING GROUP
SPARKFORD YEOVIL SOMERSET ENGLAND
distributed in the USA by
HAYNES PUBLICATIONS INC
861 LAWRENCE DRIVE
NEWBURY PARK
CALIFORNIA 91320
USA

Acknowledgements

Thanks are due to Fiat U.K. Limited for their assistance in the supply of technical specifications and illustrations. Also to Marston Garage of Marston Magna and Dunn's Motor Group of Taunton and Exeter for their help with cars.

Castrol Limited provided lubrication data and the Champion Sparking Plug Company supplied the illustrations showing the various spark plug conditions. The bodywork repair photographs used in this manual were provided by Lloyds Industries Limited who supply 'Turtle Wax', 'Dupli-color Holts', and other Holts range products.

The patience of Brian Horsfall during the photography of the assembly sequences must not be forgotten, and Felix Nicholson's work on text and layout was, as always, invaluable.

About this manual

Its aim

The aim of this book is to help the practical motorist to get the best value from his car. It can do this in two ways. In the first instance the owner can decide what work is needed, even if he should choose to entrust that work to a garage, and in the second instance he can use the detailed instructions given in the book to carry out the work himself. Not only can the owner gain satisfaction from having done the work himself, he will also reap the benefit of saving the labour charge.

The book has drawings and descriptions to show the function of the various components so that their layout can be understood. Then the tasks are described in a step-by-step sequence so that even a novice can cope with what may have appeared a complicated job.

The jobs are described assuming only normal tools are available, and not special tools. However, a reasonable tool kit will be a worthwhile investment. Many special workshop tools produced by the manufacturer merely speed the work, and in these cases guidance is given on how to do the job without them. Where special tools are required on certain occasions, to prevent damage to components, the use of the tool is described. The author has in some instances endeavoured to find ways of improvising with materials which are usually found in the home workshop.

Using the manual

The book is divided into thirteen chapters. Each Chapter is divided into numbered Sections which are headed in **bold** type between horizontal lines. Each Section consists of serially numbered paragraphs.

There are two types of illustration: (1) Figures which are numbered according to Chapter and sequence of occurrence in that Chapter; (2) Photographs which have a reference number in their caption. All photographs apply to the Chapter in which they occur so that the reference figure pinpoints the pertinent Section and paragraph number.

Procedures, once described in the text, are not normally repeated. If it is necessary to refer to another part of the manual the reference will be given in Chapter number, Section number and, if necessary, paragraph number. Cross-references given without the use of the word 'Chapter' apply to Sections and/or paragraphs in the same Chapter (eg. 'see Section 8' means also 'in this Chapter').

When the left or right side of the car is mentioned it is as if looking forward from the rear of the car.

Great effort has been made to ensure that this book is complete and up-to-date. However, it should be realised that manufacturers continually modify their cars, even in retrospect.

Whilst every care is taken to ensure that the information in this manual is correct, no liability can be accepted by the authors or publishers for loss, damage or injury caused by any errors in, or omissions from, the information given.

Contents

Fiat 124S saloon 1971

Buying spare parts
and vehicle identification numbers

Buying spare parts

Spare parts can be obtained from many sources, for example: Fiat garages, other garages and accessory shops, and motor factors. Our advice regarding spare parts is as follows:

Officially appointed Fiat garages - This is the best source of parts which are peculiar to your car and otherwise not generally available (eg. complete cylinder heads, internal gearbox components, badges, interior trim etc). It is also the only place you should buy your parts if your car is still under warranty; non-Fiat components may invalidate the warranty. To be sure of obtaining the correct parts it will always be necessary to give the storeman your car's engine and chassis number, and if possible take the old part along for positive identification. Remember that many parts are available on a factory exchange scheme - any parts returned should always be clean! It obviously makes good sense to go to the specialists on your car for this type of part for they are best equipped to supply you.

Other garages and accessory shops - These are often very good places to buy material and components needed for the maintenance of your car (eg. oil filters, spark plugs, fan belts, oils and grease, touch-up paint, filler paste etc). They also sell general accessories, usually have convenient opening hours, charge lower prices and can often be found not far from home.

Motor factors - Good factors will stock all of the more important components which wear out relatively quickly (eg. clutch components, pistons, valves, exhaust systems, brake cylinders/pipes/hoses/seals/shoes and pads, etc). Motor factors will often provide new or reconditioned components on a part exchange basis - this can save a considerable amount of money.

Vehicle identification numbers

As already stated, when ordering new parts it is essential that the storeman has full information about your particular model of Fiat. He cannot guarantee to supply you with the correct part unless you give him information including the model, chassis number and if necessary the engine number.

The Fiat 124 has three places on it which give identification details.

The *Identification plate* is secured to the right side of the engine compartment on early models or to the body cross panel in part of the radiator on later models. This gives the chassis type and number, the engine type, the spares number and, on later models, a further number to do with optional extras or variations which may be fitted.

The *engine type and serial number* is stamped on the cylinder block. This can be either on the front face just above the timing chain cover on early models or on the left side just forward of the oil level dipstick hole on later models.

The *chassis type and number* is also given elsewhere. On early models it is stamped on the panel below the identification plate. In later versions it is stamped on the air intake panel at the rear of the engine compartment on the right hand side.

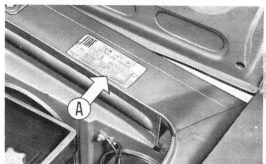

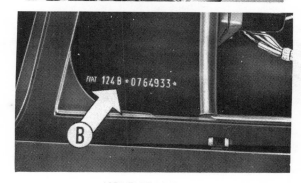

1971 FIAT 124S

A Identification Plate
B Chassis Type and number
Early models shown at top

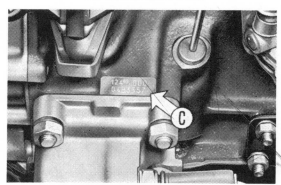

C Engine Number
Early models shown on the left

Tools and working facilities

Introduction

A selection of good tools is a fundamental requirement for anyone contemplating the maintenance and repair of a motor vehicle. For the owner who does not possess any, their purchase will prove a considerable expense, offsetting some of the savings made by do-it-yourself.

However, provided the tools purchased are of a good quality, they will last for many years and prove an extremely worthwhile investment.

To help the owner to decide which tools are needed to carry out the various tasks detailed in this manual, we have compiled three lists of tools under the following headings: Maintenance and minor repair; Repair and overhaul, and Special. The newcomer to practical mechanics should start off with the 'Maintenance and minor repair' tool kit and confine himself to the simpler jobs around the vehicle. Then, as his confidence and experience grows, he can undertake more difficult tasks, buying extra tools as, and when, they are needed. In this way, a 'Maintenance and minor repair' kit can be built up into a 'Repair and overhaul' tool kit over a considerable period of time without any major cash outlays. The experienced do-it-yourselfer will have a tool kit good enough for most repair and overhaul procedures and will add tools from the 'Special' category when he feels the expense is justified by the amount of use to which these tools will be put.

It is obviously not possible to cover the subject of tools fully here. For those who wish to learn more about tools and their use there is a book entitled 'How to Choose and Use Car Tools' available from the publishers of this manual.

Maintenance and minor repair tool kit

The tools given in this list should be considered as a minimum requirement if routine maintenance, servicing and minor repair operations are to be undertaken. We recommend the purchase of combination spanners (ring one end, open-ended the other); although more expensive than open-ended ones, they do give the advantages of both types of spanner.

Combination spanners - 10, 11, 13, 14, 17 mm
Adjustable spanner - 9 inch
Engine sump/gearbox/rear axle drain plug key (where applicable)
Spark plug spanner (with rubber insert)
Spark plug gap adjustment tool
Set of feeler gauges
Brake adjuster spanner (where applicable)
Brake bleed nipple spanner
Screwdriver - 4 in. long x ¼ in. dia. (plain)
Screwdriver - 4 in. long x ¼ in. dia. (crosshead)
Combination pliers - 6 inch
Hacksaw, junior
Tyre pump
Tyre pressure gauge
Grease gun (where applicable)
Oil can
Fine emery cloth (1 sheet)
Wire brush (small)
Funnel (medium size)

Repair and overhaul tool kit

These tools are virtually essential for anyone undertaking any major repairs to a motor vehicle, and are additional to those given in the Basic list. Included in this list is a comprehensive set of sockets. Although these are expensive they will be found invaluable as they are so versatile - particularly if various drives are included in the set. We recommend the ½ in. square drive type, as this can be used with most proprietary torque wrenches. If you cannot afford a socket set, even bought piecemeal, then inexpensive tubular box spanners are a useful alternative.

The tools in this list will occasionally need to be supplemented by tools from the Special list.

Sockets (or box spanners) to cover range 6 to 27 mm
Reversible ratchet drive (for use with sockets)
Extension piece, 10 inch (for use with sockets)
Universal joint (for use with sockets)
Torque wrench (for use with sockets)
'Mole' wrench - 8 inch
Ball pein hammer
Soft-faced hammer, plastic or rubber
Screwdriver - 6 in. long x 5/16 in. dia. (plain)
Screwdriver - 2 in. long x 5/16 in. square (plain)
Screwdriver - 3 in. long x 1/8 in. dia. (electrician's)
Pliers - electrician's side cutters
Pliers - circlip (internal and external)
Cold chisel - ½ inch
Scriber (this can be made by grinding the end of a broken hacksaw blade)
Scraper (this can be made by flattening and sharpening one end of a piece of copper pipe)
Centre punch
Pin punch
Hacksaw
Valve grinding tool
Allen keys
Selection of files
Wire brush (large)
Axle stands
Jack (strong scissor or hydraulic type)

Special tools

The tools in this list are those which are not used regularly, are expensive to buy, or which need to be used in accordance with their manufacturers' instructions. Unless relatively difficult mechanical jobs are undertaken frequently, it will not be economic to buy many of these tools. Where this is the case, you could consider clubbing together with friends (or a motorists club) to make a joint purchase, or borrowing the tools against a deposit from a local garage or tool hire specialist.

The following list contains only those tools and instruments freely available to the public, and not those special tools produced by the vehicle manufacturer specifically for its dealer network. You will find occasional references to these manufacturers' special tools in the text of this manual. Generally, an alternative method of doing the job without the vehicle manufacturers' special tool is given. However, sometimes there is no alternative to using them. Where this is the case and the relevant tool cannot be bought or borrowed you will have to entrust the work to a franchised garage.

Valve spring compressor
Piston ring compressor
Balljoint separator
Universal hub/bearing puller
Impact screwdriver
Micrometer and/or vernier gauge
Carburettor flow balancing device (where applicable)
Dial gauge
Stroboscopic timing light
Dwell angle meter/tachometer
Universal electrical multi-meter
Cylinder compression gauge
Lifting tackle
Trolley jack
Light with extension lead

Buying tools

For practically all tools, a tool factor is the best source since he will have a very comprehensive range compared with the average garage or accessory shop. Having said that, accessory shops often offer excellent quality tools at discount prices, so it pays to shop around.

Remember you don't have to buy the most expensive items on the shelf, but it is always advisable to steer clear of the very cheap tools.

There are plenty of good tools around, at reasonable prices, so ask the manager or proprietor of the shop for advice before making a purchase.

Care and maintenance of tools

Having purchased a reasonable tool kit, it is necessary to keep the tools in a clean and serviceable condition. After use, always wipe off any dirt, grease and metal particles, using a clean, dry cloth, before putting the tools away. Never leave them lying around after they have been used. A simple tool rack on the garage or workshop wall, for items such as screwdrivers and pliers is a good idea. Store all normal spanners or sockets in a metal box. Any measuring instruments, gauges, meters, etc., must be carefully stored where they cannot be damaged or become rusty.

Take a little care when the tools are used. Hammer heads inevitably become marked and screwdrivers lose the keen edge on their blades from time to time. A little timely attention with emery cloth or a file will soon restore items like this to a good serviceable finish.

Working facilities

Not to be forgotten when discussing tools, is the workshop itself. If anything more than routine maintenance is to be carried out, some form of suitable working area becomes essential.

It is appreciated that many an owner mechanic is forced by circumstances to remove an engine or similar item, without the benefit of a garage or workshop. Having done this, any repairs should always be done under the cover of a roof.

Wherever possible, any dismantling should be done on a clean, flat workbench or table at a suitable working height.

Any bench needs a vice; one with a jaw opening of 4 in (100 mm) is suitable for most jobs. As mentioned previously, some clean, dry storage space is also required for tools, as well as the lubricants, cleaning fluids, touch-up paints and so on which soon become necessary.

Another item which may be required, and which has a much more general usage, is an electric drill with a chuck capacity of at least 5/16 in (8 mm). This, together with a good range of twist drills, is virtually essential for fitting accessories such as wing mirrors and reversing lights.

Last, but not least, always keep a supply of old newspapers and clean, lint-free rags available, and try to keep any working area as clean as possible.

Spanner jaw gap comparison table

Jaw gap (in.)	Spanner size
0.250	1/4 in. AF
0.275	7 mm AF
0.312	5/16 in. AF
0.315	8 mm AF
0.340	11/32 in. AF/1/8 in. Whitworth
0.354	9 mm AF
0.375	3/8 in. AF
0.393	10 mm AF
0.433	11 mm AF
0.437	7/16 in. AF
0.445	3/16 in. Whitworth/1/4 in. BSF
0.472	12 mm AF
0.500	1/2 in. AF
0.512	13 mm AF
0.525	1/4 in. Whitworth/5/16 in. BSF
0.551	14 mm AF
0.562	9/16 in. AF
0.590	15 mm AF
0.600	5/16 in. Whitworth/3/8 in. BSF
0.625	5/8 in. AF
0.629	16 mm AF
0.669	17 mm AF
0.687	11/16 in. AF
0.708	18 mm AF
0.710	3/8 in. Whitworth/7/16 in. BSF
0.748	19 mm AF
0.750	3/4 in. AF
0.812	13/16 in. AF
0.820	7/16 in. Whitworth/9/16 in. BSF
0.866	22 mm AF
0.875	7/8 in. AF
0.920	1/2 in. Whitworth/9./16 in. BSF
0.937	15/16 in. AF
0.944	24 mm AF
1.000	1 in. AF
1.010	9/16 in. Whitworth/5/8 in. BSF
1.023	26 mm AF
1.062	1 1/16 in. AF/27 mm AF
1.100	5/8 in. Whitworth/11/16 in. BSF
1.125	1 1/8 in. AF
1.181	30 mm AF
1.200	11/16 in. Whitworth/3/4 in. BSF
1.250	1 1/4 in. AF
1.259	32 mm AF
1.300	3/4 in. Whitworth/7/8 in. BSF
1.312	1 5/16 in. AF
1.390	1 3/16 in. Whitworth/15/16 in. BSF
1.417	36 mm AF
1.437	1 7/16 in. AF
1.480	7/8 in. Whitworth/1 in. BSF
1.500	1 1/2 in. AF
1.574	40 mm AF/15/16 in. Whitworth
1.614	41 mm AF
1.625	1 5/8 in. AF
1.670	1 in. Whitworth/1 1/8 in. BSF
1.687	1 11/16 in. AF
1.811	46 mm AF
1.812	1 13/16 in. AF
1.860	1 1/8 in. Whitworth/1 1/4 in. BSF
1.875	1 7/8 in. AF
1.968	50 mm AF
2.000	2 in. AF
2.050	1 1/4 in. Whitworth/1 3/8 in. BSF
2.165	55 mm AF
2.362	60 mm AF

Routine maintenance

Although any car will probably 'go' for a considerable time without doing anything to it in the way of maintenance, there is no doubt that prevention is certainly less costly than cure. Those who boast that they never lift the bonnet and never have any trouble are probably spending a fortune in fuel and oil and driving an unsafe vehicle with no performance.

Maintenance tends to get less frequent and less regular as the car gets older and changes owners more frequently.

Modern cars — the Fiat 124 included — are designed and built with a large percentage of components which have a certain life and are then renewed. Consequently the approach to maintenance is no longer a matter of wading in with the oil can and grease gun. In fact on the Fiat 124 there are no grease nipples

at all on the early models. One was introduced later at the front end of the propeller shaft. Apart from this grease is used only in the generator, starter motor and front wheel bearings — all 12 or 18 month service intervals.

Modern maintenance can be divided into two categories, one part for safety, the other for performance and economy. The former requires inspection and perhaps action. The latter requires regular checks and action. The maintenance routines given below give frequency on a time basis. The intervals are minimum for a mileage of 1000 miles or less per month on average. Consistent mileage in excess of 1000 per month might call for a shorter maintenance interval. Where necessary the maintenance procedures are explained after the schedules. Otherwise the relevant chapter in the book giving the details is referred to.

Safety maintenance schedule

STEERING

Front suspension arm ball joints - Check for wear	3 months
Steering tie-rod ball joints - Check for wear	3 months
Steering gear - Check worm to roller play and worm shaft bearings - Adjust if necessary	3 months
Front wheel bearings - Check endfloat and adjust if necessary	3 months

BRAKES

Hydraulic fluid reservoir in level - Check	1 month
Handbrake efficiency - Check and adjust	3 months
Brake pad material thickness - Check	6 months
Hydraulic lines, hoses, master cylinder and wheel calipers - Examine for leaks or corrosion	6 months
Renew hydraulic fluid in system by bleeding right through	3 years

Note: A significant drop in the fluid reservoir level or any other indication of fluid leakage is a danger signal. A complete and thorough examination of the hydraulic system should be made.

SUSPENSION

Tyres - Inflation pressure check	Weekly
Tyres - Wear and damage check	As suspect
Dampers - Check for leakage and malfunction	3 months
Front and rear suspension arm pivot bushes	6 months

Removal of cover plate under filter cartridge

Safety maintenance procedures

STEERING – See Chapter 11.

BRAKES

Hydraulic fluid reservoir level. Raise the bonnet. The hydraulic fluid reservoir is mounted on the bulkhead. Clean round the filler cap before removing it and top up to the indicated level with the approved fluid if necessary. (See recommended lubricants schedule). For other brake matters see Chapter 9.

SUSPENSION

See Chapter 11.

Efficiency and performance maintenance schedule

ENGINE

Lubricating oil - Top up to level	Weekly
Drain, renew filter and refill with fresh oil	3 months
Fan belt - Check tension and adjust if necessary	1 month
Battery - Electrolyte level check	Weekly
Distributor - Check contact points gap	
Adjust or renew	3 months
Lubricate	3 months
Air cleaner - Renew paper element	6 months (If dusty atmosphere more often)
Valve clearances - Check and adjust	6 months
Spark plugs - Remove, clean and reset	3 months
Renew	12 months
Carburettor - Check throttle cable linkage and lubricate	6 months
Carburettor - Clean jets and filters	6 months
Crankcase emission control system - Clean pipes, vent valve and flame trap	12 months

FRONT SUSPENSION

Front wheel bearings - Repack with grease	12 months

GEARBOX

Check oil level and top up if necessary	6 months
Drain and refill with fresh oil	18 months

CLUTCH

Check pedal free travel	6 months

PROPELLER SHAFT AND REAR AXLE

Grease front propeller shaft splined yoke (later models)	18 months
Check axle oil level and top up as necessary	6 months
Drain rear axle and refill with fresh oil	18 months

Efficiency and performance maintenance procedures

ENGINE
Lubricating Oil

When the engine has been stopped for at least 2 minutes, and is standing on level ground, remove the dipstick. The level mark should be between 'Min' and 'Max'. Add oil through the filler in the valve rocker cover, allowing time for the oil to drain down before checking the level again.

When changing the oil the engine should be warmed up first. Then unscrew the sump drain plug and drain the oil into a container which should hold at least a gallon or 4 litres to avoid overflow.

The filter cartridge is located at the left front of the engine

Removal of filter cartridge

Greasing the filter cartridge sealing ring

Putting in engine oil

and to remove it the metal undertray must first be taken off by undoing the securing screws. To remove the filter cartridge use a chain wrench which can be improvised from a length of chain and a screwdriver. Grease the rubber seal of the new filter cartridge and screw it home firmly but no more than hand tight.

Clean and replace the sump drain plug making sure the washer is in good condition. Refill the engine with 7 pints/3.75 litres of fresh oil. Run the engine to check that the filter seal does not leak and re-check the oil level again later.

Fan Belt — See Chapter 2
Battery — See Chapter 10
Distributor — See Chapter 4. For lubrication put one or two drops of engine oil into the hole just below the spindle cam.
Air Cleaner — See Chapter 3
Valve Clearances — See Chapter 1
Spark Plugs — See Chapter 4
Carburettor — See Chapter 3
Crankcase Emission Control System — See Chapter 3.

FRONT WHEEL BEARINGS — See Chapter 11.

GEARBOX
Lubricating Oil
With the car standing level and having been at rest for at least 2—3 minutes remove the level plug on the right hand side of the gearbox casing. The oil should be level with the hole and the easiest way to check this is to add oil from an oil gun or dispenser pack until it overflows. When draining the oil warm the gearbox up with a good run first and then remove the level plug and the drain plug from the bottom cover plate. Let it drip for at least 15 minutes. Replace the drain plug and refill with 2.2/5 pints/1.35 litres of the recommended oil.

CLUTCH PEDAL FREE TRAVEL — See Chapter 5.

PROPELLER SHAFT AND REAR AXLE — Lubrication
On later models (68/69) only there is a grease nipple on the front end of the propeller shaft front section. Inject one or two shots of the recommended grease from a grease gun.
The rear axle oil level checking and draining procedure is the same as for the gearbox. The refill quantity is 1¼ pints/0.70 litres).

Gearbox level plug

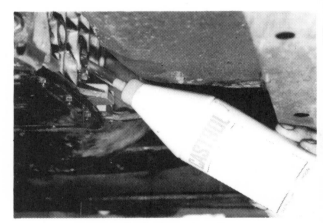
Putting in gearbox oil

Rear axle level plug (A) and drain plug (B)

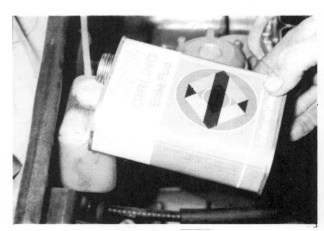
Putting brake fluid into the reservoir

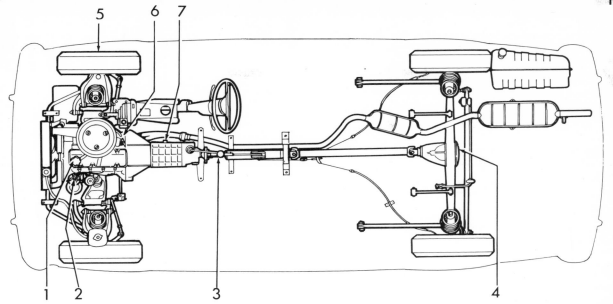

Lubrication diagram

1   Engine oil filler cap - sump 6.6 pints/3.75 litres

2   Distributor - one or two drops

3   Propeller shaft splines (late models)

4   Rear axle filler plug - 2½ pints/0.70 litres

5   Front wheel bearings - see text

6   Starter motor - see text

7   Gearbox filler plug - 2.4 pints/1.35 litres

Recommended lubricants and fluids

LOCATION	TYPE	CASTROL PRODUCT
ENGINE SUMP	Multi-grade engine oil	Castrol GTX
GEARBOX	Multi-grade engine oil	Castrol GTX
REAR AXLE	Hypoid gear oil 90 EP	Castrol Hypoy B
STEERING BOX	Hypoid gear oil 90 EP	Castrol Hypoy B
DISTRIBUTOR	Engine or light oil	Castrol GTX
FRONT WHEEL BEARINGS	Lithium based medium grease	Castrol LM Grease *
GENERATOR BEARINGS	Medium grease	Castrol LM Grease *
STARTER BUSHES	Engine or light oil	Castrol GTX
PROPELLER SHAFT SPLINES	Medium grease with molybdenum	Castrol MS3
BRAKE MASTER CYLINDER	Hydraulic fluid SAE 70 R 3	Castrol Girling Brake Fluid
ANTIFREEZE	BS1 3151/3152	Castrol Antifreeze

*Castrol Spheerol AP3 is the ideal grease for these bearings but it is obtainable through FIAT agents only.
Use engine oil or Castrol Everyman to lubricate locks and hinges.

Chapter 1 Engine

Contents

Specifications

Engine - General

	124	124S
Type...	4 cylinder in line, ohv pushrod operated	
Bore	73 mm	80 mm
Stroke	71.5 mm	71.5 mm
Displacement	1197 cc	1438 cc
Maximum bhp DIN	60 @ 5,600 rpm	70 @ 5,400 rpm
Maximum torque DIN	64.4 ft lbs @ 3,400 rpm	80.9 ft lbs @ 3,300 rpm
Compression ratio..	8.8 : 1	9 : 1
Firing order..	1 – 3 – 4 – 2	
No.1 cylinder location	Front of engine	
Compression pressure..	170 lbs/sq in	

Camshaft and bearings

Camshaft drive...	Duplex endless chain
Bearings...	3 renewable shells
Camshaft journal diameter - front	48.033 – 48.058 mm
- centre..	43.833 – 43.858 mm
- rear	36.875 – 36.9 mm
Cam lift...	8.625 mm

Connecting rods and big end bearings

Bearing type	Split shell
Big end bore	48.630 — 48.646 mm
Small end bore	21.940 — 21.960 mm
Bearing shell thickness	1.531 — 1.538 mm
Gudgeon pin interference fit	0.101 — 0.042 mm
Big end bearing clearance (new)	0.026 — 0.076 mm

Crankshaft and main bearings

Bearing type	Split shell
Standard journal diameter	50.775 — 50.795 mm
Bearing to journal clearance (new)	0.050 — 0.095 mm
Crankshaft end float	0.055 — 0.265 mm
Thrust washers	2 part ring on inner face of rear main bearing

Cylinder block and crankcase

Type	Cast iron - cylinders cast integrally
Oversize bores	.2 mm, .4 mm, .6 mm
Tappet diameter	21.978 — 21.996 mm
Tappet clearance	.007 — .043 mm

Cylinder head and valves

Type	Aluminium
Valve guide bore - inlet	8.022 mm — 8.040 mm
- exhaust	8.029 mm — 8.047 mm
Valve stem to guide clearance - inlet	.022 — .055 mm
- exhaust	.029 — .062 mm
Valve seat angle	45°
Valve face angle	45° 30'
Valve head diameter - inlet	34.5 mm
Valve seat contact width - inlet	1.6 — 1.7 mm
- exhaust	1.9 — 2.0 mm
Valve lift	8.625 mm
Outer valve springs - free length	50 mm
- loaded length	32.7 mm with 30.7 Kg
Inner valve springs - free length	39.2 mm
- loaded length	28.7 mm with 15.4 Kg
Valve timing - inlet opens	25° BT DC
(Rocker clearance - inlet closes	59° ABDC
at 0.375 mm) - exhaust opens	65° BBDC
- exhaust closes	19° ATDC

Valve rocker clearance (cold):

1438 cc	0.20 mm
1197 cc	0.15 mm

Pistons and piston rings

Piston clearance in cylinder bore (new)	.060 — .080 mm
Piston ring gap in bore - top	0.30 — 0.45 mm
- centre and lower	0.20 — 0.35 mm
Piston ring clearance in groove - top	0.045 — 0.077
- centre	0.015 — 0.055
- bottom	0.020 — 0.052

Piston diameter (measured at 52,25 mm from crown at right angles to gudgeon pin)	124	124S
	Class A 72.960 — 72.970 mm	79.930 — 79.940 mm
	Class C 72.980 — 72.990 mm	79.950 — 79.960 mm
	Class E 73.00 — 73.010 mm	79.970 — 79.980 mm

Oversize pistons available	0.2 mm, 0.4 mm, 0.6 mm
Gudgeon pins	Interference fit in small end of connecting rod
Gudgeon pin diameter - Div 1	21.970 — 21.974 mm
- Div 2	21.974 — 21.978 mm
- Div 3	21.978 — 21.982 mm
Oversize pins available	+ 0.2 mm

Lubrication system

Oil pump

Gears to housing clearance	0.11 — 0.18 mm

Gears to cover face	0.020 – 0.105 mm
Oil pressure relief valve spring - free length	40.2 mm
- minimum length and loading	21 mm at 5 Kg
Oil pressure...	64 to 86 p.s.i.
Engine oil capacity (from dry)	4.2 litres (7.4 Imp pints)
Sump refill capacity	3.75 litres (6.6 Imp pints)

Torque wrench settings

Flywheel mounting screw	8 Kgm/58 ft lbs
Cylinder head bolts	8 Kgm/58 ft lbs
Connecting rod cap nuts...	5 Kgm/36 ft lbs
Main bearing cap bolts	8 Kgm/58 ft lbs
Rocker shaft standard nut	4 Kgm/29 ft lbs
Camshaft sprocket screw..	5 Kgm/36 ft lbs

1. General description

Both 124 and 124S versions of the 4 cylinder ohv pushrod engine are basically the same. The increased power of the 'S' is due to its larger capacity achieved by a larger bore.

The design of the engine is conventional. The crankshaft runs in five main bearings and the overhead inclined valves are operated by a chain driven camshaft, tappets and pushrod through rockers pivoting on a shaft mounted on the aluminium cylinder head. The valve seats are cast iron inserts. The cylinder block is cast iron and the cylinders are bored directly into it.

Pistons are fitted with 3 rings – 1 compression and 2 oil control. The gudgeon pin is a floating fit in the piston and an interference fit in the connecting rod small end.

The oil pump is the gear type draining from a sump. It is driven by a special drive sleeve in mesh with a skew gear on the camshaft. This sleeve has a splined internal bore and also drives the distributor.

The engine is supported together with the transmission unit at three places; one on each side of the engine between the crankcase and the body side rails and underneath the gearbox by a crossmember bolted to the underframe.

The lubrication system is pressurized. The oil circulates under pressure from the gear type pump which draws oil from the sump and forces it through a full flow filter. The oil pressure is gauged after it has passed through the filter. From the filter it flows to a longitudinal gallery cast in the crankcase and five branches from this gallery run direct to the main crankshaft bearings. Oilways in the crankshaft allow oil to pass to the connecting rod big end bearings. From the main bearings oil also passes from further oilways to the three camshaft bearings.

From the centre camshaft bearing oil passes through another oilway vertically through the cylinder head into the hollow rocker shaft. This acts as a gallery and oil feeds out to lubricate the rocker arms.

Oil pressure is lost at this point, and the oil drains back down from the head through the pushrod apertures to the sump. It lubricates the tappets and cams on the way. Maintenance of oil pressure is dependent on the tolerances of the bearings and journals the viscosity of the oil and the efficiency of the pump. A relief valve in the pump prevents excess pressure from cold oil damaging the filter and a relief valve in the filter permits oil to continue circulating if the filter gets blocked.

2. Major operations with engine in place

The following work may be conveniently carried out with the engine in place:

1 Removal and replacement of the cylinder head assembly.
2 Removal and replacement of the clutch assembly.
3 Removal and replacement of the engine front mountings.
The following work can be carried out with the engine in place,

but is inadvisable unless there are very special reasons:
4 Removal and replacement of the sump (the engine must be raised first).
5 Removal and replacement of big end bearings (after sump removal).
6 Removal and replacement of pistons and connecting rods (after removing cylinder head and sump).
7 Removal and replacement of the timing chain and sprockets (after removal of the radiator).
8 Removal and replacement of the oil pump (after removal of the sump).

3. Major operations for which the engine must be removed

1 Removal and replacement of crankshaft and crankshaft main bearings.
2 Removal and replacement of flywheel.
3 Removal and replacement of rear crankshaft oil seal.

4. Methods of engine removal

1 The engine complete with gearbox can be lifted as a unit from the engine compartment. Alternatively, the engine and gearbox can be split at the front of the bellhousing, the gearbox supported and left in position, and the engine removed. Whether or not components like the carburettor, manifolds, generator and starter are removed first depends to some extent on what work is to be done.

5. Engine removal - with gearbox

1 The do-it-yourself owner should be able to remove the engine fairly easily in about 3½ hours. It is essential to have a good hoist, and two strong axle stands if a pit is not available. Engine removal will be much easier if you have someone to help you. Before beginning work it is worthwhile to get all the accumulated debris cleaned off the engine unit at a service station which is equipped with steam or high pressure air and water cleaning equipment. It helps to make the job quicker, easier and, of course, much cleaner. Decide whether you are going to jack up the car and support it on axle stands or raise the front end on wheel ramps. If the latter, run the car up now (and chock the rear wheels) whilst you still have engine power available. Remember that with the front wheels supported on ramps the working height and engine lifting height is going to be increased.
2 Open the bonnet and prop it up to expose the engine and ancillary components. Disconnect the battery leads and lift the battery out of the car. This prevents accidental short circuits while working on the engine.
3 Undo the nuts and bolts from the bonnet hinges and lift the

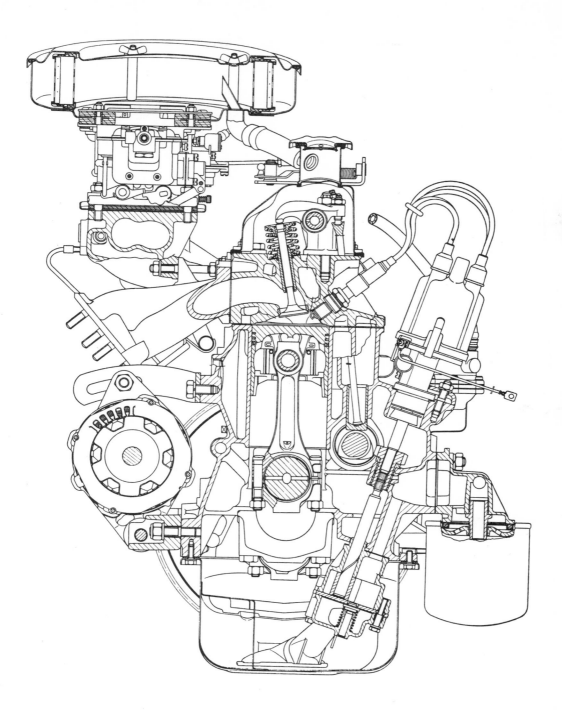

Fig.1.1. Engine cross section - lateral. (Downdraught carburettor fitted)

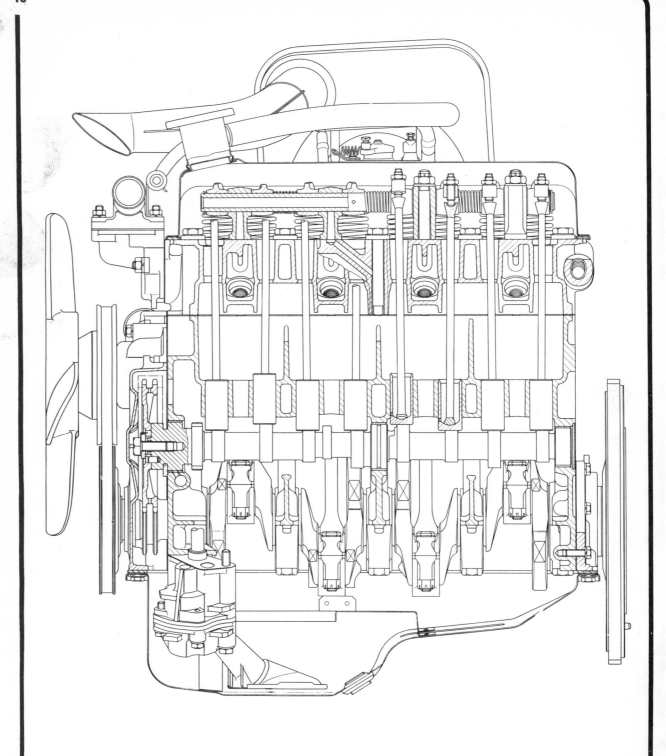

Fig.1.2. Engine cross section - longitudinal. (Side draught carburettor fitted)

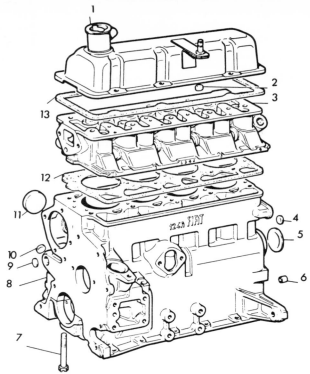

Fig.1.3. Crankcase, cylinders and cylinder head (static components only)

1 Rocker cover	5 Camshaft rear bearing	8 Crankcase/cylinder	11 Plug
2 Plug	plug	block	12 Head gasket
3 Cylinder head	6 Dowel	9 Plug	13 Rocker cover
4 Gallery plug	7 Bearing cap bolt	10 Plug	gasket

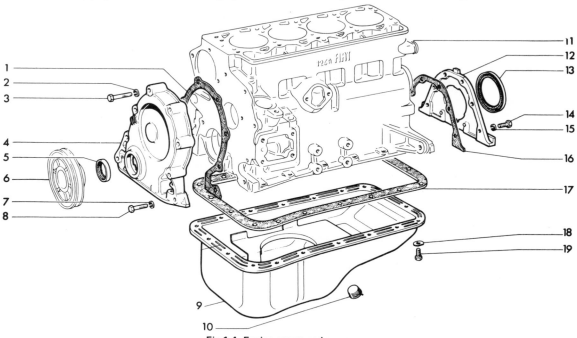

Fig.1.4. Engine covers and sump

1 Gasket	6 Crankshaft pulley	11 Cylinder block	15 Lockwasher
2 Lockwasher	7 Lockwasher	12 Crankcase rear	16 Gasket
3 Screw	8 Screw	cover	17 Sump gasket
4 Timing chain cover	9 Sump	13 Oil seal	18 Washer
5 Oil seal	10 Drain plug	14 Screw	19 Sump screw

bonnet off. Place it somewhere safe where it will not be knocked over or bumped into. Remove also the undertrays beneath the engine.

4   Drain the cooling system.

5   Remove the sump drain plug and drain the oil out of the engine into a container (an old 1 gallon oil tin with the side cut out).

6   Drain the oil from the gearbox.

7   Disconnect the HT and LT leads from the coil to the distributor.

8   Disconnect the leads to the generator, starter motor, low oil pressure indicator and water temperature sender units.

9   Disconnect the accelerator rod from the relay lever and the choke cable from the carburettor.

10   Disconnect the fuel line from the pump.

11   Disconnect the exhaust pipe from the manifold by removing the four nuts.

12   Disconnect the water hoses connecting the radiator to the engine and also those connecting the heater to the engine.

13   Disconnect the radiator hose to the auxiliary tank.

14   Remove the radiator by undoing the two upper screws and sliding it off the lower support bracket before lifting it out.

15   Remove the air cleaner from the carburettor.

16   From inside the car remove the cover round the base of the gear lever and also remove the lever as described in Chapter 6.

17   Under the car undo the three bolts holding the flexible coupling to the mainshaft and move the shaft to one side.

18   Undo the speedometer drive knurled ring from one side of the gearbox.

19   Disconnect the clutch cable from the operating lever and draw the cable out through the clutch bellhousing.

20   Undo the exhaust pipe support clip from the rear of the transmission.

21   Support the gearbox with a jack and remove the supporting crossmember from underneath it.

22   Now sling the engine to whatever lifting device you are using and support the weight. Undo the engine mounting nuts, the upper one on the right and the lower one on the left. This will enable the studs to disengage easily from the body mountings (photos). It is important to sling the engine fairly well forward so that when lifted the whole unit will tilt at an acute angle for lifting out. At the same time there should be no possibility of the unit slipping out of the sling. Make sure also that there is sufficient head room to lift the unit out.

23   Lift steadily and carefully watching that the lifting slings do not strain against any ancillaries on the engine which could be damaged.

6. Engine removal - without gearbox

1   Begin by following the instructions in Section 5 from paragraphs 1—15 inclusive.

2   Remove the three bolts securing the starter motor to the transmission unit. Disconnect also the starter motor leads. It will be necessary to remove the heat shield also from the exhaust manifold.

3   Remove the four bolts securing the flywheel cover to the front of the transmission.

4   Support the front end of the gearbox on a jack and remove the four bolts holding it to the crankcase. An articulated socket adaptor piece will be needed to reach two of these.

5   Take the weight of the engine using a hoist and if necessary raise the jack beneath the gearbox so that it too, is just supported. Undo the engine mounting stud nuts, as described in Paragraph 21 of the previous Section.

6   Raise the engine to just clear the mountings, and raise the jack beneath the gearbox at the same time so that it is still just supported. Ease the engine forward to disengage it from the gearbox input shaft, then lift it up and out. Do not allow the engine (or gearbox) weight to be taken on the gearbox input shaft during the removal procedure.

7. Engine dismantling - general

1   Owners who dismantle a lot of engines will probably have a stand on which to mount them, but most will make do with a work bench. This should be large enough on which to spread the inevitable bits and pieces and tools, and strong enough to support the engine weight. If the floor is the only possible place, try and ensure that the engine rests on a hardwood platform, or similar, rather than concrete (or beaten earth!!).

2   Spend some time on cleaning the unit. If you have been wise this will have been done before the engine was removed, at a service bay. Good solvents such as 'Gunk' will help to 'float' off caked dirt/grease under a water jet. Once the exterior is clean, dismantling may begin. As parts are removed clean them in petrol or paraffin (do not immerse parts with oilways in paraffin. Paraffin, which could possibly remain in oilways, would dilute the oil for initial lubrication after reassembly).

3   Where components are fitted with seals and gaskets it is always best to fit new ones - but do NOT throw the old ones away until you have the new ones to hand. A pattern is then available if they have to be specially made. Hang them on a convenient hook.

4   In general it is best to work from the top of the engine downwards. In any case support the engine firmly so that it does not topple over when you are undoing stubborn nuts and bolts.

5   Always place nuts and bolts back together in their components or place of attachment if possible - it saves so much confusion later. Otherwise put them in small, separate pots or jars so that their groups are easily identified.

8. Engine dismantling - ancillary components

1   If you are obtaining a replacement reconditioned engine all ancillaries must come off first - just as they will if you are doing a thorough engine inspection/overhaul yourself. These are:

Dynamo	(Chapter 10)
Distributor	(Chapter 4)
Thermostat and cover	(Chapter 2)
Oil filter	(Section 8)
Carburettor	(Chapter 3)
Inlet manifold	(Section 8)
Exhaust manifold	(Section 8)
Water pump	(Chapter 2)
Fuel pump	(Chapter 3)
Engine mounting brackets	(Section 8)

2   If you are obtaining what is called a 'short engine' (or 'half-engine') comprising cylinder block, crankcase, crankshaft, pistons, and connecting rods all assembled, then the cylinder head, flywheel, sump and oil pump will need removal also.

3   Remove all the ancillaries according to the removal instructions for them described in the chapters and sections as indicated in paragraph 1.

4   To remove the oil filter cartridge simply unscrew it. If it is tight put a piece of chain around it and a screwdriver locked in the links to act as a type of grip.

5   Both inlet and exhaust manifolds can be taken off after removing the carburettor and the seven securing nuts and washers.

6   The oil filter support can be removed also by unscrewing the four nuts.

7   The engine mounting brackets are simply bolted to the crankcase. They can be removed without taking the engine from the car if the engine is supported and raised a little.

9. Valve rocker assembly - removal

1   Undo the rocker cover screws and take off the cover.

5.21A. Undoing the upper right hand engine mounting nut

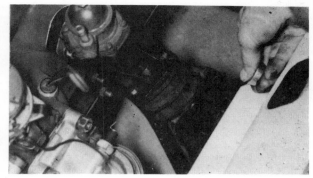

5.21B. Undoing the lower left engine mounting nut

6.6. Hoisting the engine. Note that no tilt is needed

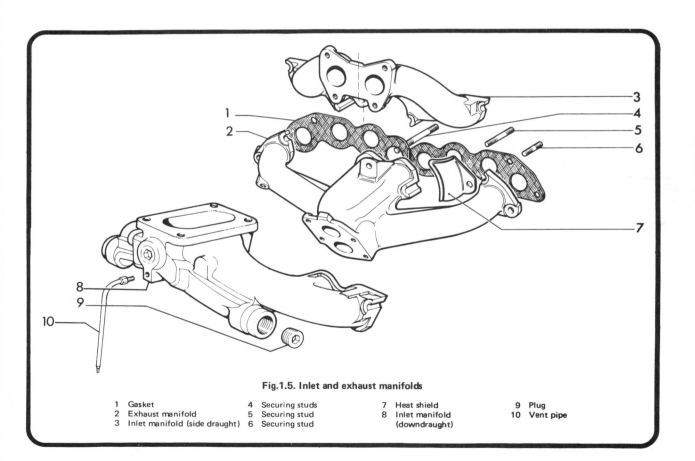

Fig.1.5. Inlet and exhaust manifolds

1	Gasket	4	Securing studs	7	Heat shield	9	Plug
2	Exhaust manifold	5	Securing stud	8	Inlet manifold	10	Vent pipe
3	Inlet manifold (side draught)	6	Securing stud		(downdraught)		

2 The rocker gear is held by four nuts which secure the support standards over four studs. Slacken the four nuts evenly a little at a time and then lift the whole assembly off.

10. Cylinder head removal

1 Assuming that the engine has not been taken from the car proceed as follows:
2 Disconnect both battery leads.
3 Drain the cooling system.
4 Remove the hoses from the water pump.
5 Remove the carburettor air cleaner unit.
6 Remove the valve rocker gear.
7 Disconnect the HT leads from the spark plugs.
8 Disconnect the carburettor connections (accelerator, choke, and fuel line).
9 Disconnect the lead to the water temperature sender unit.
10 Remove the carburettor (not essential but less likely to get damaged).
11 Lift out the pushrods.
12 Slacken off the holding down bolts in the reverse sequence of that shown for tightening and remove them.
13 Lift off the head. If it sticks then it is possible (with the engine in the car) to re-connect the battery so that cylinder compression will force the seal. Do not try and force anything between head and block or damage will result. Hit the side of the head with a soft faced heavy mallet if necessary.

11. Valves - removal

1 Remove the cylinder head.
2 The valves are located by a collar on a compressed spring which grips two collets (or a split collar) into a groove in the stem of the valve. The spring must be compressed with a special G clamp in order to release the collets and the valve. Place the specially shaped end of the clamp over the spring collar with the end of the screw squarely on the face of the valve. Screw up the clamp to compress the spring and expose the collets on the valve stem. Sometimes the collar sticks and the clamp screw cannot be turned. In such instances, with the clamp pressure still on, give the head of the clamp (over the spring) a tap with a hammer, at the same time gripping the clamp frame firmly to prevent it slipping off the valve.

Take off the two collets, release the clamp, and the collar and spring can be lifted off. The valve can then be pushed out through its guide and removed. If the end of the valve sticks at the guide when removing it, it is due to burring. Carefully grind off the corner of the stem to permit it to pass through the guide. If you force it through it will score the guide way. Make sure that each valve is kept in a way that its position is known for replacement. Unless new valves are to be fitted each valve MUST go back where it came from. The springs, collars and collets should also be kept with their respective valves. A piece of card with eight holes punched in is a good way to keep the valves in order.

12. Valve guides

If the valves are a very slack fit in the guides calling for renewal of the guides new guides may be fitted. The circlip is removed from the top of the guide and they are then drifted out from the valve port side with a stepped drift. New guides are driven in from the top of the cylinder head - also with a stepped drift. Great care must be taken to ensure that they are driven in 'clean' to start with and that the drift is so shaped that it cannot spread or split the guide. It is possible for the guides to distort slightly when being fitted and it may be necessary to ream them to prevent binding on the valve stem.

This job calls for proper tools and experience and is best entrusted to a competent fitter. Otherwise costly damage may be caused to the cylinder head.

13. Sump - removal

The engine should be out of the car in order to remove the sump. Otherwise disconnect the front engine mountings and jack the engine up until sufficient clearance is available to remove it once the securing screws are taken out.

With the engine out, it is better to wait until the cylinder head is removed. Then invert the engine and undo the set screws holding the sump to the crankcase and lift it off. If the cylinder head is not being removed (for example if the oil pump only is being removed) the engine should be placed on its side.

14. Crankshaft pulley, timing cover, sprockets and chain - removal

1 The timing gear is accessible with the engine in the car but unless the sump is removed first, the sump gasket will have to be broken and a section replaced. This is not ideal but can be done with careful attention to the re-sealing of the timing case lower end to the sump, on replacement. It will be necessary to remove the radiator and the fan belt as described in Chapter 2. Then remove the radiator grille for ease of access.
2 Unlock the tab washer and undo the large nut which holds the fan belt driving pulley to the crankshaft. It will be necessary to prevent the crankshaft from turning, by locking the flywheel with a bar in the starter ring teeth against one of the dowel pegs in the end of the crankcase.
3 Another way is to block one of the crankshaft journals with a piece of wood against the side of the crankcase. With the engine in the car, the pulley may also be removed. Put the car in gear while undoing the bolt.
4 The pulley should pull off easily. If not, lever it off with two screwdrivers at 180° to each other. Take care not to damage either the pulley flange or the timing case cover which is made only of light alloy.
5 Remove the bolts holding the timing case cover in place, and also the four sump screws from its lower edge. Then take it off.
6 Remove the bolt, lockwasher and plain washer from the camshaft sprocket and then lift the sprocket off the locating peg on the end of the camshaft. The sprocket and chain can then be disengaged and removed.
7 The sprocket on the camshaft is a fairly tight keyed fit. If it is necessary to take it off a puller may be needed.

15. Pistons, connecting rods and big end bearings - removal

1 As it is necessary to remove the cylinder head and the sump from the engine in order to remove pistons and connecting rods, the removal of the engine is the logical thing to do first. With the engine on the bench and the cylinder head and sump removed, stand the block inverted (with crankshaft uppermost).
2 Each connecting rod and its bearing cap is matched, and held by two high tensile steel bolts. Before anything else, mark each connecting rod and cap with its cylinder number and relationship - preferably with the appropriate number of dabs of paint. Using punch or file marks may be satisfactory, but it has been known for tools to slip - or the marks even to cause metal fatigue in the connecting rod. Once marked, undo the bearing cap bolts using a good quality socket spanner. Lift off each bearing cap and put it in a safe place. Carefully turn the engine on its side. Each piston can now be pushed out from the block by its connecting rod. Clean a small area on the front of each piston crown and place an indicative dab of paint. Do not use a punch, or file marks, on the pistons under any circumstances. The shell bearings in the connecting rods and caps can be removed simply by pressing the edge of the end opposite the

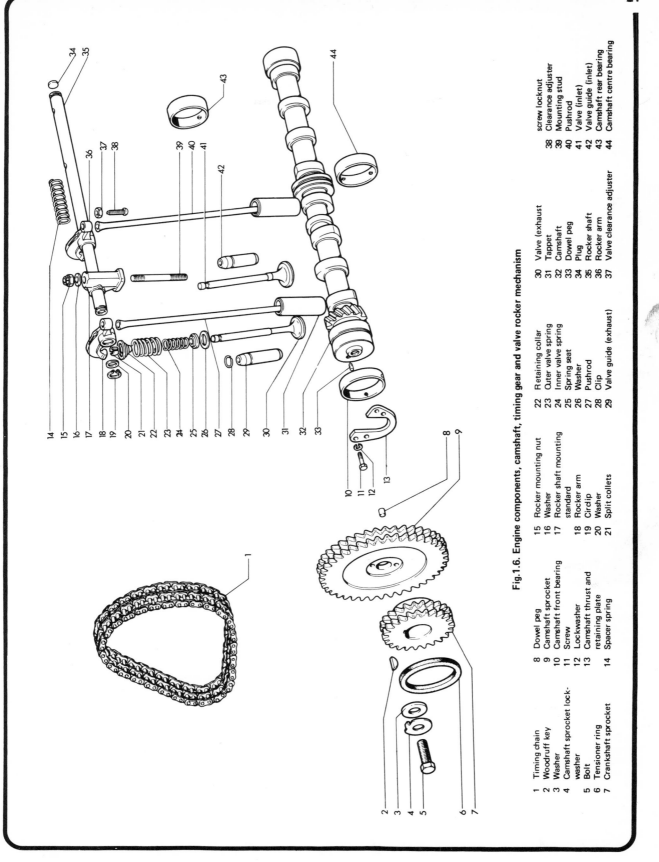

Fig.1.6. Engine components, camshaft, timing gear and valve rocker mechanism

1 Timing chain
2 Woodruff key
3 Washer
4 Camshaft sprocket lock-washer
5 Bolt
6 Tensioner ring
7 Crankshaft sprocket
8 Dowel peg
9 Camshaft sprocket
10 Camshaft front bearing
11 Screw
12 Lockwasher
13 Bolt
14 Spacer spring
15 Rocker mounting nut
16 Washer
17 Rocker shaft mounting standard
18 Rocker arm
19 Circlip
20 Washer
21 Split collets
22 Retaining collar
23 Outer valve spring
24 Inner valve spring
25 Spring seat
26 Washer
27 Pushrod
28 Clip
29 Valve guide (exhaust)
30 Valve (exhaust)
31 Tappet
32 Camshaft
33 Dowel peg
34 Plug
35 Rocker shaft
36 Rocker arm
37 Valve clearance adjuster
38 Clearance adjuster screw locknut
39 Mounting stud
40 Pushrod
41 Valve (inlet)
42 Valve guide (inlet)
43 Camshaft rear bearing
44 Camshaft centre bearing

notch in the shell and they will slide round to be lifted out. Note from where each comes.

16. Gudgeon pins

The gudgeon pins float in the piston and are an interference fit in the connecting rods. This 'interference fit' between gudgeon pin and connecting rod, means that heat is required (230—260°C) before a pin can be satisfactorily replaced in the connecting rod. If it is necessary to replace either the piston or connecting rod, we strongly recommend that the assembly of the two be entrusted to someone with experience. Misapplied heat can ruin one, or all, of the components very easily.

17. Piston rings - removal

Unless new rings are to be fitted for certain, care has to be taken that rings are not broken on removal. Starting with the top ring (all rings are to be removed from the top of the piston) ease one end out of its groove and place a piece of steel band (shim, old feeler gauge blade, strip of cocoa tin!) behind it.

Then move the metal strip carefully round behind the ring, at the same time nudging the ring upwards so that it rests on the surface of the piston above, until the whole ring is clear and can be slid off. With the second and third rings which must also come off the top, arrange the strip of metal to carry them over the other grooves.

Note where each ring has come from (pierce a piece of paper with each ring showing 'top 1', 'middle 1' etc).

18. Flywheel - removal

1 The flywheel can be removed with the engine in the car but it is not recommended, and the following procedures prevail when the engine has been lifted out:
2 Remove the clutch assembly (Chapter 5).
3 Jam the crankshaft in position with a piece of wood and undo the six bolts in the centre of the flywheel.
4 Using a soft headed mallet, tap the periphery of the flywheel progressively all round, drawing it off the crankshaft boss. Do not allow it to assume a skew angle as the fit on the flange is at very close tolerances to maintain proper balance and concentricity with the crankshaft. Make sure it is well supported so that it does not drop.

19. Oil pump - removal

1 Remove the engine from the car (preferably - although one may detach the sump with the engine in place if the engine is disconnected from the front mountings and jacked up).
2 Remove the sump.
3 Undo the bolts securing the pump and suction pipe unit to the crankcase and withdraw the pump.

20. Camshaft - removal

1 Remove the engine from the car.
2 Remove the sump, timing gear cover, timing chain and sprockets, oil pump distributor and then driving gear.
3 Remove the fuel pump.
4 If the cylinder head has been removed stand the engine inverted - if not lie it on its right hand side and rotate the camshaft several times to push the tappets out of the way.
5 Undo the two bolts retaining the thrust plate and slide the thrust plate out.
6 The camshaft can now be drawn out, and care must be taken that it is manoeuvred past the tappets without damage to either

the cams or the tappets. This will be easy if the engine is completely inverted. If, however, it is lying on its side with the tappets in such a position that they could fall out under their own weight, more care is necessary. In the event it would be advisable to prop the engine so that the tappets cannot fall out of their bores. Take care also not to damage the camshaft bearings with the edges of the cams as the shaft is withdrawn.

21. Tappets - removal

The tappets can be lifted out of their bores in the crankcase after the cylinder head has been removed.

22. Crankshaft and main bearings - removal

1 With the engine removed from the car, remove the sump, oil pump, timing chain and sprockets, and flywheel. If the cylinder head is also removed so much the better as the engine can be stood firmly in an inverted position. Take off the rear cover plate incorporating the seal.
2 Remove the connecting rod bearing caps. This will already have been done if the pistons are removed.
3 Using a good socket wrench, remove the two cap bolts from each of the main bearing caps.
4 Lift off each cap carefully noting its position.
5 Grip the crankshaft at each end and lift it out. Remove the shell bearings from the crankcase and bearing caps and also the semicircular thrust washers.

23. Crankshaft - examination and renovation

1 Examine all the crankpins and main bearing journals for signs of scoring or scratches. If all surfaces are undamaged, check next that all the bearing journals are round. This can be done with a micrometer or caliper gauge, taking readings across the diameter at six or seven points for each journal. If you do not own, or know how to use, a micrometer, take the crankshaft to your local engineering works and ask them to 'mike it up' for you.
2 If the crankshaft is ridged or scored, it must be reground. If the ovality exceeds 0.05 mm/.002 inches on measurement, but there are no signs of scoring or scratching on the surfaces, regrinding may be necessary. It would be advisable to ask the advice of the engineering works to whom you would entrust the work of regrinding in such instances.
3 Check also that the oilway plugs are secure (photo).

24. Big end (connecting rod) bearings and main bearings - examination and renovation

1 Big end bearing failure is normally indicated by a pronounced knocking from the crankcase and a slight drop in oil pressure. Main bearing failure is normally accompanied by vibration, which can be quite severe at high engine speeds, and a more significant drop in oil pressure. Oil pressure drop can only be verified, of course, if a gauge is fitted.
2 The shell bearing surfaces should be matt grey in colour with no sign of pitting or scoring.
3 Replacement shell bearings are supplied in a series of thicknesses dependent on the degree of regrinding that the crankshaft requires, which is done in multiples of 0.25 mm. So depending on how much it is necessary to grind off, bearing shells are supplied as 0.25 mm undersize and so on. The engineering works regrinding the crankshaft will normally supply the correct shells with the reground crank.
4 If an engine is removed for overhaul, it is worthwhile renewing big end bearings and main bearings as a matter of course. This will

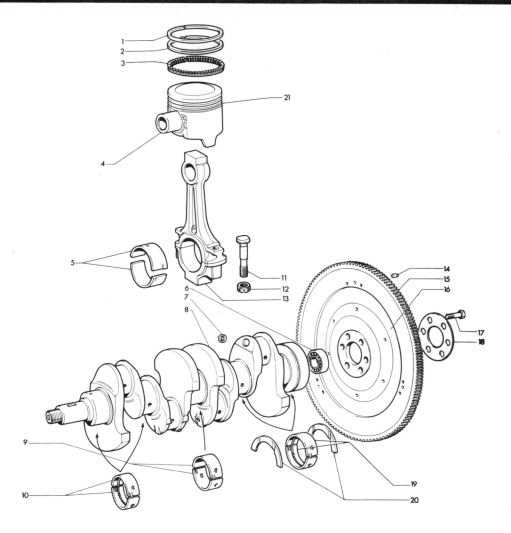

Fig.1.7. Crankshaft, pistons and connecting rods

1 Top compression ring
2 Lower compression ring
3 Oil control ring
4 Gudgeon pin
5 Big end bearing shells
6 Roller bearing for gearbox input shaft
7 Crankshaft oilway plug
8 Crankshaft
9 Centre main bearing shells (no 3)
10 Nos 1 and 2 main bearing shells
11 Connecting rod cap bolt
12 Nut
13 Connecting rod
14 Clutch cover dowel peg
15 Flywheel starter ring gear
16 Flywheel
17 Flywheel securing bolt
18 Spacer washer
19 Nos 4 and 5 main bearing shells
20 Crankshaft endfloat thrust washers
21 Piston

23.3. The pointer shows a crankshaft oilway sealing plug

add many thousands of miles to the life of the engine before any regrinding of crankshafts is necessary. Make sure that bearing shells renewed are standard dimensions if the crankshaft has not been reground.

25. Cylinder bores - examination and renovation

1 The bores must be checked for ovality, scoring, scratching and pitting. Starting from the top, look for a ridge where the top piston ring reaches the limit of its upward travel. The depth of this ridge will give a good indication of the degree of wear. It can be checked with the engine in the car and the cylinder head removed. Other indications are excessive oil consumption and a smoky exhaust.

2 Meausre the bore diameter across the block and just below any ridge. This can be done with an internal micrometer. Compare this with the diameter of the bottom of the bore, which is not subject to wear. If no micrometer measuring instruments are available, use a piston from which the rings have been removed, and measure the gap between it and the cylinder wall with a feeler gauge. Another way of measuring the bore to determine the need for rebore, is to measure the difference in the gap of a piston ring below and above the ridge. The differences divided by three will give an indication of the bore wear.

3 If the difference in bore diameters at top and bottom is 0.15 mm/.006 inches or more, then the cylinders need reboring. If less than .010 inch, then the fitting of new and special rings to the pistons may cure the trouble.

4 If the cylinders have already been bored out to their maximum, it is possible to have liners fitted.

26. Pistons and rings - examination and renovation

1 Examine the pistons (with the rings removed as described in Section 17) for signs of damage on the crown and around the top edge. If any of the piston rings have broken, there could be quite noticeable damage to the grooves, in which case the piston must be renewed. Deep scores in the piston walls also call for renewal. If the cylinders are being rebored, new oversize pistons and rings will be needed anyway. If the cylinders do not need reboring and the pistons are in good condition, only the rings need to be checked.

Pistons should be measured across the diameter at right angles to the gudgeon pin - 52 mm/2 inches down from the piston crown.

2 To check the existing rings, place them in the cylinder bore and press each one down in turn to the bottom of the stroke. In this case a distance of 65 mm. from the top of the cylinder will be satisfactory. Use an inverted piston to press them down square. With a feeler gauge, measure the gap for each ring which should be as given in the 'Specifications' at the beginning of this Chapter. If the gap is too large, the rings will need renewal.

3 New pistons are not usually fitted in an un-rebored block. If they are the precautions for fitting new rings should be considered as indicated in the following paragraphs.

4 When new rings are fitted in untouched bores the top ring normally has a cutaway step — a 'ridge - dodger' ring — to prevent the top ring fouling any ridge which there may be in the bore. If the top ring does not have such a feature then the ridge should be scraped or ground away. If this is not done the ring will probably break when it hits the ridge.

5 New rings should be placed in the bores as described in paragraph 2, and the gap checked. Any gaps which are too small should be increased by filing one end of the ring with a fine file. Be careful not to break the ring as they are brittle (and expensive). On no account make the gap less than specification. If the gap should close when under normal operating temperatures, the ring will break.

6 The groove clearance of new rings in old pistons should be within the specified tolerances. If it is not enough, the rings could stick in the piston grooves causing loss of compression.

27. Camshaft and camshaft bearings - examination and renovation

1 With the camshaft removed, examine the bearings for signs of obvious wear and pitting. If there are signs, then the three bearings will need renewal. This is not a common requirement, and to have to do so is indicative of severe engine neglect at some time. As special removal and replacement tools are necessary to do this work properly, it is recommended that it is done by a 'specialist'. Check that the bearings are located properly so that the oilways from the bearing housings are not obstructed.

2 The camshaft itself should show no marks on either the bearing journals or the profiles. If it does, it should be renewed. Check that the overall height of each cam from base to peak is within specification. If not, the camshaft should be renewed.

3 Examine the skew gear for signs of wear or damage. If this is badly worn it will mean renewing the camshaft.

4 The thrust plate (which also acts as the locating plate) should not be ridged or worn in any way. If it is, renew it.

28. Timing chain and sprockets - examination and renovation

The timing chain is kept at correct tension by centrifugally operated bob weights attached to the links and also a flexible ring insert between the two rows of sprocket teeth. If the chain is noisy due to slackness the chain and sprockets should all be renewed. To renew part only will not give satisfactory results.

29. Valve rocker arms and pushrods - examination and renovation

1 The rockers should have no noticeably radial play on the shaft and the end of the rocker arm which bears on the valve stem should be flat. Provided the shaft itself is not worn a new rocker can be put on the shaft.

2 The pushrods must be straight - renew any that are not. Also the ends of the pushrods must be hemispherical and not scored or ridged.

30. Tappets - examination and renovation

Examine the bearing surfaces of the tappets which lie on the camshaft. Any indentation in these surfaces, or any cracks, indicate serious wear and the tappets should be renewed. Thoroughly clean them out, removing all traces of sludge. It is most unlikely that the sides of the tappets will prove worn, but, if they are a very loose fit in their bores and can readily be rocked, they should be exchanged for new units. It is unusual to find wear in the tappets, and it is likely to occur only at very high mileages, or in cases of neglect. If tappets are worn, examine the camshaft carefully as well.

31. Connecting rods - examination and renovation

1 It is possible, but not likely, that a previous owner may have misguidedly filed the caps to take up slack. If so then the offending rods must be renewed. Check the alignment of the rods visually and if in doubt get them checked on a proper jig.

32. Flywheel starter teeth - examination and renovation

1 If the teeth on the flywheel are badly worn, or if some are missing, then it will be necessary to remove it and fit a new one. This is not a normal area of serious wear. The teeth should last the life of the engine. (N.B. Some early models may have a detachable ring gear which a specialist can replace).

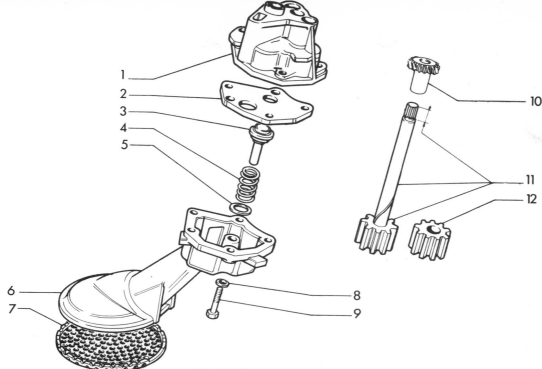

Fig.1.8. Oil pump - components

1 Pump body	4 Spring	7 Strainer	10 Drive gear
2 Cover	5 Spring seat	8 Washer	11 Pump gear and shaft
3 Pressure relief valve	6 Suction arm	9 Body screw	12 Driven pump gear

33. Oil pump - examination and renovation

1 If the oil pump is worn, it is best to purchase an exchange re-conditioned unit, as to rebuild the oil pump is a job that calls for engineering shop facilities.

2 To check if the pump is still serviceable, first check if there is any slackness in the spindle bushes, and then remove the bottom cover held by three bolts.

3 Then check the two gears (the impellers) and the inside of the pump body for wear with the aid of a feeler gauge. Measure (a) the gearwheels radial clearance (blade inserted between the end of the gearwheel teeth and the inside of the body), (b) the gearwheel end clearance (place a straight edge across the bottom flange of the pump body and measure with the feeler blades the gap between the straight edge and the sides of the gearwheel). The correct clearances are listed in the 'Specifications'.

4 Fit a replacement pump if the clearances are incorrect.

34. Decarbonisation

1 Modern engines, together with modern fuels and lubricants, have virtually nullified the need for the engine to have a 'de-coke' which was common enough only a few years ago. Carbon deposits are formed mostly on the modern engine only when it has to do a great deal of slow speed, stop/start running, for example, in busy traffic and city traffic conditions. If carbon deposit symptoms are apparent, such as pinking or pre-ignition and running on after the engine has been switched off, then a good high speed run on a motorway or straight stretch of road is usually sufficient to clear these deposits out. It is beneficial to any motor car to give it a good high speed run from time to time.

2 There will always be some carbon deposits, of course, so if the occasion demands the removal of the cylinder head, for some reason or another, it is a good idea to remove the carbon deposits when the opportunity presents itself. Carbon deposits in the combustion chambers of the cylinder head can be dealt with as described under the section heading 'Cylinder head - inspection and renovation'. The other carbon deposits which have to be dealt with are those on the crowns of the pistons. This work can easily be carried out with the engine in the car, but great care must be taken to ensure that no particles of dislodged carbon fall either into the cylinder bores and down past the piston rings or into the water jacket orifices in the cylinder block.

3 Bring the first piston to be attended to to the top of its stroke and then using a sheet of strong paper and some self adhesive tape, mask off the other three cylinders and surrounding block to prevent any particles falling into the open orifices in the block. To prevent small particles of dislodged carbon from finding their way down the side of the piston which is actually being decarbonised, press grease into the gap between the piston and the cylinder wall. Carbon deposits should then be scraped away carefully with a flat blade from the top of the crown of the piston and the surrounding top edge of the cylinder. Great care must be taken to ensure that the scraper does not gouge away into the soft aluminium surface of the piston crown.

4 A wire brush, either operated by hand or a power drill should not be used if decarbonising is being done with the engine still in the car. It is virtually impossible to prevent carbon particles being distributed over a large area and the time saved by this method is very little.

5 In addition to the removal of carbon deposits on the pistons, it is a good time also to make sure that traces of gasket or any sealing compound are removed from the mating face of the cylinder block top face.

6 After each piston has been attended to, clean out the grease and carbon particles from the gap where it has been pressed in. As the engine is revolved to bring the next piston to the top of its stroke for attention, check the bore of the cylinder which has just been

decarbonised and make sure that no traces of carbon or grease are adhering to the inside of the bore.

35. Valves, valve seats and valve springs - examination and renovation

1 Examine the heads of the valves for pitting and burning, especially the heads of the exhaust valves. The valve seatings should be examined at the same time. If the pitting on valve and seat is very slight, the marks can be removed by grinding the seats and valves together with coarse, and then fine, valve grinding paste.

2 Where bad pitting has occurred to the valve seats it will be necessary to recut them and fit new valves. This latter job should be entrusted to the local Fiat agency or engineering shop. In practice it is very seldom that the seats are so badly worn. Normally, it is the valve that is too badly worn for replacement, and the owner can easily purchase a new set of valves and match them to the seats by valve grinding.

3 Valve grinding is carried out as follows: Smear a trace of coarse carborundum paste on the seat face and apply a suction grinder tool to the valve head. With a semi-rotary motion, grind the valve head to its seat (photo), lifting the valve occasionally to redistribute the grinding paste. When a full matt even surface finish is produced on both the valve seat and the valve, then wipe off the paste and repeat the process with fine carborundum paste, lifting and turning the valve to redistribute the paste as before. A light spring placed under the valve head will greatly ease this operation. When a smooth unbroken ring of light grey matt finish is produced, on both valve and valve seat faces, the grinding operation is complete. It is important though that the seat widths of the grinding do not exceed specification. If they do the valve will need renewal and the seat recutting by a specialist.

4 Scrape away all carbon from the valve head and the valve stem. Carefully clean away every trace of grinding compound, taking great care to leave none in the ports or in the valve guides. The simplest way is to flush with paraffin and then hose out with water.

5 Check that all valve springs are intact. If any one is broken, all should be replaced. Check that the free height of the springs is within specifications. If some springs are not within specification, replace them all. Springs suffer from fatigue and it is a good idea to replace them even if they look all right.

36. Cylinder head - examination

1 With the valves removed and all carbon deposits cleaned away, the valve seats must be examined for signs of cracking or pitting. Mild pitting can be cured by grinding in the valves with carborundum paste, but any hair line cracks or severe ridging and pitting mean that at least the seats will need recutting or renewing. This is a specialist task. Cracks visible anywhere else in the head, mean that it must be scrapped.

2 The head must be perfectly flat where it joins the cylinder block. Use a metal straight edge at various positions along and across the head to see if it is warped in any way. The least one can expect from a warped head is persistent blowing of gaskets and loss of coolant.

3 Check the valve guides (Section 12).

4 See that all water passages are clear and scrape away any visible hard deposits. Note that a chemical de-scaler might be worth using after the engine is reassembled.

5 Make sure also that the other mating flange surfaces (for manifolds etc) are clean, flat and unpitted.

37. Engine reassembly - general

1 To ensure maximum life with minimum trouble from a rebuilt engine, not only must everything be correctly assembled, but everything must be spotlessly clean, all the oilways must be clear, locking washers and spring washers must always be fitted where indicated and all bearing and other working surfaces must be thoroughly lubricated during assembly.

2 Before assembly begins renew any bolts or studs, the threads of which are in any way damaged, and whenever possible use new spring washers.

3 Apart from your normal tools, a supply of clean rag, an oil can filled with engine oil (an empty plastic detergent bottle thoroughly cleaned and washed out, will do), a new supply of assorted spring washers, a set of new gaskets, and a torque spanner, should be collected together.

38. Crankshaft - replacement

1 Ensure that the crankcase is thoroughly clean and that all oilways are clear. If possible blow the drillings out with compressed air.

2 Clean the crankshaft in the same fashion and then inject engine oil into the crankshaft oilways.

3 Fit the halves of the five main bearing shells with the crankcase so that the notches engage in the cut-outs. Note that the centre shell has no oil groove in it (photos). With new bearings soak them in paraffin and wipe them dry before fitting to clear any surface preservative. When in position oil them with clean engine oil.

4 The crankshaft endfloat/thrust washers are semi-circular and one fits each side of the crankcase No 5 (rear) bearing housing. The thrust washer grooves should face outwards. Hold the washers in position with a dab of grease (photos).

5 Lower the crankshaft into position taking care not to dislodge the thrust washers.

6 The main bearing caps are all Identifiable , Nos 2—5 being centre punched 1—4, and No 1 cap having no marks (photo). Clean the caps and fit the shells remembering that the plain bearing goes in the centre. Replae the caps having lubricated the journals. The caps should all face the same way - lining up the marks and with the bearing locating notches opposite those in the crankcase (photo).

7 Tighten down all the cap bolts evenly, one bearing at a time to the specified torque of 58 ft lbs/8 kgm (photo). After each one turn the crankshaft to check that there is no binding. If there is, something is wrong so check before going further.

39. Pistons and connecting rods - reassembly

As mentioned in Section 16 the connecting rods and gudgeon pins are an interference fit requiring heat to enable them to be correctly assembled. This work should be entrusted to someone with the necessary experience and equipment. It is important that the piston and connecting rod are assembled the proper way round to ensure that the offset of the piston is on the thrust side of the cylinder. The offset side of the piston is on the same side as the oil jet hole which is bored into the shoulder of the rod. This offset/jet hole should point towards the left side of the cylinder wall. There is a second oil hole in the rear face of the connecting rod also.

40. Piston ring - replacement

1 Ensure that the piston and piston rings have been inspected and renewed in accordance with the procedures described in Section 26.

2 Check that the ring grooves are completely clean.

3 Fit the rings over the top of the piston, starting with the bottom oil control ring.

4 The ring may be spread with the fingers sufficiently to go around the piston, but it could be difficult getting the first ring past the other grooves. It is well worth spending a little time cutting a strip of thin tin plate from any handy can, say 1 inch side and slightly shorter in length than the piston circumference. Place the ring round this and then slide the strip with the ring on it over the piston, until the ring can be conveniently slipped off into its groove.

5 Follow in the same way with the other two rings - making sure

35.3. Grinding an exhaust valve into its seat

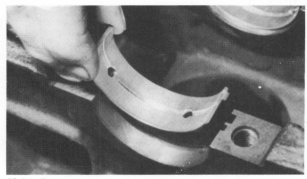

38.3A. Fitting a main bearing shell into the crankcase

38.3B. The centre main bearing shell has no oil groove

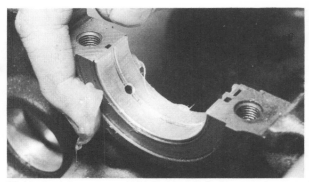

38.4A. Applying grease to hold the crankshaft thrust washer in position

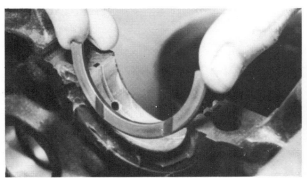

38.4B. Fitting one of the crankshaft thrust washers at the side of No.5 main bearing

38.6A. Main bearing caps showing the identifying marks

38.6B. Fitting a main bearing cap

38.7. Tightening a main bearing cap bolt

40.5. The lower of the two compression rings has a step in its lower edge - (indicated)

that they are the right way up. The second ring has a cut away lower edge (photo).
6 The words 'TOP' or 'BOTTOM' which may be marked on the rings indicate which way up the ring goes in its groove in the piston, i.e. the side marked 'TOP' should face the top of the piston, and does not mean that the ring concerned should necessarily go into the top groove.

41. Piston - replacement in cylinder

1 The pistons, complete with connecting rods and new shell bearings, can be fitted to the cylinder bores in the following sequence:
2 With a wad of clean rag wipe the cylinder bores clean. If new rings are being fitted, any surface oil 'glaze' on the walls should be removed by rubbing with a very fine abrasive. This can be a very fine emery cloth, or a fine cutting paste as used for rubbing down paintwork. This enables new rings to bed into the cylinders properly which would otherwise be prevented, or at least delayed for a long time. Make sure that all traces of abrasive are confined to the cylinder bores and are completely cleaned off before assembling the pistons into the cylinders. Then oil the pistons, rings, and cylinder bores generously with engine oil. Space the piston ring gaps equally around the piston.
3 The pistons, complete with connecting rods, are fitted to their bores from above. Fit the shell bearing into the connecting rod first engaging the notch in the cut-out (photo).
4 As each piston is inserted into its bore, ensure that it is the correct piston/connecting rod assembly for that particular bore. The oil drilling in the connecting rod shoulder faces the thrust side (left) of the cylinder (photo). The matching numbers of the connecting rod and cap face the other side of the cylinder.
5 The piston will only slide into the bore as far as the oil control ring. It is then necessary to compress the piston rings into a clamp (photo). Gently tap the piston into the cylinder bore with a wooden or plastic hammer. If a proper piston ring clamp is not available, then a suitable Jubilee clip may be tried. Some bottom oil control rings are very flexible and may protrude from certain types of clamp so watch out for these.
6 If new pistons and rings are being fitted to a rebored block, the clearances are very small and care has to be taken to make sure that no part of a piston ring catches the edge of the bore before being pressed down. They are very brittle and easily broken. For this reason it is acceptable practice to chamfer the lip of the cylinder very slightly to provide a lead for the rings into the cylinder. The chamfer should be at an angle of 45° and should not be cut back too much. If some form of hose clip is being used to compress the piston rings, it may be found that the screw housing prevents the clip from lying exactly flush with the cylinder head. Here again watch carefully to ensure that no part of the ring slips from under the control of the clamp.

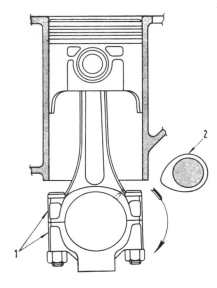

Fig.1.9. Diagram to indicate piston/connecting rod assembly position in cylinder relative to camshaft to obtain offset on the correct side. Viewed from front of engine.

1 Position of connecting rod and cap mating marks
2 Camshaft

42. Connecting rod to crankshaft - reassembly

1 If the old bearings are nearly new and are being refitted, then ensure they are replaced in their correct locations on the correct rods.
2 Generously lubricate the crankpin journals with engine oil, and turn the crankshaft so that the crankpin is in the most advantageous position for the connecting rod to be drawn on to it.
3 Wipe the connecting rod bearing cap and back of the shell bearing clean, and fit the shell bearing in position ensuring that the locating tongue at the back of the bearing engages with the locating groove in the connecting rod cap (photo).
4 Make sure the cap fits the correct rod by checking the matching marks (photo).
5 Generously lubricate the shell bearing and offer up the connecting rod bearing cap to the connecting rod (photo).
6 Fit the connecting rod nuts on oiled threads and tighten them with a torque spanner to 36 lbs ft/5 kgm.
7 Oil the cylinder bores well for initial lubrication.

43. Tappet/camshaft - replacement

1 Wipe the camshaft bearing journals clean and lubricate them generously with engine oil. Ensure the small oil hole in the centre of the camshaft is clear.
2 Insert the camshaft into the crankcase gently, taking care not to damage the camshaft bearings with the cams (photo).
3 Replace the camshaft locating plate (photo), and tighten down the two retaining bolts and washers.
4 Tappets should be replaced in their respective bores, lubricated well, after the camshaft has been replaced. See that the oil drain holes in them are clear (photo).

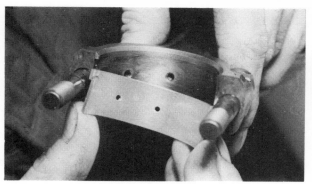

41.3. Fitting a big end bearing shell into a connecting rod

41.5. Putting the piston/connecting rod into the cylinder having clamped the piston rings

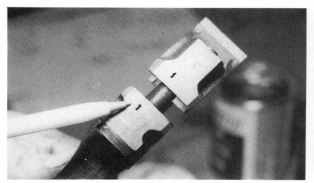

42.4. Each connecting rod and cap has corresponding marks

42.5. Fitting a big end bearing cap with a new bearing shell on to the connecting rod

42.6. Tightening the big end bearing cap nuts

43.2. Replacing the camshaft into the crankcase.

43.3. Fitting the camshaft thrust/retaining plate

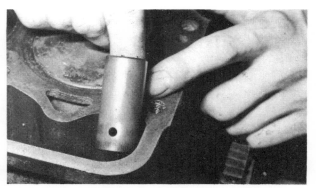

43.4. Replacing a cam follower (tappet) into the crankcase

44. Timing sprocket, timing chain and cover - replacement

1 This section describes the replacement procedure as part of the general overhaul of the engine, and assumes that the engine is removed from the car. If, however, the timing gear has been removed with the engine in the car, the following additional points should be noted when refitting the timing case. The sump gasket is made of a resilient material so when the timing chain cover is removed it should remain intact and be sufficiently compressible to re-use. If it has been stuck down then it will be necessary to find a new piece of gasket when re-fitting the cover.

2 It is advisable to fit a new oil seal into the timing case, so first of all drive out the old one.

3 Place the new seal in position with the lip facing the inside of the cover.

4 Drive the seal home with a block of wood and a mallet. It is possible to do this work with the cover fitted to the engine and the engine in the car. Only the crankshaft pulley needs to be taken off.

5 The crankshaft sprocket should have a serviceable tension ring between the two sets of teeth and then be driven on to the crankshaft lining up with and engaging the key (photos).

6 Fit the chain onto the camshaft sprocket. Turn the crankshaft so that the line up mark on the sprocket points as near as possible to the centre line of the camshaft. Turn the camshaft so that the locating peg points as near as possible to the centre line of the crankshaft.

7 Place the camshaft sprocket in position so that the dimple in its outer edge, the line up mark on the crankshaft sprocket and the centre lines of both the crankshaft and camshaft all line up. Do this carefully because if it is one tooth out the engine performance will be seriously affected.

8 Replace the lockwasher with one finger in the smaller hole of the camshaft sprocket and refit the securing bolt (photo). Tighten the bolt to 36 ft lbs/5 kgm and bend up the other lock tab.

9 Replace the cover with a new gasket and put back all the screws (including those from the front edge of the sump if the engine is still in the car) finger tight. It is best to tighten them all after the crankshaft pulley wheel has been replaced.

45. Crankshaft rear oil seal and retaining plate - replacement

1 Fit a new seal into the cover with the lip facing inwards and see that the seal has an arrow pointing in the direction in which the shaft will rotate (photo). If incorrect then you have the wrong seal.

2 With a new gasket, fit the cover over the rear of the crankshaft having first made certain that the flange is lubricated with engine oil (photo).

46. Oil pump - replacement

1 Before fitting the pump it is as well to check first that the bushing for the drive gear inside the crankcase is in good condition (photo).

2 This can be done by replacing the pump/distributor drive gear, using a suitable guide rod, and verifying that there is no excessive play (photo).

3 Place the mounting bolts through the oil pump, and offer the pump up to the crankcase, remembering to fit the new gasket between the mating faces (photos).

47. Sump replacement

1 Put the new gasket in position and do not use any form of sealing compound on it. Place the sump in position (photos).

2 Replace all the securing screws with special washers. The washers should have their convex/serrated sides towards the bolt heads.

3 Tighten all screws evenly and not too tightly. If the timing chain cover has been removed do not tighten the front screws until the crankshaft pulley has been positioned and the timing chain cover screws tightened.

44.5A. A rubber ring is fitted between the crankshaft sprocket teeth to assist chain tensioning

44.5B. Putting the crankshaft sprocket onto the crankshaft

44.7A. Replacing the camshaft sprocket and timing chain together

44.7B. Lining up the marks (arrowed) and the two shaft centre lines with a straight edge

44.8. Tightening the camshaft sprocket securing nut

45.1. The seal in the rear cover plate has an arrow (indicated) in the direction of shaft rotation

45.2. Fitting the crankshaft rear cover plate and oil seal

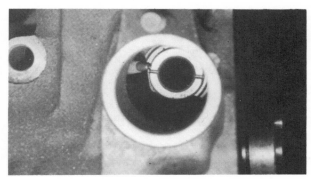

46.1. View of the oil pump/distributor drive gear bushing in the crankcase, looking down through the distributor mounting hole

46.2. Replacing the oil pump/distributor drive gear into its bushing using a guide rod - in this case the engine oil dipstick

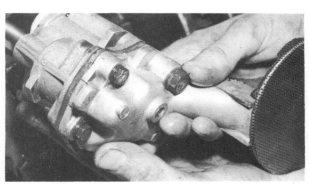

46.3A. Replacing the oil pump ....

46.3B.......... not forgetting that a gasket is fitted

47.1A. Positioning the sump gasket

47.1B. Putting the sump in position

48. Crankshaft pulley wheel - replacement

1 Fit the pulley on to the keyed nose of the crankshaft (photo).
2 Replace the special lockwasher so that the slot engages one of the webs. Refit the special nut (photo). Tighten the nut to 88 lb ft/12 kgm. This can be done when the engine is back in the car and prevented from turning by engaging a gear.

49. Flywheel - replacement

1 The flywheel has a dimple mark near the edge on the clutch side (photo). This should be at 12 o'clock when Nos 1 and 4 pistons are at TDC.

48.2. Refitting the special lockwasher and securing nut for the crankshaft pulley

49.2A. Fitting the flywheel to the crankshaft

48.1. Replacing the crankshaft pulley

2 Place the flywheel carefully in position on the end of the crankshaft and replace the special washer and six securing bolts. Tighten the bolts evenly to 58 lbs ft/8 kgm. (photos).

50. Valves and valve springs - reassembly to cylinder head

1 Gather together all the new or reground valves and ensure that if the old valves are being replaced they will return into their original positions.
2 Ensure that all valves and springs are clean and free from carbon deposits and that the ports and valve guides in the cylinder head have no carbon dust or valve grinding paste left in them.
3 Fit the steel discs which form the lower bearing surface of the springs against the cylinder head (photo).

49.1. On the clutch face of the flywheel a dimple (indicated) is at 12 o'clock with Nos.1 and 4 pistons at TDC to obtain the correct balance point

49.2B. Replacing the special washer and flywheel securing screws

50.3. Replacing the steel disc before the valve springs

50.5A. Replacing the inner and outer valve springs

50.5B. Putting the upper spring seat in position

50.5C. Compressing the valve springs with the clamp screw on the valve head

50.6. With the springs clamped the collets are replaced

51.1. Fitting the oil filter cartridge adaptor housing

4   Place the valve in the guide - having smeared the stem with molybdenum paste or oil first.

5   Fit the inner and outer valve springs and the retainer collar and compress the springs with a suitable tool until the grooved part of the valve stem is clear of the retainer (photos).

6   Fit the two split collets, tapered lid inwards so that they engage the valve stem recesses snugly. Use a dab of grease to hold them in place if necessary.

7   Release the compressor and watch the two collets stay put. Tap the valve stem end with a mallet after assembly just to ensure that all is properly settled.

51. Oil filter adaptor - replacement

1   Always refit a new gasket and mount the unit on the studs in the crankcase with the filter cartridge mounting facing the bottom of the engine.

52. Cylinder head - replacement

1   With the valves and springs reassembled, examine the head to make sure that the mating face is perfectly clean and smooth and that no traces of gasket or other compound are left. Any scores, grooves or burrs should be carefully cleaned up with a fine file.

2   Examine the face of the cylinder block in the same way as the head. Make sure that the tappets are clean and in position in their bores.

3   Most head gaskets indicate which side is the top, but on the Fiat 124 there can be no confusion as it is not symmetrical, there being one odd hole at the front end (photo).

4   Place the gasket in position on the block and lower the head onto it (photo). Replace all the cylinder head bolts.

5   Proceed with a torque wrench to tighten down the bolts ¼ − ½ turn at a time in the progressive order as indicated in Fig.

1.10 (photo). The tightening sequence should continue until each bolt is down to a torque of 58ft lbs/8 kgm. If, in the early stages, any one bolt is obviously slacker than the rest, it should be tightened equal to the others even if it may require a turn or so out of sequence. The whole point of the procedure is to keep the tightening stresses even over the whole head, so that it goes down level and undistorted.

53. Valve rocker shaft assembly - replacement

1   Replace the eight pushrods through the head so that the lower ends engage the tappet recesses (photo).

2   Place the rocker assembly over the head and line up the four mounting standards over the studs and lower it (photo). It will not go all the way down as some valves will have opened under pressure from the rockers.

3   Engage the ends of the pushrods into the rocker arms and then tighten down the four securing nuts and washers a little at a time so that the whole assembly goes down evenly. It is quite good pratice to slacken off the valve clearance adjuster locknuts at this stage and back off the screws.

4   Tighten the nuts finally to 29 ft lbs/4 kgm (photo).

54. Valve clearances - adjustment

1   Clearances should be set as soon as the rocker shaft is reassembled, it is so easy to forget. After the engine has been installed and run for a while they should be checked again.

2   Recommended clearances are as given in the Specifications for all valves.

3   There are differnet ways of ensuring the valves are in the correct position for clearance setting. A simple way is to turn the engine until No.1 cylinder is at TDC on the inlet/exhaust stroke. This can be ascertained by seeing that the exhaust valve is almost fully

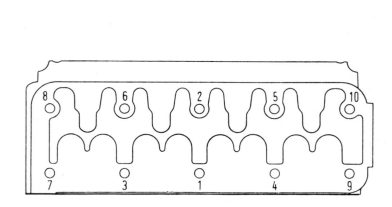

Fig. 1.10. Cylinder head bolt tightening sequence

52.4. Placing the cylinder head gasket on the cylinder block. Note the odd hole (arrowed) at the front of the gasket

52.5. Replacing the cylinder head

52.6. Tightening the cylinder head bolts

53.1. Putting back the pushrods through the cylinder head

53.2. Replacing the rocker shaft assembly on to the cylinder head

53.4. Tightening the rocker shaft assembly securing nuts

closed and the inlet valve just beginning to open. When No 1 cylinder is in this position both valves for No 4 are set up to check clearances. The arrangement is reciprocal for Nos 1 and 4 cylinders and Nos 2 and 3 cylinders in the same way. Alternatively some may find it easier to follow the table below which gives an individual checking order which involves minimum turning of the engine. No 1 valve is the front valve of the engine on No 1 cylinder.

Valve fully open	Valve clearance to check
No 8	No 1 (exhaust)
No 6	No 3 (inlet)
No 4	No 5 (exhaust)
No 7	No 2 (inlet)
No 1	No 8 (exhaust)
No 3	No 6 (inlet)
No 5	No 4 (exhaust)
No 2	No 7 (inlet)

4 To adjust the screw undo the locknut with a ring spanner just enough to enable the screw to be turned using another small spanner.
5 Place the .015 mm feeler blade between the rocker arm and the valve stem and turn the adjusting screw until the feeler blade can be moved with a slight drag. Hold the screw and tighten the locknut with the feeler blade still in position. Check that the feeler blade still has the same drag (photo).

55. Inlet and exhaust manifolds - replacement

1 When refitting the inlet and exhaust manifolds, which are bolted together and fit as a complete assembly, the carburettor should not be attached otherwise the centre securing bolt is inaccessible for tightening (photo). Place the gaskets on the studs making sure the mating faces are clean (photo).
2 Before fitting the manifolds the heater water pipe which runs behind them must be loosely positioned. Do not tighten the water pipe securing nuts until after the manifolds are secure. The rear of the pipe is held by a clip to one of the manifold studs.

56. Engine assembly - final details

The ancillaries which were removed at the first stage of dismantling may all be replaced before the engine is put back in the vehicle. One possible exception is the carburettor which is somewhat vulnerable and relatively fragile. Details of removal and replacement of these items are dealt with in the appropriate chapters as mentioned in Section 8 of this Chapter. It is much easier to fit the dynamo and fan belt at this stage and similarly to set the static ignition timing which is necessary when replacing the distributor.

If you have not removed the two undertray panels at the front of the engine compartment refit the oil filter cartridge before replacing the engine - (otherwise one of the undertrays will have to be removed to change it).

57. Engine - replacement

1 Whether or not the engine was removed together with the gearbox it is simpler to replace them separately. The propeller shaft coupling is not quite so straightforward as in some other makes. Even though the propeller shaft front support strap and centre coupling housing will need releasing and moving to one side this is still the most convenient method.
2 Sling the engine so that it stays horizontal when lifted and lower it into position on the mountings. It is not necessary to tip it and a slight turn sideways in the early stages of lowering will enable it to clear the top edge of the engine compartment.
3 When the mounting bolts are secure the engine will stay in position when released from the sling.
4 If the engine is being refitted with the gearbox in place it is important that no strain is imposed on the gearbox input shaft when centering it into the clutch cover assembly. It may be necessary to wiggle the engine about a little but if the clutch assembly has been correctly assembled (see Chapter 5) there should be little difficulty.

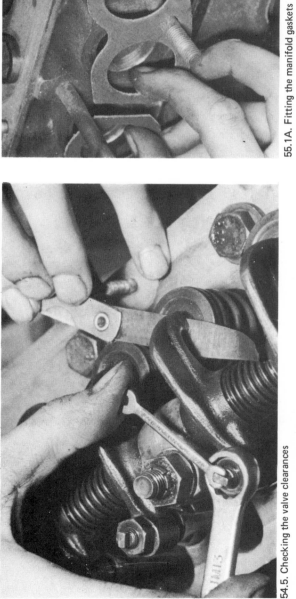

54.5. Checking the valve clearances

55.1A. Fitting the manifold gaskets

55.2. Refitting the manifolds to the cylinder head. Note that the heater water pipe (arrowed) has been positioned first

55.1B. Note the lower centre manifold securing nut which cannot be fitted with the carburettor in position

58. Fault finding

When investigating starting and unven running faults do not be tempted into a snap diagnosis. Start from the beginning of the check procedure and follow it through. It will take less time in the long run. Poor performance from an engine in terms of power and economy is not normally diagnosed quickly. In any event the ignition and fuel systems must be checked first before assuming any further investigation needs to be made.

Symptom	Reason/s	Remedy
Engine will not turn over when starter switch is operated	Flat battery Bad battery connections Bad connections at solenoid switch and/or starter motor	Check that battery is fully charged and that all connections are clean and tight.
	Starter motor jammed	Rock the car back and forth with a gear engaged. If this does not free pinion remove starter.
	Defective solenoid	Remove starter to repair solenoid.
	Starter motor defective	Remove and overhaul starter motor.
Engine turns over normally but fails to fire and run	No spark at plugs	Check ignition system according to procedures given in Chapter 4.
	No fuel reaching engine	Check fuel system according to procedures given in Chapter 3.
	Too much fuel reaching the engine (flooding)	Check the fuel system.
Engine starts but runs unevenly and misfires	Ignition and/or fuel system faults	Check the ignition and fuel systems as though the engine had failed to start.
	Incorrect valve clearances	Check and reset clearances.
	Burnt out valves Blown cylinder head gasket	Remove cylinder head and examine and overhaul as necessary.
	Worn out piston rings Worn cylinder bores	Remove cylinder head and examine pistons and cylinder bores. Overhaul as necessary.
Lack of power	Ignition and/or fuel system faults	Check the ignition and fuel systems for correct ignition timing and carburettor settings.
	Incorrect valve clearances	Check and reset the clearances.
	Burnt out valves Blown cylinder head gasket	Remove cylinder head and examine and overhaul as necessary.
	Worn out piston rings Worn cylinder bores	Remove cylinder head and examine pistons and cylinder bores. Overhaul as necessary.
Excessive oil consumption	Oil leaks from crankshaft rear oil seal, timing cover gasket and oil seal, rocker cover gasket, oil filter gasket, sump gasket, sump plug washer	Identify source of leak and renew seal as appropriate.
	Worn piston rings or cylinder bores resulting in oil being burnt by engine (smoky exhaust is an indication)	Fit new rings or rebore cylinders and fit new pistons, depending on degree of wear.
	Worn valve guides and/or defective valve stem seals	Remove cylinder heads and recondition valve stem bores and valves and seals as necessary.
Excessive mechanical noise from engine	Wrong valve to rocker clearances	Adjust valve clearances.
	Worn crankshaft bearings Worn cylinders (piston slap).	Inspect and overhaul where necessary.
	Slack or worn timing chain and sprockets	Renew all timing mechanism.
Unusual vibration	Fan blade broken off	Break off another fan blade to balance fan until renewal is possible.
	Broken engine/gearbox mounting	Renew mounting.
	Misfiring on one or more cylinders	Check ignition system.

Chapter 2 Cooling system

Contents

Specifications

Type...	Pressurised, pump assisted circulation with thermostat temperature control
Capacity	7.5 litres (1.6 gallons)
Radiator - leak test pressure..	14 psi
- radiator pressure cap opens at	13—15 psi
Fan belt - V pulley drive	Tension permits depression of 10—15 mm/.4—.6 ins with 10 kg/22 lbs pressure midway between the generator and fan pulleys
Thermostat - starts to open	85° — 89°C (185 — 192°F)
- fully open	100°C (212°F)
Water pump - centrifugal type	
Impeller interference fit on shaft	0.017 mm — 0.060 mm
Fan pulley hub interference fit on shaft	0.012 mm — 0.060 mm
Clearance between impeller blades and body..	1 mm

1. General description

The engine cooling water is circulated through the cooling passages in the engine block and radiator by a centrifugal pump driven by the fan belt. A multi-bladed fan forces air through the radiator to assist cooling at low road speeds or high engine revolutions. The system is pressurized to increase the boiling temperature and the radiator cap is spring loaded to relieve this pressure when it exceeds 15 psi. With normal expansion from heating water leaves the system through the radiator cap into an expansion bottle. When the liquid contracts on cooling, the fluid is drawn back into the system from the expansion tank.

A thermostat is incorporated to restrict circulation until normal running temperature (85° — 89°C) has been reached.

The heater which is standard on all models, is fed by a hot water pipe from the cylinder head water jacket.

The cooling system circulation is as follows:—

From the cylinder head (the hottest part) hot water goes via the thermostat elbow (open thermostat) to the top of the radiator. It passes down the radiator and goes out through the bottom hose to the pump. The pump forces water into the block and it then goes up to the head and the cycle starts again. The water for the heater radiator is taken off by a separate pipe from the rear of the cylinder head and returns to the inlet side of the pump by another pipe - the idea being to keep this water as hot as possible.

When the thermostat is closed, restricting the outlet from the cylinder head, the pump does not circulate the water. (Being a centrifugal pump it does not build up pressure).

On later models a by-pass thermostat was introduced. The reason for this was so that the water in the cylinder head and block could circulate within the engine only, rather than stay static until the thermostat began to open. This results in more uniform heat distribution at the warm up stage. In this system the water from the cylinder head takes the line of least resistance back to the pump which is via the by-pass pipes.

The thermostat is housed in the three-way junction and when cold blocks the bottom radiator hose. When hot it blocks the by-pass pipe from the head. When the water heats up and the thermostat moves the water circulates through the top radiator hose, down through the radiator and up to the other side of the thermostat and to the pump.

2. Cooling system - draining, flushing and filling

1 With the car on level ground drain the system as follows:—
2 If the engine is cold, remove the filler cap from the radiator by turning the cap anticlockwise. If the engine is hot, having just been run, then turn the filler cap very slightly until the pressure in the system has had time to disperse. Use a rag over the cap to protect your hand from escaping steam. If, with the engine very hot, the cap is released suddenly, the drop in pressure can result in the water boiling. With the pressure released, the cap can be removed.
3 If antifreeze is in the radiator drain it into a clean bucket or bowl

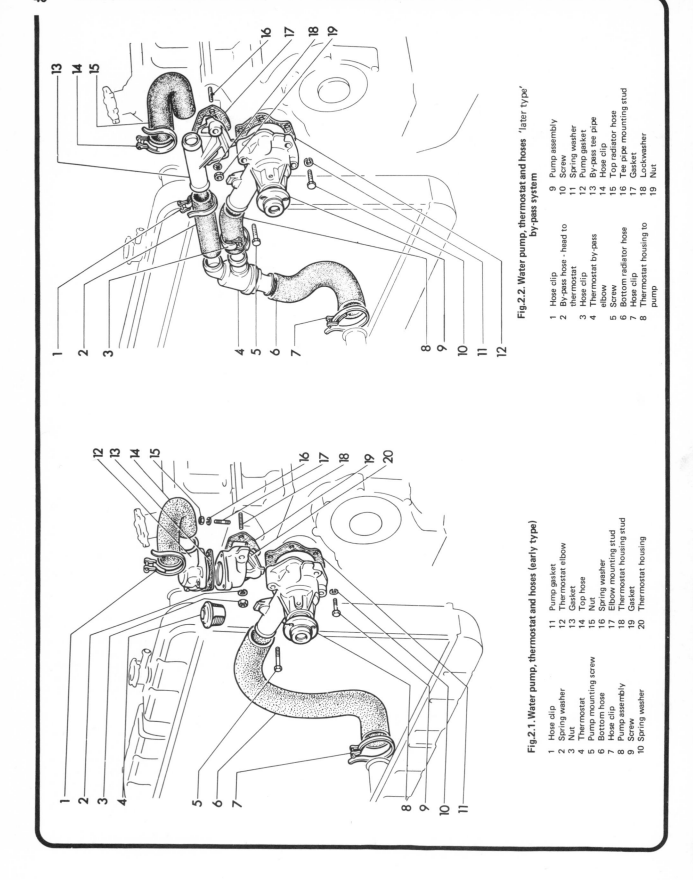

Fig.2.2. Water pump, thermostat and hoses 'later type' by-pass system

1	Hose clip	9	Pump assembly
2	By-pass hose - head to	10	Screw
	thermostat	11	Spring washer
3	Thermostat	12	Pump gasket
4	Thermostat by-pass	13	By-pass tee pipe
	elbow	14	Hose clip
5	Screw	15	Top radiator hose
6	Bottom radiator hose	16	Tee pipe mounting stud
7	Hose clip	17	Gasket
8	Thermostat housing to	18	Lockwasher
	pump	19	Nut

Fig.2.1. Water pump, thermostat and hoses (early type)

1	Hose clip	11	Pump gasket
2	Spring washer	12	Thermostat elbow
3	Nut	13	Gasket
4	Thermostat	14	Top hose
5	Pump mounting screw	15	Nut
6	Bottom hose	16	Spring washer
7	Hose clip	17	Elbow mounting stud
8	Pump assembly	18	Thermostat housing stud
9	Screw	19	Gasket
10	Spring washer	20	Thermostat housing

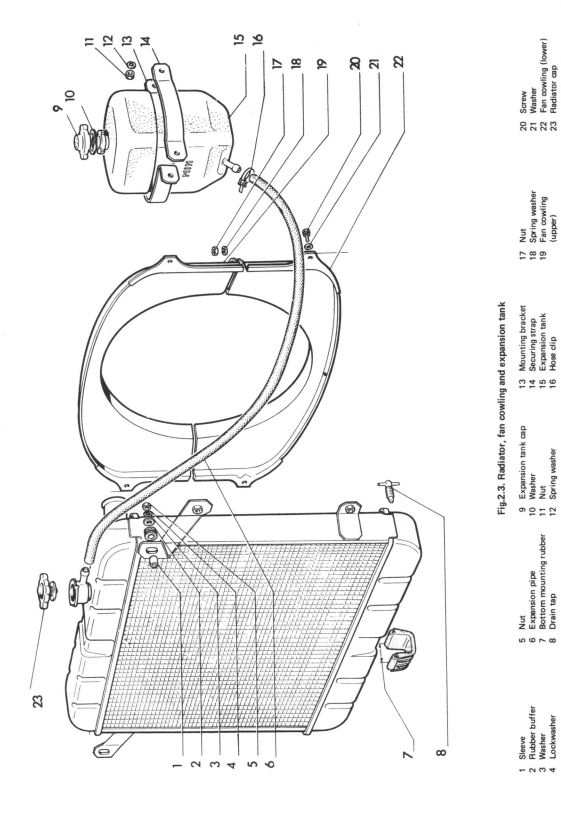

Fig.2.3. Radiator, fan cowling and expansion tank

1	Sleeve	5	Nut	
2	Rubber buffer	6	Expansion pipe	
3	Washer	7	Bottom mounting rubber	
4	Lockwasher	8	Drain tap	

9	Expansion tank cap	13	Mounting bracket	17	Nut	20 Screw
10	Washer	14	Securing strap	18	Spring washer	21 Washer
11	Nut	15	Expansion tank	19	Fan cowling	22 Fan cowling (lower)
12	Spring washer	16	Hose clip		(upper)	23 Radiator cap

for re-use.

4 Open the two drain taps. The radiator drain tap is on the bottom of the radiator tank and the engine drain tap is halfway down the rear right hand side of the cylinder block.

5 When the water has finished running, probe the drain tap orifices with a short piece of wire to dislodge any particles of rust or sediment which may be blocking the taps and preventing all the water draining out. The cylinder block tap is very prone to blockage and may need removal altogether (photo).

NOTE: Opening only radiator tap will not drain the cylinder block.

6 With time the cooling system will gradually lose its efficiency as the radiator becomes choked with rust scales, deposits from water and other sediment. To clean the system out, remove the radiator cap and drain tap and leave a hose running in the radiator cap orifice for ten to fifteen minutes.

7 Where the system is suspected of being choked with scale of one sort or another it is best to give it a treatment with one of the many proprietary chemical descaling compounds which are on the market. Check that whichever one you choose is suitable for use with aluminium cylinder heads.

8 When filling the system use clean water (mixed with antifreeze as appropriate - see Section 6) and fill slowly to minimise air locks. Some may take the trouble to use only distilled water or rain water. This will greatly reduce the rate of any deposit formation. Fill the radiator right up to the top and replace the cap. Then fill the expansion bottle about 75 mm/3 inches above the minimum mark.

3. Radiator - removal, inspection, cleaning and replacement

1 Drain the cooling system as described in Section 2.
2 Undo the clip which holds the top water hose to the header tank and pull it off. Unclip and pull off the bottom hose.
3 Remove the two nuts, one on each side at the top of the radiator, which secure it to the body (photo). Take care of the washers, spacers and buffer pads.
4 Lift the radiator out - the bottom is located in a channel (photo).
5 Clean out the inside of the radiator by flushing as described in Section 3. When the radiator is out of the car, it is well worthwhile to invert it for reverse flushing. Clean the exterior of the radiator by hosing down the matrix (honeycomb cooling material) with a strong water jet to clear away embedded dirt and insects which will impede the air flow. If it is thought that the radiator may be partially blocked, it is best to first flush it with a chemical solution while still in the car. If this does not have any effect flush water through and check that water flows through it at a reasonable rate. Five gallons should go through in about half a minute.
6 Leaks which are on the exterior can usually be repaired by soldering but leaks in the vertical tubes are not so accessible. A temporary leak stopper can be obtained by using a proprietary additive to the cooling liquid or by blocking up the offending area of radiator with mastic or filler paste. Beyond this though there is little alternative than a new radiator.
7 Replacement of the radiator is a reversal of the removal procedure. Check that the hoses are not cracked or brittle with age. Fit new ones if they are. Some owners prefer to fit screw type worm drive hose clips in place of the type fitted. Whichever is used do not over-tighten them.

4. Thermostat - removal, testing and replacement

1 To remove the thermostat, partially drain the cooling system (four pints is enough), loosen the upper radiator hose at the thermostat elbow end and pull it off the elbow. (Early types only - see paragraph 8 for later models).
2 Unscrew the two set and spring washers from the thermostat housing and lift the housing and gasket away.
3 Remove the thermostat and suspend it by a piece of string in a

saucepan of cold water together with a thermometer. Neither the thermostat nor the thermometer should touch the bottom of the saucepan, to ensure a false reading is not given.

4 Heat the water, stirring it gently with the thermometer to ensure temperature uniformity, and note when the thermostat begins to open. The temperature at which this should happen is given in the 'Specifications'.

5 Discard the thermostat if it opens too early. Continue heating the water until the thermostat is fully open. Then let it cool down naturally. If the thermostat will not open fully in boiling water, or does not close down as the water cools, then it must be exchanged for a new one. If a thermostat is unserviceable it is better to run without one rather than with one which is faulty.

6 If the thermostat is stuck open when cold, this will be apparent when removing it from the housing.

7 Replacing the thermostat is a reversal of the removal procedure. Remember to use a new gasket between the thermostat housing elbow and the thermostat. Renew the thermostat elbow if it is badly corroded.

8 On later models which are fitted with the by-pass system, the thermostat acts as a two-way valve - and as a mixer. It is enclosed in the three-way connection of the hose from the base of the radiator to the pump inlet and cylinder head outlet hoses. When cold the thermostat shuts off the bottom radiator hose and the pump draws water only from the cylinder head hose. As the engine warms up so the thermostat shuts off the cylinder head hose and all water is drawn through the radiator.

To check this thermostat remove the three-way connection from the hoses and see that it seats on the lower valve when cold, and on the upper valve when hot (near boiling point). The whole connection should be immersed in near boiling water to check the latter. If faulty the whole assembly must be renewed.

5. Water pump - removal, dismantling and replacement

1 Partially drain the cooling system.
2 Slacken the dynamo securing bolts and remove the fan belt (Section 7).
3 Detach the hoses from the pump body and undo also the bolts holding the fan and pulley hub to the shaft (photo).
4 Undo the two nuts securing the heater return pipe flange (photo), and take out the four bolts holding the body to the cylinder block.
5 Draw the pump off the cylinder block.
6 Renewal of pump parts is possible, but in view of the time and relative cost it must be decided whether or not to fit a new unit.
7 To dismantle the pump the impeller and pulley hub have to be drawn off the shaft with a suitable puller. They are held by interference fit - no keys or splines.
8 The bearing and shaft are one assembly and can only be renewed as such. After removal of the set screw in the body which locates the bearing casing in position the shaft and bearing assembly can be driven out.
9 New parts are fitted in the reverse order. Line up the bearing hole to suit the set screw aperture in the pump body when driving the new bearing/shaft assembly into position. Fit new packing behind the bearing.
10 The impeller should be pressed on to the shaft until there is no more or less than a 1 mm gap between the blades and pump body. If the press fit is not tight enough (interference of .017 — .060 mm/ .0007—.002 ins) then it may work loose.
11 Press the fan pulley hub on similarly.
12 Refit the pump to the cylinder block using a new gasket and a suitable sealing compound such as 'Hermetite Golden'. Reconnect the hoses, refit the fan and pulley hub and replace and adjust the fan belt.

2.5. Removing the cylinder block drain tap

3.3. Removing a radiator securing nut

3.4. Lifting the radiator out

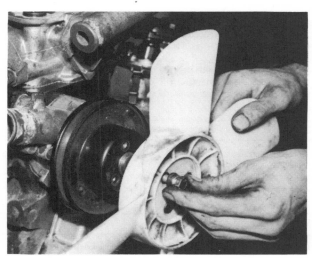

5.3A. Removing the fan

5.3B. Removing the fan pulley

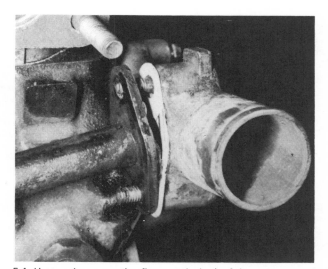

5.4. Heater pipe connecting flange at the back of the water pump. In this photo the manifolds have been removed from the engine. The flange nuts can be removed but the pipe cannot unless the manifolds are off

6. Antifreeze solution

1 Where temperatures are likely to drop below freezing point, the coolant system must be adequately protected by the addition of antifreeze. Even if you keep the engine warm at night it is possible for water to freeze in the radiator with the engine running in very cold conditions - particularly if the engine cooling is being adequately dealt with by the heater. The thermostat stays closed and the radiator water does not circulate.

2 It is best to drain the coolant completely and flush out the system first. Then treat it with a chemical descaling liquid as described earlier. Antifreeze is itself a searching cleaning agent and if it is put into a dirty system it will work as a descaler and require flushing out. It can be used as a cleaner but is more expensive.

3 Most proprietary antifreeze marketed is suitable for aluminium engines but make sure. The amount required in solution varies little between makes and is always marked on the container. As a guide the table gives the quantities needed for various protective levels based on the Fiat 124 system capacity of 7.5 litres/12.8 pints.

%	Quantity	Complete protection
25	1.9 litres/3.2 pints	−11°C
35	2.6 litres/4.5 pints	−19°C
45	3.4 litres/5.8 pints	−29°C

4 Mix the antifreeze with half the total water capacity and pour it in. Top up with clean water and run the engine up to normal working temperature with the heater water valve on.

7. Fan belt - removal, replacement and adjustment

1 If the fan belt is worn, or has stretched unduly, it should be replaced. The most usual reason for replacement is breakage in service and every wise motorist will carry a spare.

2 Even though the belt may have broken and fallen off, go through the removal routine which is first of all to loosen the two generator pivot bolts and the nut on the adjusting link. Then move the generator inwards. Take the old belt off the three pulleys.

3 Put a new belt over the pulleys.

4 The generator must now be used as a tensioner in effect, by pulling it away from the engine and locking it in the required position. This can call for some sustained effort unless the pivot bolts are slackened only a little so that the generator is quite stiff to move. A lever between the generator and block can help, but do not apply any pressure to the rear end shield of an alternator of the cover may break.

5 The tension of the belt midway between the alternator and water pump pulleys should be 10−15 mm/3/8−5/8 inch under thumb pressure (photo). If in doubt it is better to be a little slack than tight. Only slipping will occur if it is too slack. If too tight, damage can be caused by excessive strain on the pulley bearings.

6 When the adjustment is right, tighten all the mounting bolts.

7 With a new belt, check the tension 250 miles after fitting.

8 Periodic checking of the belt tension is necessary and there is no hard and fast rule as to the most suitable interval, because fan belts do not necessarily stretch or wear to a pre-determined schedule. Assuming most owners check their own oil and water regularly, it is suggested as a good habit to check the fan belt tension every time the bonnet goes up. It takes only a second.

8. Water temperature gauge warning light

1 If the red indicator light on the instrument panel comes on at any time overheating is being caused due to loss of coolant or malfunction of the engine or cooling system. Diagnose the fault without delay.

2 To check that the warning circuit is working correctly pull off the lead from the temperature transmitter switch which is screwed into the front of the cylinder head.

3 Switch on the ignition and touch the end of the lead to the cylinder block. The warning lamp should light. If it does not the most likely reason is a faulty sender switch.

9. Fault finding

Fault	Reason/s	Remedy
Loss of coolant	Leak in system	Examine all hoses, connections, drain taps, radiator and heater for leakage when the engine is cold, then when hot and under pressure. Tighten clips, renew hoses and repair radiator as necessary.
Loss of coolant from radiator into expansion bottle	Defective radiator pressure cap Overheating Blown cylinder head gasket causing excess pressure in cooling system forcing coolant past radiator cap into expansion bottle Cracked block or head due to freezing	Examine, renew if necessary. Check reasons for overheating. Remove cylinder head for examination.
Overheating	Insufficient coolant in system Water pump not turning properly due to slack fan belt Kinked or collapsed water hoses causing restriction to circulation of coolant Faulty thermostat (not opening properly) Engine out of tune Blocked radiator either internally or externally Cylinder head gasket blown forcing coolant out of system New engine not run-in	Top up radiator and expansion bottle. Tighten fan belt. Renew hose as required. Fit new thermostat. Check ignition and carburettor settings. Flush out and clean cooling fins. Remove head and renew gasket. Adjust engine speed until run-in.
Engine running too cool	Missing or faulty thermostat	Fit new thermostat.

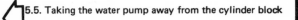
5.5. Taking the water pump away from the cylinder block

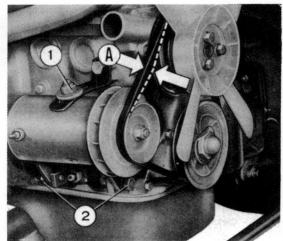

7.5. Fan belt tension adjustment
1. Adjustment clamp nut
2. Generator pivot bolts
A. Belt deflection - 10—15 mm under 10 kgs/22 lbs

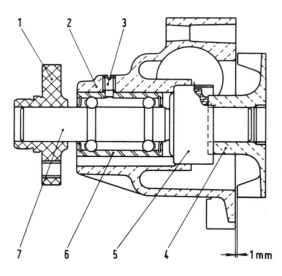

1mm

Fig.2.4. Water pump - longitudinal cross section

1	Fan pulley hub	3	Spindle bearing locating	4	Impeller	6	Bearing cage
2	Pump body		screw	5	Seal gland	7	Shaft

Chapter 3 Fuel system and carburation

Contents

Specifications

Fuel pump

Type...	Mechanical - operated by lever from camshaft eccentric

Carburettors

		124		124S
Make	Weber 32 DCOF	Solex 32 PHH/6		Weber 32 DHS 1
Type...	Fixed double choke side draught			
		(both chokes)	1st choke	2nd choke
Bore	32 mm	32 mm	32 mm	32 mm
Choke	23 mm	23 mm	23 mm	23 mm
Main jet...	1.10 mm	1.15 mm	1.30 mm	1.35 mm
Idle jet	0.45 mm	0.50 mm	0.45 mm	0.80 mm
Start jet	Butterfly valve	1.15 mm	Throttle choke	
Main air metering jet	1.65 mm	1.65 mm	1.70 mm	1.60 mm
Idle air metering jet	1.80 mm	1.80 mm	1.70 mm	0.70 mm
Accelerator pump discharge nozzle	0.40 mm	0.40 mm	0.40	—
Needle valve seat	1.50 mm	1.60 mm	1.75 mm	
Float weight	15 grams	9 grams	11 grams	
Fuel level height (float to cover incl gasket)*	3 mm	special gauge	6 mm	

* See text

Fuel tank - capacity	39 litres/8.6 gallons

1. General description

The system is conventional and consists of a fuel tank mounted in the luggage compartment (boot) at the right hand side. A mechanical fuel pump mounted on the crankcase and driven by an eccentric on the camshaft draws fuel from the tank and delivers it to the float chamber of the carburettor. A fuel filter is incorporated in the fuel pump.

At least four models of carburettor have been developed and fitted over the years and it is not possible for this manual to deal in great depth with all of them. Principally they are either dual throat side draught fixed choke type and dual throat progressive downdraught type. These can have been made by either Solex or Weber. The three types dealt with are those which are most likely to be found on UK import cars. It must be pointed out that later versions have certain pre-settings built-in for purposes of exhaust emission control. These carburettors are calibrated by the manufacturer and only they have the calibrated equipment needed. Although the emission controls are not in force in the UK, at the time of writing, the manufacturers use the same carburettors with the same pre-

settings (but without the full necessary paraphernalia for the control system). As far as the do-it-yourself owner is concerned therefore, we must warn him against tampering because the results could prove very expensive. The adjustments and degree of dismantling indicated are as far as he should ever need to go; and it is most unlikely that these will be necessary often.

Later models with downdraught progressive choke carburettors have a vacuum operated second choke throttle flap. These can easily be identified by the vacuum unit mounted on the side of the carburettor which is linked to the throttle spindle. These should not be tampered with otherwise the whole carburettor can be thrown off balance.

2. Air filter - removal and servicing

1 To change the filter element and clean the interior of the housing it is necessary only to remove the wing nut(s) and cover plate (photo). The old element can be taken out (photos) and the interior wiped out. Element renewal is normally required after 6000 miles, but in dusty or industrially polluted conditions it may be necessary

2.1A. Removing air filter cover on a sidedraught carburettor

2.1B. Removing air filter element from sidedraught carburettor

2.1C. Cover removed from air filter on downdraught carburettor

2.2A. Sidedraught filter housing stiffening plate being removed

2.2B. Downdraught filter housing stiffening plate being removed. Note that the choke flaps are shut

2.3. Undoing additional screw securing downdraught air filter housing

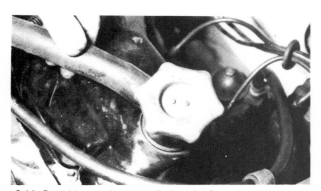

2.4A. Detaching crankcase ventilation pipe from the rocker cover

2.4B. Detaching crankcase ventilation pipe from the carburettor (sidedraught)

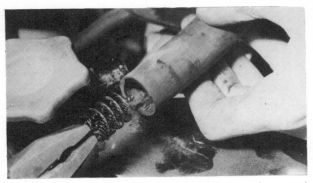

2.4C. Removing an oil separation element from the crankcase ventilation pipe

2.5A. Taking the air cleaner unit away (sidedraught)

2.5B. Lifting the air claner unit away (downdraught)

3.2A. Accelerator cable and mounting bracket

3.2B. Accelerator cable end fixture to bellcrank

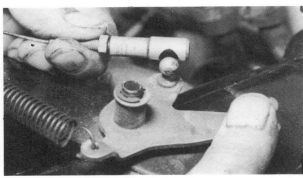

3.2C. Accelerator cable end fixture clip

3.6A. Cold start cable attachment points on Solex sidedraught carburettor

3.6B. Cold start cable attachment (arrowed) Weber 32 DHS downdraught carburettor

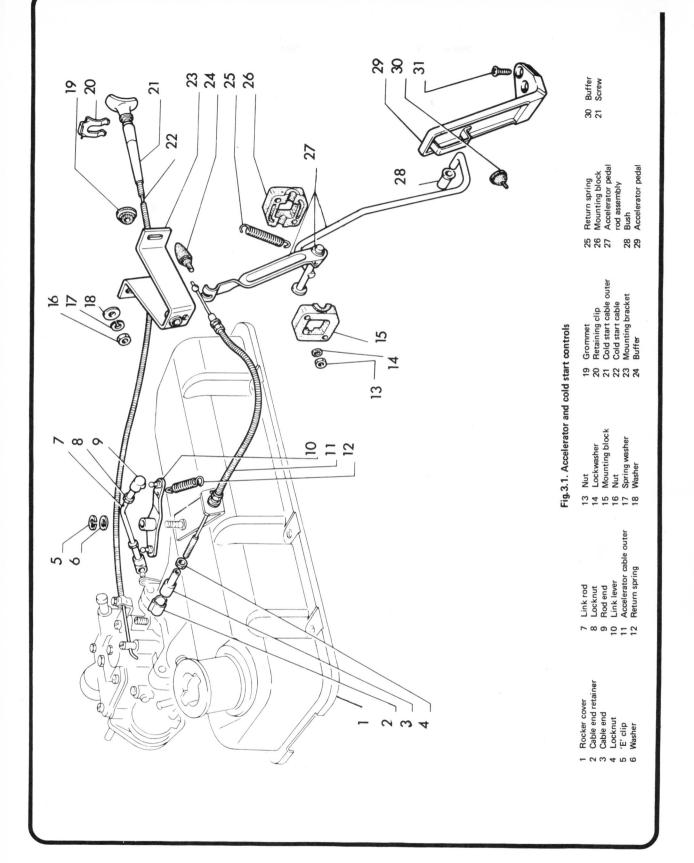

Fig.3.1. Accelerator and cold start controls

1 Rocker cover
2 Cable end retainer
3 Cable end
4 Locknut
5 'E' clip
6 Washer

7 Link rod
8 Locknut
9 Rod end
10 Link lever
11 Accelerator cable outer
12 Return spring

13 Nut
14 Lockwasher
15 Mounting block
16 Nut
17 Spring washer
18 Washer

19 Grommet
20 Retaining clip
21 Cold start cable outer
22 Cold start cable
23 Mounting bracket
24 Buffer

25 Return spring
26 Mounting block
27 Accelerator pedal
   rod assembly
28 Bush
29 Accelerator pedal

30 Buffer
31 Screw

more often. It is important not to run with a choked filter or without one at all. Either of these conditions will upset the mixture balance of the carburettor.

2 The filter housing units may be removed from the carburettor after the element has been taken out. Take off the four securing nuts and lift out the retaining plate and the sealing washer behind it (photos). In the case of downdraught carburettors it is important to prevent anything falling into the carburettor choke tubes so pull out the choke cable to close the flaps as shown.

3 On downdraught carburettors there is an additional bolt securing the filter cover hot air inlet pipe to the engine which must also be removed (photo).

4 The crankcase ventilation system pipes to the rocker cover and carburettor should also be detached (photos). Note that the larger pipe may incorporate an oil separator element (photo). This, together with the pipes should be flushed clean with paraffin prior to re-assembly.

5 The filter element housings may then be lifted off (photos).

3. Accelerator and cold start controls - description and adjustment

1 The accelerator is cable operated from the foot pedal to a lever and link rod mounted on the rocker cover. The cable and link rod are both adjustable and it is important that this adjustment is correct. Normally it would only be necessary to check it when the cable is renewed or the carburettor has been removed.

2 Replacement of the accelerator cable is a straightforward operation. The pedal end hooks into position and the carburettor end is located on a bracket and to a bellcrank mounted on the rocker cover (photos).

3 With the air cleaner removed check that the throttle flaps are fully open when the accelerator pedal is depressed. At the same time adjust the cable so that the accelerator pedal is at the bottom limit of its travel when the throttle is open. In other words the cable and lever must not act as the stop to the pedal travel.

4 When the accelerator pedal is released the throttle flaps must close completely (after the throttle stop screw has been backed off). Adjustment may call for alteration of the link rod setting. Cable lengths may vary.

5 Sticking of the throttle is mostly due to the cable. If it is kinked or curved through too sharp a bend its free movement may be affected. A broken strand can also cause the trouble. In such cases the cable must be renewed.

6 The cold start control is a single wire operating either a disc type cold start device on the Solex or a conventional flap spindle on the Weber (photos). In either case it is essential that the outer cable is clamped so that the cold start spindle or arm movement moves through its full arc and that when the choke control is pushed home the cold start device returns to its normal running position.

4. Solex C32 PHH/6 carburettor - description and adjustment

1 The Solex side draught dual throat carburettor is ostensibly two single choke carburettors made in one unit with a common float chamber. Each throat (or choke) is identical and feeds a pair of cylinders. The throttle flaps are on a common spindle. Each throat of the carburettor has its own set of fuel jets with the exception of the idling jet which feeds both. An auxiliary venturi is placed concentrically within the main venturi.

Regarding each throat as a separate carburettor the principle of operation is as follows: At full throttle opening the depression (low pressure) in the throat draws a fuel/air mixture from the discharge tube.

The fuel/air mixture has been emulsified in the emulsion tube prior to reaching the discharge tube. The fuel has reached the emulsion tube through the main jet from the float chamber. When the engine is cold operation of the 'choke', as it is normally called, (incorrectly in this case because it does not operate a strangler flap

in the throat) opens up a supplementary fuel passage permitting a far larger proportion of fuel to air, to be drawn into the discharge tube.

At idling speed when the throttle flap is closed there is no mixture drawn through the discharge tube, so mixture is drawn through the idler orifice in the side of the throat. This orifice is positioned on the engine side of the throttle flap. Two progression holes bleed air into the idler mixture passage from the other side of the throttle flaps. These progression holes act as mixture feed orifices as the throttle flap opens further and until the main jet takes over.

In addition there is an accelerator pump. When the accelerator is depressed sharply for quick acceleration, this pump delivers more neat fuel immediately to supplement what would otherwise be too weak a fuel mixture at the very start of acceleration. There is also a crankcase ventilation valve details of which are dealt with in Section 10.

2 Adjustments are limited and necessary only to ensure a satisfactory idling speed. The float chamber fuel level is most unlikely to alter and would only normally need checking after fitting a new needle valve or where the carburettor had been dismantled and mishandled. Before making any adjustments on the carburettor see that the accelerator and choke controls are correctly adjusted as described in Section 3.

3 Idling speed is adjusted by both the throttle stop screw and the mixture adjusting screw. With the engine warm and running set the throttle stop screw so that the engine ticks over at a fast idle speed (photo).

4 Then adjust the mixture screw to the position where the engine is running its fastest (photo). Then back off the throttle stop screw and re-adjust the mixture control again and continue doing this until a smooth tickover is obtainable. Do not try and set the tickover too slow. This is an engine which works in the higher revolution ranges and is not designed to tickover very slowly.

The checking and setting of the fuel level in the float chamber involves dismantling and is dealt with in the next section.

5. Solex C32 PHH/6 carburettor - removal and dismantling

1 Remove the air cleaner assembly.

2 Disconnect the throttle linkage by disengaging the link rod from the throttle lever at the carburettor.

3 Remove the four nuts that hold the carburettor to the inlet manifold and remove the heat shield (photo).

4 Carefully draw the assembly off and remove the gaskets and insulator (photos).

5 Dismantling of the carburettor should only be carried out if necessary. If the engine is out of tune make quite sure that the obvious parts of the ignition circuit and the valve clearances are correct first. See that the throttle spindle bushes are not worn. If they are, the carburettor is worn out and no amount of dismantling can cure it unless the casting is re-bushed.

6 Before any dismantling begins it is wise to get a gasket set. If any of them is stuck and consequently damaged during disassembly it must be renewed. It is no good trying to 'bodge' carburettor gaskets.

7 Removal of the top cover screws gives access to the floats, float chamber and needle valve. If the fuel level is suspected of being faulty - particularly on a carburettor which has seen a lot of service the first thing to do is change the needle valve anyway. Unless you have access to the special float and needle valve setting gauges determination of the correct fuel level is impractical. It is best to check that the floats are not punctured. Fit the new needle valve with the same number of washers under it as before and replace the cover.

8 With the small top cover only removed, the two main air metering jets are accessible and the two idler jets. Take care not to let the screwdriver slip if these are removed and use only an air blast for cleaning them.

9 Removal of the bottom cover gives access to the accelerator pump

5.3. Removing Solex carburettor heat shield

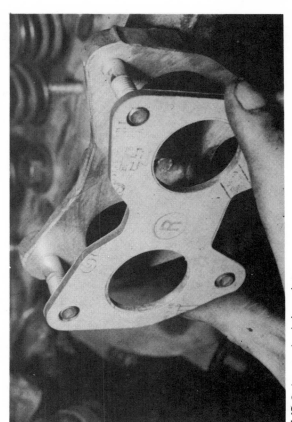

5.4B. Carburettor insulating gasket

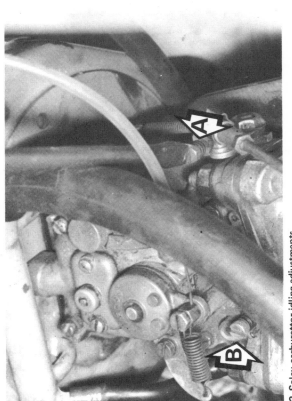

4.3. Solex carburettor idling adjustments
A Throttle stop screw
B Volume control screw

5.4A. Removing Solex carburettor

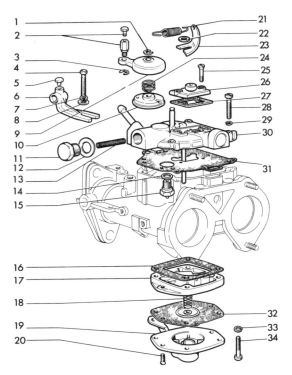

Fig.3.2. Solex C32 PHH/6 carburettor, covers, diaphragms and gaskets

1	'E' clip	10	Cold start disc valve	19	Bottom cover	27	Gasket
2	Cold start cable clamp	11	Plug	20	Cover screw	28	Screw
3	'E' clip	12	Washer	21	Cold start return	29	Spring washer
4	Screw	13	Filter gauze		spring	30	Top cover
5	Clamp screw	14	Washer	22	Washer	31	Gasket
6	Cable outer guide	15	Needle valve	23	Spring stay	32	Accelerator pump
7	Spring washer	16	Gasket	24	Disc spring		diaphragm
8	Washer	17	Bottom plate	25	Jet cover screw	33	Spring washer
9	Cover	18	Spring	26	Jet cover	34	Screw

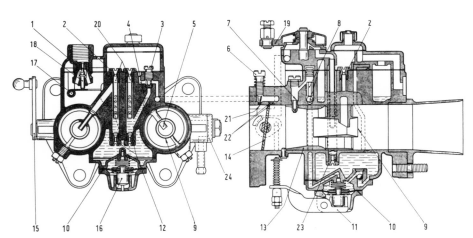

Fig.3.3. Solex C32 PHH/6 carburettor - Lateral and longitudinal sections

1	Needle valve	7	Accelerator pump dis-	13	Primary venturi	21	Idle mixture port
2	Main air correction		charge nozzle	14	Throttle valve	22	Idle transfer ports
	jet	8	Pump delivery valve	15	Throttle control lever	23	Choke jet
3	Idle jet	9	Auxiliary venturi	16	Pump diaphragm pin	24	Recirculation duct of
4	Float	10	Accelerator pump	17	Float pivot pin		crankcase gases
5	Discharge tube		diaphragm	18	Valve needle		
6	Idle mixture volume	11	Pump control lever	19	Choke control lever		
	control screw	12	Main jets	20	Emulsion tubes		

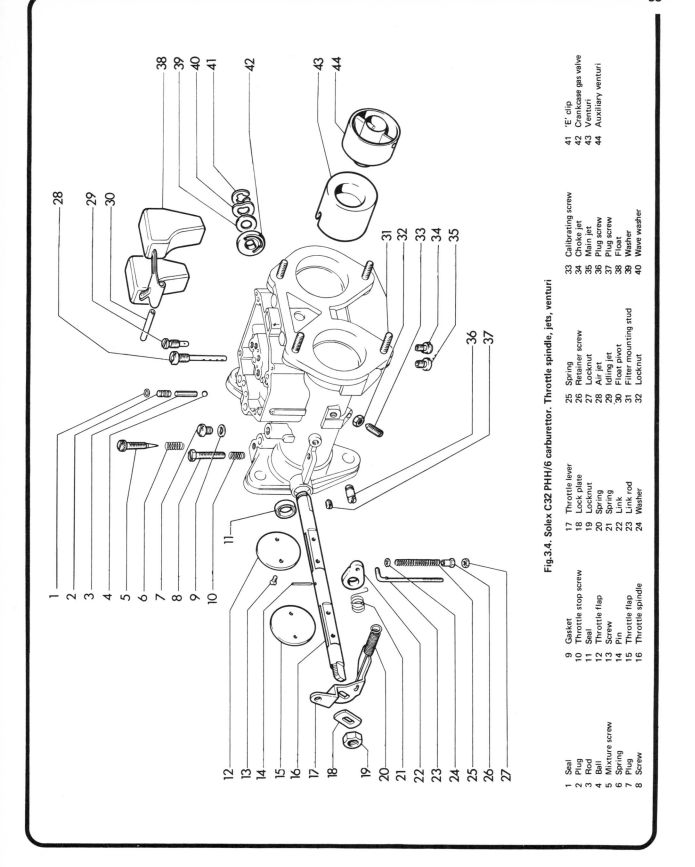

Fig.3.4. Solex C32 PHH/6 carburettor. Throttle spindle, jets, venturi

1	Seal	9	Gasket	17	Throttle lever	25	Spring	33	Calibrating screw	41	'E' clip
2	Plug	10	Throttle stop screw	18	Lock plate	26	Retainer screw	34	Choke jet	42	Crankcase gas valve
3	Rod	11	Seal	19	Locknut	27	Locknut	35	Main jet	43	Venturi
4	Ball	12	Throttle flap	20	Spring	28	Air jet	36	Plug screw	44	Auxiliary venturi
5	Mixture screw	13	Screw	21	Spring	29	Idling jet	37	Plug screw		
6	Spring	14	Pin	22	Link	30	Float pivot	38	Float		
7	Plug	15	Throttle flap	23	Link rod	31	Filter mounting stud	39	Washer		
8	Screw	16	Throttle spindle	24	Washer	32	Locknut	40	Wave washer		

and diaphragm under these is the single common starting jet and the two main fuel jets.

10 Any further dismantling of the carburettor is not recommended.

6. Weber 32 DCOF carburettor - description and adjustment

The dual throat Weber carburettor is similar in most respects to the Solex and the principle of operation is the same. The main obvious difference is that all the jets are accessible from under the top cover and the floats, instead of pivoting inside the main body, are hinged on to the top cover.

The other difference is in the cold start. A conventional flap is used in the choke tube operated by a lever. Adjustments are few. The fuel level is set by the floats which involves some dismantling and is mentioned in the next section.

The choke flap and throttle flap are inter-linked to provide easy cold starting. When the choke is operated the throttle is opened the required amount depending on the degree of choke setting. Independent adjustment between throttle and choke is necessary and there is no provision for any. It is important that when the choke cable is pushed fully home that the flap takes up a position parallel with the axis of the choke tube.

Slow running adjustment is accomplished by adjustment of the throttle stop screws and mixture control screws as on the Solex carburettor.

7. Weber 32 DCOF carburettor - removal and dismantling

1 Removal of the carburettor is the same as for the Solex although one should bear in mind that it is not necessary to take the carburettor from the engine in order to remove the top cover. Once again it must be emphasised that dismantling is to be discouraged as the settings are very easily upset. A set of new gaskets should be obtained.

2 Access to the jets and float chamber is by removal of the top cover after taking out the four securing screws. The float level can be checked readily without any special gauges. With the needle valve closed the top of the float should be 3 mm from the under side of the cover with the gasket fitted. It is important to ensure that the arm of the float only touches the end of the needle valve lightly otherwise the clamping device with the ball end could be depressed inadvertently. The float pivot return hook should restrict movement in the other direction so that the top of the float is 11.5 mm from the under side of the cover. If any adjustment by bending is necessary great care is needed to ensure equal alteration of both float halves. Check also that the arm still operates the needle valve smoothly and the floats do not bind against the sides of the float chamber.

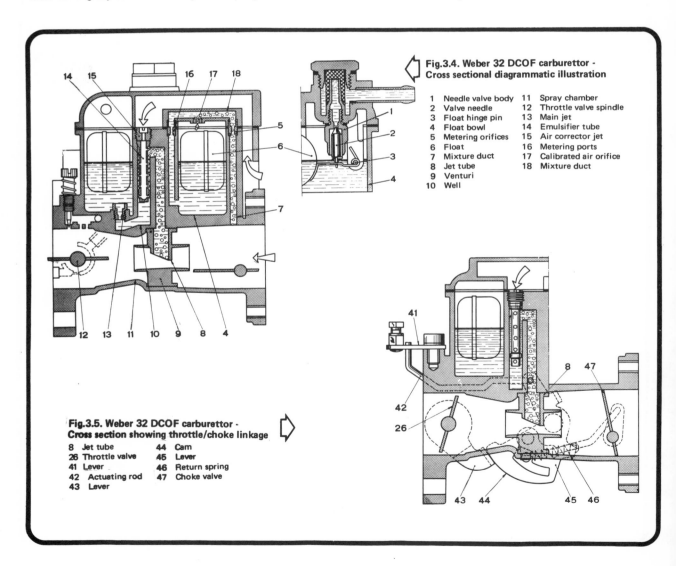

Fig.3.4. Weber 32 DCOF carburettor - Cross sectional diagrammatic illustration

1	Needle valve body	11	Spray chamber
2	Valve needle	12	Throttle valve spindle
3	Float hinge pin	13	Main jet
4	Float bowl	14	Emulsifier tube
5	Metering orifices	15	Air corrector jet
6	Float	16	Metering ports
7	Mixture duct	17	Calibrated air orifice
8	Jet tube	18	Mixture duct
9	Venturi		
10	Well		

Fig.3.5. Weber 32 DCOF carburettor - Cross section showing throttle/choke linkage

8	Jet tube	44	Cam
26	Throttle valve	45	Lever
41	Lever	46	Return spring
42	Actuating rod	47	Choke valve
43	Lever		

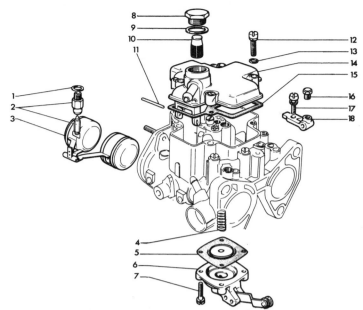

Fig.3.6. Weber 32 DCOF carburettor. Covers and gaskets

1	Washer	6	Cover	11	Pivot pin	16	Clamp screw
2	Needle valve	7	Screw	12	Screw	17	Screw
3	Float	8	Plug	13	Washer	18	Cable bracket
4	Spring	9	Gasket	14	Top cover		
5	Diaphragm-accelerator pump	10	Filter	15	Gasket		

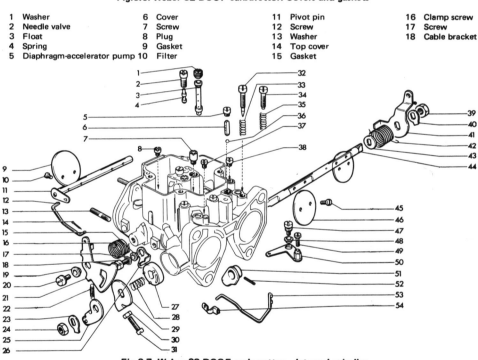

Fig.3.7. Weber 32 DCOF carburettor - Jets and spindles

1	Air jet	15	Bush	29	Lever	43	Washer
2	Jet holder	16	Spring	30	Locknut	44	Throttle spindle
3	Emulsion tube	17	Washer	31	Screw	45	Screw
4	Idling jet	18	Screw	32	Mixture screw	46	Throttle flap
5	Screw	19	Bush	33	Spring	47	Screw
6	Rod	20	Screw	34	Stop screw	48	Bush
7	Valve	21	Intermediate lever	35	Spring	49	Clamp screw
8	Main jet	22	Spring	36	Ball	50	Choke bellcrank
9	Choke flap	23	Lock washer	37	Screw	51	Cam
10	Screw	24	Locknut	38	Screw	52	Roll pin
11	Choke spindle	25	Lever	39	Locknut	53	Link rod
12	Link rod	26	Lever	40	Lock washer	54	Clip
13	Filter mounting stud	27	Crankcase gas valve	41	Throttle lever		
14	Split pin	28	Spring	42	Spring		

8. Weber 32 DHS 1 carburettor - description and adjustment

1 The double choke downdraught carburettor is quite different from the dual throat sidedraught types. Whereas the former is effectively two carburettors in one casting - each throat supplying a pair of cylinders, the double choke downdraught has two throats but each supplies all four cylinders. The second choke 'comes in' when the engine demands, and consequently the depression in the venturi of the primary choke call for it. The pressure differential is amplified by a finely balanced valve which operates the secondary throttle valve. A mechanical link prevents the secondary throttle from opening until the primary is almost fully open.

2 It will be appreciated that such a carburettor only gives of its best when the rest of the engine - compression pressures and ignition timing particularly - is as it should be. Attempts to rectify basic engine mixture by messing about with this type of carburettor are doomed to failure.

3 Cold starting rich mixtures are obtained by butterfly choke valves.

4 The only adjustment for slow running is by the two volume control screws. On all but the earliest models the throttle stop screw is set and locked for reasons explained in the General description section at the beginning of the Chapter. This throttle stop screw must not be disturbed (photo).

9. Weber 32 DHS 1 carburettor - removal and dismantling

1 Dismantling must be limited to removal of the top cover for float/fuel level checking.

2 Remove the air filter cover and element and remove the four nuts securing the filter housing, not forgetting to disconnect the emission pipes.

3 Disconnect the fuel pipe and choke spindle linkage. After removing the securing screws the top cover may be lifted off.

4 The procedure for setting the floats is the same as is described for the 32 DCOF model in Section 7, but notice that instead of clearances of 4 mm and 11.5 mm they are 6 mm and 14 mm respectively.

5 To remove the carburettor completely from the manifold disconnect the throttle linkage also and undo the four mounting stud nuts.

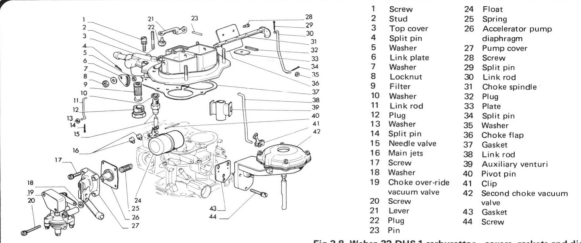

1	Screw	24	Float
2	Stud	25	Spring
3	Top cover	26	Accelerator pump
4	Split pin		diaphragm
5	Washer	27	Pump cover
6	Link plate	28	Screw
7	Washer	29	Split pin
8	Locknut	30	Link rod
9	Filter	31	Choke spindle
10	Washer	32	Plug
11	Link rod	33	Plate
12	Plug	34	Split pin
13	Washer	35	Washer
14	Split pin	36	Choke flap
15	Needle valve	37	Gasket
16	Main jets	38	Link rod
17	Screw	39	Auxiliary venturi
18	Washer	40	Pivot pin
19	Choke over-ride	41	Clip
	vacuum valve	42	Second choke vacuum
20	Screw		valve
21	Lever	43	Gasket
22	Plug	44	Screw
23	Pin		

Fig.3.8. Weber 32 DHS 1 carburettor - covers, gaskets and diaphragms

Fig.3.9. Weber 32 DHS 1 carburettor
A Vacuum control and link for over-riding the manual choke flap control when in closed position
B Throttle stop screw which should not be touched

Fig.3.10. Weber 32 DHS 1 carburettor
A Vacuum control and link for secondary throttle
B Operating arm for manual choke flap control

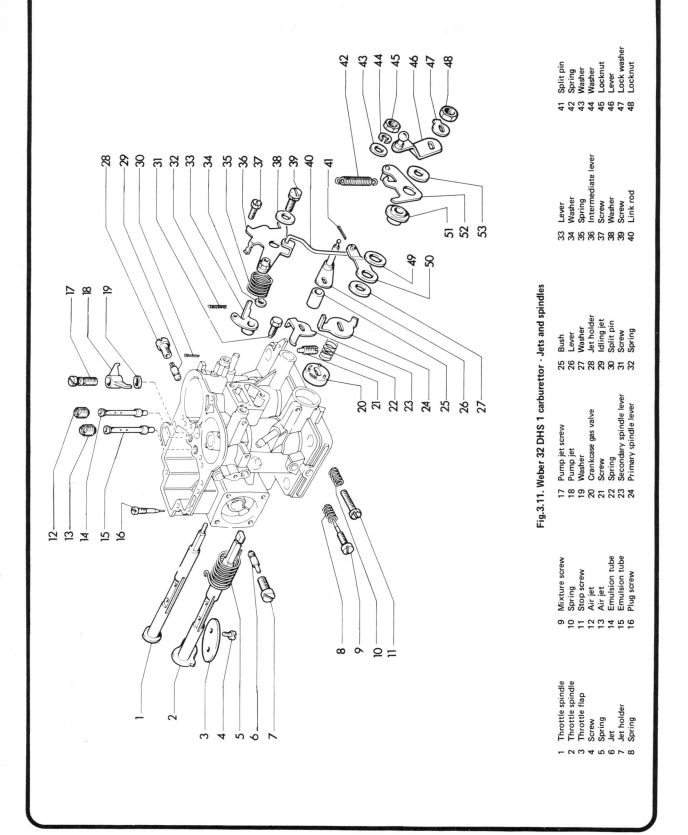

Fig.3.11. Weber 32 DHS 1 carburettor - Jets and spindles

1	Throttle spindle	9	Mixture screw	17	Pump jet screw	25	Bush	33	Lever	41	Split pin
2	Throttle spindle	10	Spring	18	Pump jet	26	Lever	34	Washer	42	Spring
3	Throttle flap	11	Stop screw	19	Washer	27	Washer	35	Spring	43	Washer
4	Screw	12	Air jet	20	Crankcase gas valve	28	Jet holder	36	Intermediate lever	44	Washer
5	Spring	13	Air jet	21	Screw	29	Idling jet	37	Screw	45	Locknut
6	Jet	14	Emulsion tube	22	Spring	30	Split pin	38	Washer	46	Lever
7	Jet holder	15	Emulsion tube	23	Secondary spindle lever	31	Screw	39	Screw	47	Lock washer
8	Spring	16	Plug screw	24	Primary spindle lever	32	Spring	40	Link rod	48	Locknut

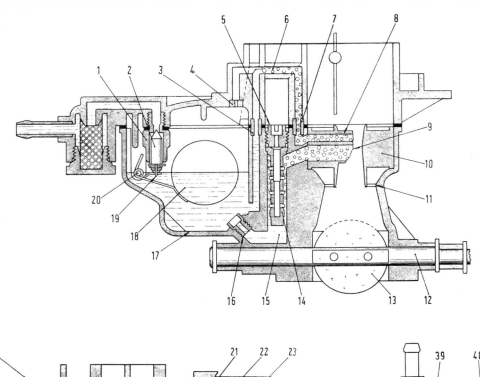

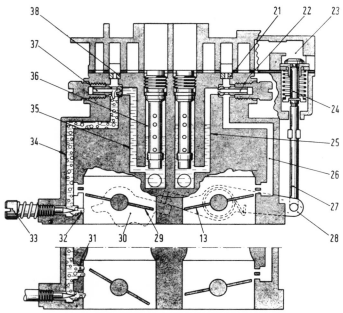

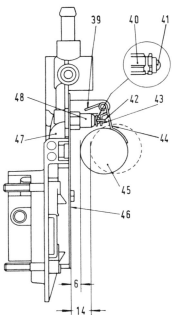

Fig.3.12. Weber 32 DHS 1 carburettor - Cross sections and diagram of float setting

1	Needle valve	13	Secondary throttle	25	Fuel passage duct	37	Idle jet
2	Needle	14	Emulsion tube	26	Mixture passage duct	38	Calibrated bushing
3	Calibrated bushing	15	Main well	27	Link	39	Lug
4	Calibrated vent	16	Main jet	28	Lever	40	Needle
5	Air correction jet	17	Bowl	29	Primary throttle	41	Movable ball
6	Mixture passage	18	Float	30	Lever	42	Needle return hook
7	Calibrated bushing	19	Needle return hook	31	Progression orifices	43	Tang
8	Mixture passage	20	Float pivot pin	32	Idle port	44	Float arm
9	Discharge nozzle	21	Calibrated bushing	33	Idle mixture adjusting screw	45	Float
10	Auxiliary venturi	22	Idle jet	34	Mixture passage duct	46	Gasket
11	Primary venturi	23	Vapors vent	35	Fuel passage duct	47	Cover
12	Throttle shaft	24	Vapors vent valve	36	Emulsion well	48	Needle valve

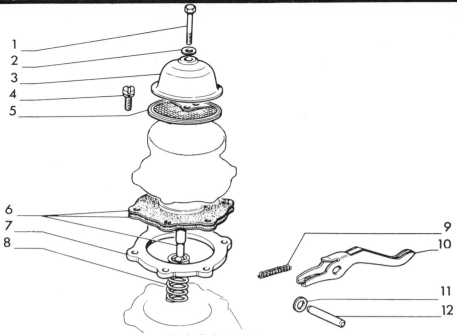

Fig.3.13. Fuel pump

1	Cover retaining screw	4	Body screw	7	Plate	10	Operating lever
2	Gasket	5	Filter	8	Spring	11	Washer
3	Cover	6	Diaphragm	9	Spring	12	Pivot pin

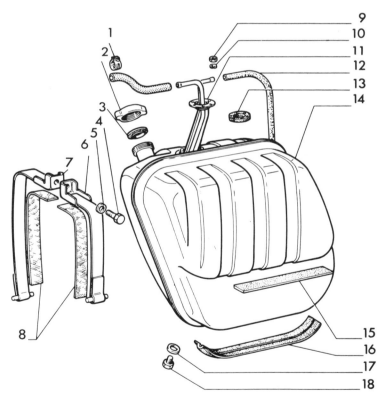

Fig.3.14. Fuel tank and fittings (Saloon)

1	Outlet pipe clip	6	Short strap	11	Outlet and vent pipe	15	Padding strip
2	Filler cap	7	Long strap		assembly	16	Insulation strip
3	Washer	8	Insulation	12	Vent pipe extension	17	Washer
4	Strap bolt	9	Nut	13	Gasket	18	Drain plug
5	Washer	10	Spring washer	14	Tank		

10. Closed circuit crankcase ventilation system and valves

1 All models are fitted with a positive crankcase ventilation/circulation system which feeds unburnt fuel and oil vapours back through the combustion chambers thereby reducing pollution into atmosphere.

2 From the oil filler cap neck on the rocker cover a pipe runs to a small manifold on the back of the air cleaner. From this three branch pipes emerge, one to each of the carburettor chokes inside the air filter and the third to a valve on the end of the carburettor throttle spindle. At idling speeds when the throttles are shut all the gases are vented into the air cleaner and intake venturis of the carburettor. As the throttle valve opens so the disc valve on the end of the spindle opens a progressively increasing aperture direct into the inlet manifold and as engine speed increases so the majority of the gases pass by this route.

3 With time the pipes and valve get gummy deposits in them and it is a good policy to clean them out each time the air filter element is changed. Flush out the pipes with petrol.

4 The valve disc is particularly susceptible to gummy deposits which could affect slow running. It is easily taken out for cleaning after removing the circlip and washers from the end of the spindle. Make sure it is put back the right way round (see Fig.3.16).

11. Fuel pump - removal, repair and replacement

1 Disconnect the two fuel lines from the pump (photo) and remove the two nuts holding the pump to the crankcase when it can be removed. Note what spacers and gaskets are fitted because these must be replaced in the same way between the pump and crankcase.

2 The pump cover (which can be removed with the pump in situ if wished) is held by a hexagon headed screw. Remove the screw and cover and lift out the filter screen with care, noting its position in relation to the pump orifices.

3 Mark the relative positions of the upper and lower halves of the pump and take out the six securing screws. Separate the two halves and examine the diaphragm for signs of holes, cracking or brittleness. To renew the diaphragm the operating lever pivot pin should be driven out and the lever withdrawn so that the diaphragm rod is disengaged from the lever.

4 Reassembly is a reversal of the dismantling procedure. Make sure that new gaskets are used and when reassembling the two halves of the pump hold the operating lever so that the diaphragm will be held flat whilst the retaining screws are tightened. When fitting the top cover use a new washer and do not overtighten the securing screw.

5 The pump should be refitted with new gaskets each side of the spacer onto the crankcase face.

6 Care should be taken to put it in position so that the lever does not get jammed on the wrong side of the camshaft.

7 After refitting the pump run the engine to make sure it is not leaking anywhere.

12. Fuel tank - removal and replacement

1 Disconnect the battery.

2 Drain the fuel by undoing the plug.

3 Remove the strap clamping screw.

4 Take off the strap and remove the guard plate above the tank.

5 Disconnect the fuel pipe and breather pipe.

6 Disconnect the earth wire and fuel gauge wire and lift the tank out, working the filler neck out of the rubber sealing grommet.

7 If the tank is suspected of leaking it may be soldered but no naked flame must be used in the process. If the tank is persistently contaminating the fuel because of deterioration of the interior flush it out as best as possible with fuel and give consideration to fitting a line filter in the flexible pipe just before the petrol pump. It is much

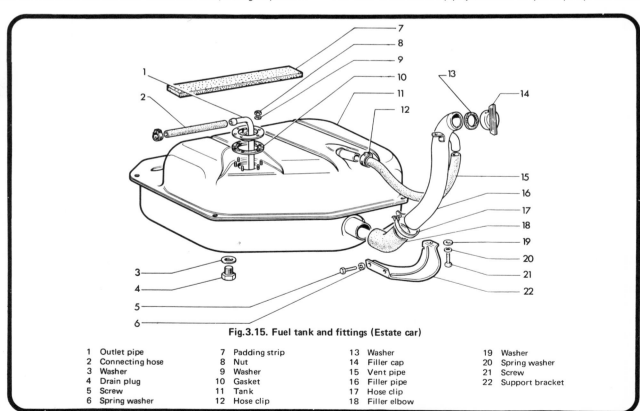

Fig.3.15. Fuel tank and fittings (Estate car)

1	Outlet pipe	7	Padding strip	13	Washer	19	Washer
2	Connecting hose	8	Nut	14	Filler cap	20	Spring washer
3	Washer	9	Washer	15	Vent pipe	21	Screw
4	Drain plug	10	Gasket	16	Filler pipe	22	Support bracket
5	Screw	11	Tank	17	Hose clip		
6	Spring washer	12	Hose clip	18	Filler elbow		

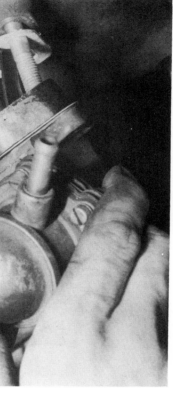

11.1. Fuel pump with outlet pipe disconnected

11.6. Fitting fuel pump with a new gasket each side of the spacer block

POSITION A

Fig.3.16. Closed circuit crankcase ventilation valve - cross section of throttle spindle and valve

A Starting position
B Running position
12 Throttle spindle
19 Gases inlet
20 Rotary valve
21 Valve slot
22 Metering orifice

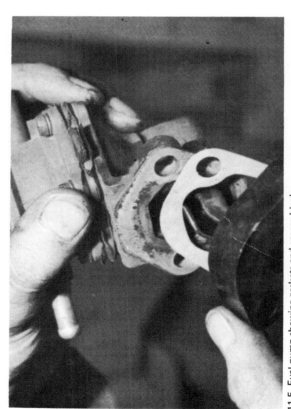

11.5. Fuel pump showing gaskets and spacer block

cheaper than a new tank and is easily fitted and readily available from accessory shops.

8 Estate car tanks are fitted flat at the rear floor and are secured by screws to the floor panel.

9 Replacement is a reversal of the removal procedure.

13. Fuel gauge tank unit - checking and removal

1 The tank unit is the most likely cause of failure of either the gauge or reserve indicator light.

2 To check the unit first remove the top tank guard plate and pull off each of the two leads, red and red/grey in turn and touch each in turn to earth with the ignition switched on. If there is a reaction from one or the other at the gauge or light then it means that that part of the sender unit is inoperative.

3 If there is still no reaction when the wires are earthed then the fault lies in the electrical system between the sender unit and gauge/indicator bulb - or with either of these two items themselves. Information about access to these is given in Chapter 10.

4 To remove the sender unit take off the leads and fuel pipe connections, undo the fixing nuts and lift it out from the tank.

14. Exhaust system - repairs and renewals

1 The exhaust system is in three sections. The front section consists of a twin outlet pipe from the exhaust manifold which converges into one. It is supported on a bracket at the rear end just before it joins the middle section. The middle section includes an expansion box at the rear end near where the pipe joins the tail section. This joint is just in front of the rear axle where the pipe rises to go over it. The middle section has no support points along its length. The rear section consists of the silencer and tail pipe. This is supported by a rubber sling at the front end of the silencer and a flexible mounting on the tail pipe.

2 It is important for any exhaust system to see that the support hangers are in good condition. If any one is broken it should be renewed immediately otherwise the unsupported weight of the system will strain and fracture the pipe and the other hangers.

3 If a new section is to be fitted the whole system should be removed unless it is easy to separate the parts in situ. Otherwise it is easy to damage or strain another section whilst struggling to get one off.

4 Assemble the system together loosely before replacing it on the car. Always fit new clamps.

5 Arrange the pipes to follow the lines of the body and tighten the manifold flange, with a new gasket, before anything else. Then fit and tighten the three hangers and finally tighten the two pipe joining clamps - Do not overtighten the pipe clamps or the tube will distort and weaken.

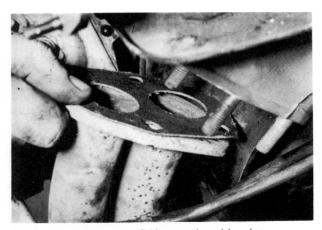

14.5A. Exhaust pipe to manifold connection with gasket

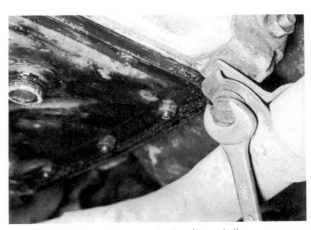

14.5B. Front exhaust pipe mounting bracket and clip

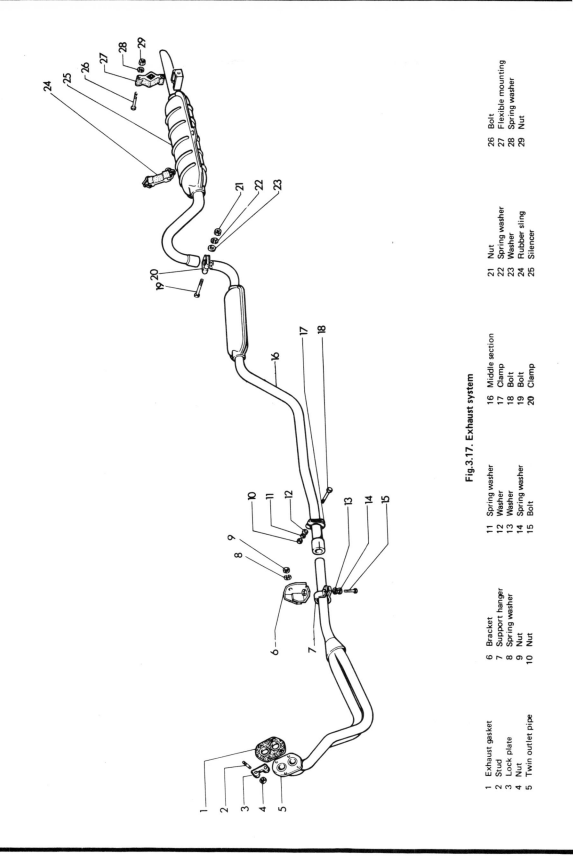

Fig.3.17. Exhaust system

1	Exhaust gasket	6	Bracket	11	Spring washer	16	Middle section	21	Nut	26	Bolt
2	Stud	7	Support hanger	12	Washer	17	Clamp	22	Spring washer	27	Flexible mounting
3	Lock plate	8	Spring washer	13	Washer	18	Bolt	23	Washer	28	Spring washer
4	Nut	9	Nut	14	Spring washer	19	Bolt	24	Rubber sling	29	Nut
5	Twin outlet pipe	10	Nut	15	Bolt	20	Clamp	25	Silencer		

Chapter 4 Ignition system

Contents

Specifications

Spark plugs...	Marelli CW 240 L
	Champion N4
(NB Marelli CW 240 LP and Champion N9Y may be fitted on some models)	
Electrode gap	0.6 — 0.7 mm/0.024 — 0.028 inch
	(0.5 — 0.6 mm/0.020 — 0.023 inch on 240 LP and N9Y plugs)
Coil	Marelli BE 200 B
	Bosch TK 12A 17
Primary winding resistance at 20°C	3.1 — 3.6 ohms
Secondary winding resistance at 20°C..	5500 — 7000 (Marelli)
	6500 — 8900 (Bosch)
Distributor - Marelli	
Firing order...	1 3 4 2
Rotation..	Clockwise
Contact points gap	0.42 — 0.48 mm/.016 — .019 inch
Contact spring pressure	550 grams/19.5 ozs
Ignition timing	
Static advance	10°
Centrifugal advance	Begins 1000 engine rpm
	10° @ 2250 engine rpm
	20° (max) @ 3550 rpm

1. General description

In order that the engine can run correctly it is necessary for an electrical spark to ignite the fuel/air mixture in the combustion chamber at exactly the right moment in relation to engine speed and load. The ignition system is based on feeding low tension voltage from the battery to the coil where it is converted to high tension voltage. The high tension voltage is powerful enough to jump the spark plug gap in the cylinders many times a second under high compression pressures, providing that the system is in good condition and that all adjustments are correct.

The ignition system is divided into two circuits, the low tension circuit and the high tension circuit.

The low tension (sometimes known as the primary) circuit consists of the battery, lead to the control box, lead to the ignition switch, lead from the ignition switch to the low tension or primary coil windings, and the lead from the low tension coil windings to the contact breaker points and condenser in the distributor.

The high tension circuit consists of the high tension or secondary coil windings, the heavy ignition lead from the centre of the coil to the centre of the distributor cap, the rotor arm, and the spark plug leads and spark plugs.

The system functions in the following manner: High tension voltage is generated in the coil by the interruption of the low tension circuit. The interruption is effected by the opening of the contact breaker points in this low tension circuit. High tension voltage is fed via the carbon brush in the centre of the distributor cap to the rotor arm of the distributor.

The rotor arm revolves anticlockwise at half engine speed inside the distributor cap, and each time it comes in line with one of the four metal segments in the cap, which are connected to the spark plug leads, the opening and closing of the contact breaker points causes the high tension voltage to build up, jump the gap from the rotor arm to the appropriate metal segment, and so via the spark plug lead to the spark plug, where it finally jumps the spark plug gap before going to earth.

The ignition is advanced and retarded automatically, to ensure the spark occurs at just the right instant for the particular load at the prevailing engine speed.

The ignition advance is controlled mechanically. The mechanical governor mechanism comprises two weights, which move out from

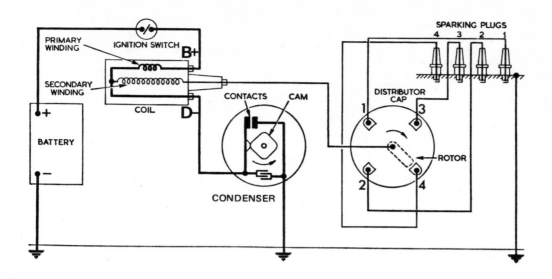

Ignition system - Schematic layout

the distributor shaft as the engine speed rises, due to centrifugal force. As they move outwards they rotate the cam relative to the distributor shaft, and so advance the spark. The weights are held in position by two springs and it is the tension of the springs which is largely responsible for correct spark advancement.

2. Contact breaker points - adjustment

1 To adjust the contact breaker points to the correct gap, first pull off the two clips securing the distributor cap to the distributor body, and lift away the cap (photo). Clean the cap inside and out with a dry cloth. It is unlikely that the four segments will be badly burned or scored, but if they are, the cap will have to be renewed.

2 Check the carbon brush located in the top of the cap to make sure that it is not broken or missing.

3 Gently prise the contact breaker points open to examine the condition of their faces. If they are rough, pitted or dirty, it will be necessary to remove them for resurfacing, or for replacement points to be fitted.

4 Presuming the points are satisfactory, or that they have been cleaned and replaced, measure the gap between the points by turning the engine over until the contact breaker arm is on the peak of one of the four cam lobes.

5 A feeler gauge of thickness 0.42—0.48 mm/.016—.019 inches should fit between the points whilst lightly touching each face.

6 If the gap varies from this amount, slacken the contact securing screw (photo).

7 Adjust the contact gap by inserting a screwdriver in the nick in the side of the fixed plate and lever it in the required direction.

8 Replace the distributor cap and clip it into place.

2.1. Removing the distributor cap

2.6. Slackening the contact points screw. Note the feeler gauge blade inserted (arrow)

3. Contact breaker points - removal and replacement

1 Remove the distributor cap.
2 Remove the two screws securing the contact points assembly to the distributor and slacken the insulated terminal in the side of the body sufficiently to release the LT lead.
3 Lift the complete contact set assembly off the pivot pin of the mounting plate.
4 If the condition of the points is not too bad, they can be reconditioned by rubbing the contacts clean with fine emery cloth or a fine carborundum stone. It is important that the faces are rubbed flat and parallel to each other so that there will be complete face to face contact when the points are closed. One of the points will be pitted and the other will have deposits on it.
5 It is necessary to completely remove the built up deposits, but not necessary to rub the pitted point right down to the stage where all the pitting has disappeared, though obviously if this is done it will prolong the time before the operation of refacing the points has to be repeated.
6 Wipe the points clean and dry and refit the assembly with the two screws. Reconnect the LT lead to the terminal.
7 Adjust the points gap as described in the previous section.

4. Condenser - removal, testing and replacement

1 The purpose of the condenser (sometimes known as capacitor) is to ensure that when the contact breaker points open there is no sparking across them which would waste voltage and cause rapid deterioration of the points.
2 The condenser is fitted in parallel with the contact breaker points. If it develops a short circuit, it will cause ignition failure as the points will be prevented from interrupting the low tension circuit.
3 If the engine becomes very difficult to start or begins to misfire whilst running and the breaker points show signs of excessive burning, then the condition of the condenser must be suspect. A further test can be made by separating the points by hand with the ignition switched on. If this is accompanied by a bright spark at the contact points it is indicative that the condenser has failed.
4 Without special test equipment the only sure way to diagnose condenser trouble is to replace a suspected unit with a new one and note if there is any improvement.
5 To remove the condenser from the distributor, take out the screw which secures it to the underside of the distributor body and slacken the insulated terminal nut enough to remove the wire connection tag.
6 When fitting the condenser it is vital to ensure that the fixing screw is secure and the condenser tightly held. The lead must be secure on the terminal with no chance of short circuiting.

5. Distributor - removal and replacement

1 Unless particular care is taken the ignition timing will be disturbed when removing the distributor. If this is to be prevented first remove the cap and turn the engine so that the rotor points towards an accurate reference point. Then mark the bottom flange of the distributor body and the adjacent block with punch marks so they may be realigned.
2 Undo the clamp securing nut and take away the clamp (photo).
3 Lift the distributor straight out (photo).
4 Provided the engine is not turned the distributor may be replaced with the rotor and marks aligned and no further adjustment is needed. Otherwise the ignition timing must be re-set as described in Section 7. When replacing the distributor do not forget the oil sealing ring (photo).

6. Distributor - inspection and overhaul

1 Apart from the contact points the other parts of a distributor which deteriorate with age and use, are the cap, the rotor, the shaft bushes, and the bob weight springs.
2 The cap must have no flaws or cracks and the 4 HT terminal contacts should not be severely corroded. The centre spring loaded carbon contact is replaceable. If in any doubt about the cap buy a new one.
3 The rotor deteriorates minimally but with age the metal conductor tip may corrode. It should not be cracked or chipped and the metal conductor must not be loose. If in doubt renew it. Always fit a new rotor if fitting a new cap.
4 The rotor is held in position by two screws and when removed the centrifugal advance mechanism is exposed (photo). There is no way to test the bob weight springs other than by checking the performance of the distributor on special test equipment, so if in doubt fit new springs anyway. If the springs are loose where they loop over the posts it is more than possible that the post grooves are worn in which case the various parts which include the shaft will need renewal. Wear to this extent would mean that a new distributor is probably the best solution in the long run. Be sure to make an exact note of both the engine number and any serial number on the distributor when ordering. When refitting the rotor note that there are two positioning lugs and recesses, one round, one square - to make sure it is replaced the proper way round.
5 If the main shaft is slack in its bushes allowing even the slightest sideways play it means that the contact points gap setting can only be a compromise because the cam position relative to the cam follower on the moving point arm is not constant. If the top of the shaft can move three thou sideways it means the points gap can vary by about the same amount. It is not practical to re-bush the distributor body unless you have a friend who can bore and bush it for you. The shaft can be removed by driving out the roll pin from the retaining collar at the bottom. (The collar also acts as an oil slinger to prevent excess engine oil creeping up the shaft).

7. Ignition timing

1 Where the relative positions of the distributor and pistons has been disturbed it is necessary to retime the static ignition setting. If the distributor has not actually been removed from the engine but only turned after slackening the clamp it is only necessary to set the points opening position as described in the later stages of the procedure hereafter described.
2 Turn the engine so that No.1 (the front) piston is at top dead centre on the compression (not the exhaust) stroke.
3 If the rocker cover is removed this can be done by noting when both valves on No.1 are closed when the mark on the inside edge of the flywheel pulley lines up with the right hand mark of the three lugs cast into the timing chain cover. Another way to get the compression stroke is to remove No.1 spark plug and feel the compression from the hole.
4 The static advance position is 10° BTDC so as the angle difference between the three timing marks on the cover is 5° the crankshaft should be turned back so that the pulley mark lines up with the left hand lug (photo).
5 The distributor contact points gap should be set before installation (it is easier for one thing), and the shaft turned so that the rotor tip points to where the No.1 terminal inside the cap would be if the cap were in position. The cap is marked on the outside with each cylinder number.
6 Without moving the shaft relative to the distributor body, replace the distributor in the crankcase. This should be done so that the contact points assembly is on the side away from the engine. Push the distributor right home so that the splines on the shaft engage with those in the drive pinion gear inside. Take care not to trap the cap clips where they cannot be lifted up.

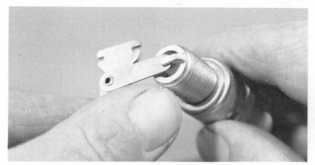

Measuring plug gap. A feeler gauge of the correct size (see ignition system specifications) should have a slight 'drag' when slid between the electrodes. Adjust gap if necessary

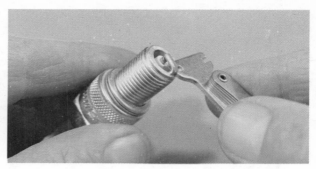

Adjusting plug gap. The plug gap is adjusted by bending the earth electrode inwards, or outwards, as necessary until the correct clearance is obtained. Note the use of the correct tool

Normal. Grey-brown deposits lightly coated core nose. Gap increasing by around 0.001 in (0.025 mm) per 1000 miles (1600 km). Plugs ideally suited to engine and engine in good condition

Carbon fouling. Dry, black, sooty deposits. Will cause weak spark and eventually misfire. Fault: over-rich fuel mixture. Check: carburettor mixture settings, float level and jet sizes; choke operation and cleanliness of air filter. Plugs can be re-used after cleaning

Oil fouling. Wet, oily deposits. Will cause weak spark and eventually misfire. Fault: worn bores/piston rings or valve guides; sometimes occurs (temporarily) during running-in period. Plugs can be re-used after thorough cleaning

Overheating. Electrodes have glazed appearance, core nose very white - few deposits. Fault: plug overheating. Check: plug value, ignition timing, fuel octane rating (too low) and fuel mixture (too weak). Discard plugs and cure fault immediately

Electrode damage. Electrodes burned away; core nose has burned, glazed appearance. Fault: initial pre-ignition. Check: as for 'Overheating' but may be more severe. Discard plugs and remedy fault before piston or valve damage occurs

Split core nose (may appear initially as a crack). Damage is self-evident, but cracks will only show after cleaning. Fault: pre-ignition or wrong gap-setting technique. Check: ignition timing, cooling system, fuel octane rating (too low) and fuel mixture (too weak). Discard plugs, rectify fault immediately

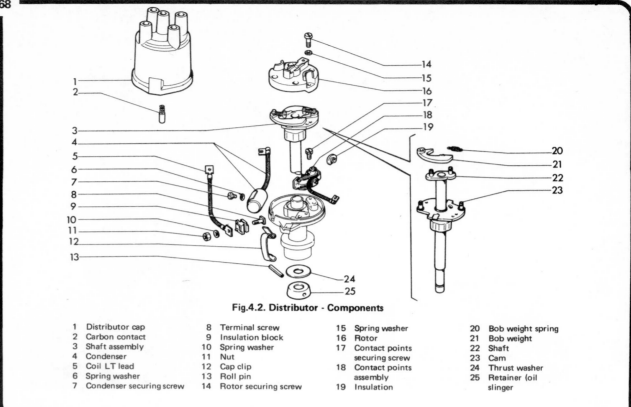

Fig.4.2. Distributor - Components

1	Distributor cap	8	Terminal screw	15	Spring washer
2	Carbon contact	9	Insulation block	16	Rotor
3	Shaft assembly	10	Spring washer	17	Contact points securing screw
4	Condenser	11	Nut	18	Contact points assembly
5	Coil LT lead	12	Cap clip	19	Insulation
6	Spring washer	13	Roll pin		
7	Condenser securing screw	14	Rotor securing screw		

20	Bob weight spring
21	Bob weight
22	Shaft
23	Cam
24	Thrust washer
25	Retainer (oil slinger)

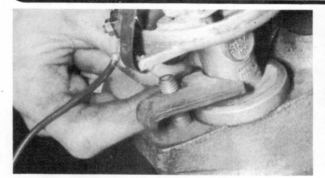

5.2. Removing distributor clamp plate

5.3. Lifting the distributor out of the crankcase

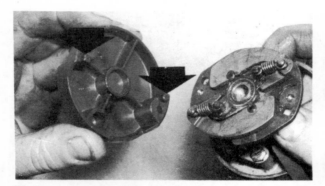

6.4. Rotor removed exposing centrifugal advance mechanism. Note round and square rotor locating lugs (arrowed)

7.4. Static ignition timing. Screwdriver indicates notch in crankshaft pulley which when aligned with lug arrowed sets No.1 piston 10° BTDC

7 Refit the clamp plate and tighten the nut sufficiently to allow the body of the distributor to be turned.

8 Turn the distributor body a little way clockwise so that the contact points are closed. Then turn it anticlockwise until the contact points are just opening. This position is most accurately measured by using a 12 volt bulb wired in parallel with the contact points. With the ignition switched on the bulb should light when the points open.

9 Another way of gauging when the points are about to open is by trapping a piece of very thin paper (cigarette paper is ideal) between the points and turning the distributor until it is released.

10 When set tighten the clamp screw, replace the cap and reconnect the plug leads making sure they are in the correct firing order 1—3—4—2. Remember that the rotor turns clockwise.

11 Final adjustment with the engine running at tickover speed can be carried out with a strobe light on the timing marks. For checking that the advance mechanism is working make another mark on the timing case cover to the left of the 10° lug. This new mark should be equivalent to two divisions away from it representing 20° BTDC and the timing should be at this at 3,550 rpm or more.

8. Spark plugs and high tension leads

1 The correct functioning of the spark plugs is vital for the correct running and efficiency of the engine. The plugs fitted as standard are listed in the 'Specifications' at the beginning of this Chapter.

2 At intervals of 3000 miles/3 months the plugs should be removed, examined, cleaned and, if worn excessively, renewed. The condition of the spark plug will also tell much about the overall condition of the engine.

3 If the insulator nose of the spark plug is clean and white, with no deposits, this is indicative of a weak mixture, or too hot a plug. (A hot plug transfers heat away from the electrode slowly - a cold plug transfers it away quickly).

4 If the tip of the insulator nose is covered with sooty black deposits, then this is indicative that the mixture is too rich. Should the plug be black and oily, then it is likely that the engine is fairly worn, as well as the mixture being rich.

5 If the insulator nose is covered with light tan to greyish brown deposits, then the mixture is correct and it is likely that the engine is in good condition and correctly tuned.

6 If there are any traces of long brown tapering stains on the outside of the white portion of the plug, then the plug will have to be renewed, as this shows that there is a faulty joint between the plug body and the insulator, and compression is being allowed to leak away, any chips or cracks also mean that the plug should be renewed.

7 Clean around the plug seats in the cylinder head before removing the plugs to prevent dirt getting into the cylinders. Plugs should be cleaned by a sand blasting machine, which will free them from carbon more thoroughly than cleaning by hand. The machine will also test the behaviour of the plugs under compression. Any plug that fails to spark at the recommended pressure should be renewed.

8 The spark plug gap is of considerable importance, as, if it is too large or too small the size of the spark and its efficiency will be seriously impaired. The spark plug gap should be set to the gap shown in the Specifications for the best results.

9 To set it, measure the gap with a feeler gauge, and then bend open, or close, the outer plug electrode until the correct gap is achieved. The centre electrode should never be bent as this may crack the insulation and cause plug failure, if nothing worse.

10 When replacing the plug see that the washer is intact and carbon free, also the shoulder of the plug under the washer. Make sure also that the plug seat in the cylinder head is quite clean.

11 Replace the leads from the distributor in the correct firing order, which is 1—3—4—2; No.1 cylinder being the one nearest the radiator.

12 The plug leads require no routine attention other than being kept clean and wiped over regularly. At intervals, say twice yearly, pull each lead off the plug in turn and also from the distributor cap. Water can seep down into these joints giving rise to a white corrosive deposit which must be carefully removed from the brass connectors at the end of each cable.

9. Fault finding

Failure of the engine to start easily, misfiring or poor acceleration and excessive fuel consumption can usually be attributed to faults in the ignition system. This of course assumes that the engine is in a reasonable condition otherwise. As with all fault diagnosis the only satisfactory method is by a logical progression and the sequence

shown should be followed where the ignition is being checked — Do not by-pass any part of this procedure unless the fault is particularly obvious and rectification of it solves the problem. Such obvious faults would be detached or broken wires.

It is assumed that the battery is charged and in good condition - otherwise tests will not be practical. It also assumes that the starter motor functions as it should and turns the engine at the proper speed.

FAULT	CHECK
No start or starts with fuss and difficulty	1 Remove HT lead from centre of distributor cap and verify that spark jumps to earth when engine is turned. If it does, fault lies in rotor arm, distributor cap, plug leads or plugs which should be checked in that order. 2 If no spark from coil HT lead check LT circuit in order: a) Disconnect at the coil the LT lead (blue/black) on the positive terminal. With a 12v bulb or voltmeter check that current is coming to the end of the lead when the ignition is switched on. If not check wiring from ignition switch. b) Remove the distributor cap. Turn the engine until the points are closed. Switch on the ignition. Hold the HT lead from the coil near a metal earth and open the points with a non-metallic article. If a spark now jumps from the end of the HT lead clean and reset the points to cure the trouble. c) If there is no spark from the HT lead but a large spark from the points when opened as in para (b) the condenser is faulty. It should be renewed. d) If there is no spark from the HT lead, and no spark large or small at the points when opened as in para (b) the winding of coil has probably failed. Repeat test with a voltmeter on the negative terminal of the coil (having reconnected the lead to the other terminal) with the ignition switched on. If there is no reading then renew the coil.
Engine starts readily but the performance is sluggish, no misfiring	1 Check the contact breaker points gap. 2 Check the plugs. 3 Check the static ignition timing. 4 Check the fuel octane rating.
Engine misfires, runs unevenly, cuts out at low revolutions only	1 Check the contact breaker gap (too large). 2 Check the plugs. 3 Check the fuel system (carburettor). 4 Check wear in distributor shaft. 5 Check condenser is securely mounted.
Engine misfires at high revolutions	1 Check the plugs. 2 Check the contact breaker gap (too small). 3 Check the fuel system (carburettor). 4 Check the distributor shaft for wear. 5 Check condenser is securely mounted.

Chapter 5 Clutch and actuating mechanism

Contents

Specifications

Type...	Dry single plate, diaphragm spring	
	124	124S
Diameter..	182 mm	200 mm
Release mechanism	Bowden cable	
Pedal free travel	25 mm/.9 inches (giving clearance of 2 mm between friction ring and release sleeve	

Torque wrench setting

Clutch cover to flywheel screws ... ...   18 ft lb/2.5 kgm

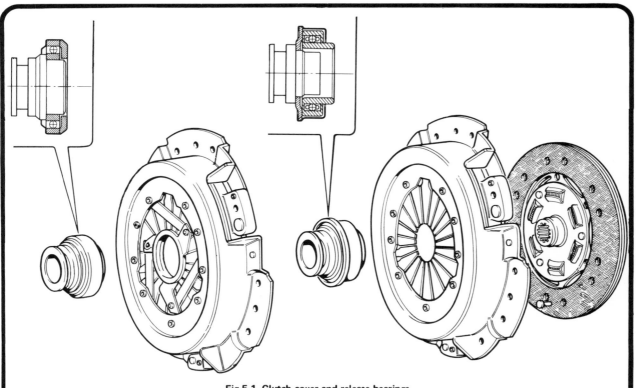

Fig.5.1. Clutch cover and release bearings

Left: Early type with thrust ring on diaphragm spring and simple thrust release bearing

Right: Later type with no thrust ring on diaphragm spring and sleeve in thrust release bearing

1. General description

The clutch consists of an integral pressure plate and diaphragm spring assembly with a single dry plate friction disc between the pressure plate assembly and the flywheel.

The bellhousing on the gearbox encloses the whole unit but only the top half of the bellhousing bolts to the engine. Consequently, there is a steel plate bolted to the lower half of the bellhousing to act as a cover.

The clutch is operated mechanically by a cable direct from the clutch pedal. This actuates a clutch release lever and thrust bearing, the lever pivoting on a ball pin inside the bellhousing and projecting through an aperture in the bellhousing opposite to the pin. Adjustment of free play is effected by a threaded ball joint at the end of the cable where it is attached to the clutch operating lever.

2. Clutch - adjustment

1 The free play in the clutch pedal cannot be determined accurately from the pedal itself. It is necessary to check the gap between the ball joint adjuster and actuating arm.
2 To measure the gap first unhook the return spring (photo). Then prop, or get someone to hold, the pedal in the fully up position.
3 Move the actuating arm until it can be felt to be up against the clutch and pull the cable to eliminate any end play there may be. Adjust the nut as necessary to obtain the gap of 15 mm/0.6 inches in between arm and adjuster (Fig.5.2).
4 Too little or no gap will wear out the thrust race prematurely. If very badly adjusted, clutch slip will occur. Too much gap will result in excessive pedal movement before the clutch disengages.
5 Do not forget to refit the return spring. If the spring is broken or disconnected it will immediately be apparent by looseness in the pedal at the top end of its travel. The clutch will work still but the actuating arm will rattle and cause wear on the thrust bearing.
6 Do not forget to tighten the locknut after adjustment is complete.

3. Clutch cable - removal and replacement

1 Remove the locknut and adjusting nut from the clutch end of the operating cable (photo).
2 Undo the nut under the water hose tee piece at the front of the cylinder head which secures the cable clip (photo).
3 Remove the cable lower end from the hole in the clutch bell-housing (photo).
4 If the pedal is now depressed the cable end will be drawn into the footwell far enough for it to be conveniently unhooked from the top of the pedal.
5 The cable assembly can then be drawn out through the bulkhead inside the engine compartment.
6 Replacement is a reversal of this procedure. Early models suffered a weak spot in the bulkhead where the cable outer is retained. This led to fracturing and consequent non-operation of the cable. Repairs can be effected by welding in a reinforcing plate (photo). It is best to get this strengthened anyway if signs of fracture appear.
7 When the cable is fitted carry out adjustments as described in Section 2.

4. Clutch assembly - removal and inspection

1 Remove the gearbox (see Chapter 6 'Gearbox removal').
2 Mark the position of the clutch cover relative to the flywheel (photo).
3 Slacken off the bolts holding the cover to the flywheel in a diagonal sequence, undoing each bolt a little at a time. This keeps the pressure even all round the diaphragm spring and prevents distortion. When all the pressure is released on the bolts, remove them, lift the cover off the dowel pegs and take it off together with the friction disc which is between it and the flywheel.
4 Examine the diaphragm spring for signs of distortion or fracture.
5 Examine the pressure plate for signs of scoring or abnormal wear.
6 If either the spring or the plate is defective it will be necessary to replace the complete assembly with an exchange unit. The assembly can only be taken to pieces with special equipment and, in any case, individual parts of the assembly are not obtainable as regular spares.
7 Examine the friction disc for indications of uneven wear and scoring of the friction surfaces. Contamination by oil will also show as hard and blackened areas which can cause defective operation. If the clearance between the heads of the securing rivets and the face of the friction lining material is less than 0.5 mm/.020 inches it would be worthwhile to fit a new disc (photo). Around the hub of the friction disc are five springs acting as shock absorbers between the hub and the friction area. These should be intact and tightly in position.
8 The face of the flywheel should be examined for signs of scoring or uneven wear and, if necessary, it will have to be renewed or reconditioned. See Chapter 1 for details of flywheel removal.

2.2. Detaching the clutch lever return spring

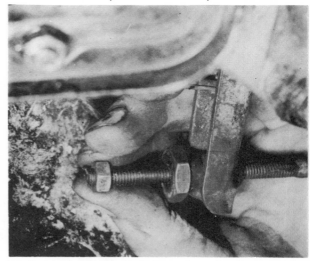

3.1. Remove the clutch cable locknut prior to the adjuster nut

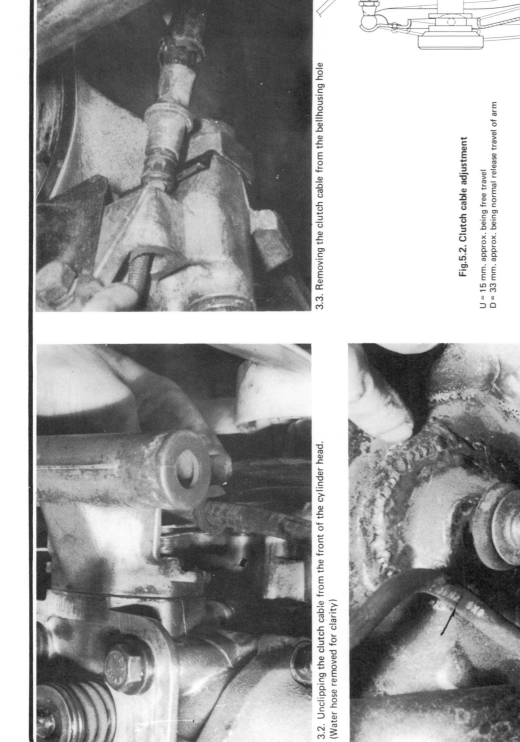

3.3. Removing the clutch cable from the bellhousing hole

Fig.5.2. Clutch cable adjustment

U = 15 mm. approx. being free travel
D = 33 mm. approx. being normal release travel of arm

3.2. Unclipping the clutch cable from the front of the cylinder head. (Water hose removed for clarity)

3.6. Clutch cable passing through the bulkhead. Note where reinforcing plate has been welded in

5. Clutch assembly - replacement

1 Replacement of the clutch cover and friction plate is the reverse of the removal procedure but not quite so straightforward, as the following paragraphs will indicate.

2 If the clutch assembly has been removed from the engine with the engine out of the car, it is a relatively easy matter to line up the hub of the friction disc with the centre of the cover and flywheel. The cover and friction plate are replaced onto the flywheel with the holes in the cover fitting over the dowels on the flywheel. The friction plate is supported with a finger while this is being done.

3 Note that the friction plate is mounted with the longer hub of the boss towards the clutch cover (photo). Usually the replacement disc is marked to prevent a mistake being made.

4 Replace the cover mounting bolts finger tight sufficiently to just grip the friction plate. Then set the friction plate in position so that the hub is exactly concentric with the centre of the flywheel and the cover assembly. An easy way of doing this is to make a temporary mandrel, using a bar from a socket set, which should fit fairly closely in the flywheel bush. Wrap a few turns of adhesive tape round the bar near the end, which will make a snug fit inside the splined boss of the friction plate. Use this as a centring device (photo). It is most important to get this right when replacing the clutch to an engine which is still in the car. Otherwise difficulty and possibly damage could occur when refitting the gearbox.

5 Tighten up the cover bolts one turn at a time in a diagonal sequence to maintain an even pressure (photo). Final torque setting should be 18 lb ft/2.5 kgm with clean dry bolt threads.

6. Clutch release arm and thrust release bearing

1 The clutch release arm and thrust bearing can only be removed after the engine and gearbox are separated.
2 The arm pivots on a ball ended stud screwed into the bellhousing and it is held in position by a spring plate clip. To get the arm off the stud it is simply pulled away (photo).
3 The thrust release ring is a sealed ball bearing and it is moved in and out by two pegs on the release lever which engage in a peripheral groove on the sleeve. When the arm is taken off over the gearbox input shaft the bearing is freed (photo).
4 Do not flush out the bearing — it will not be possible to re-pack it with grease. If the ball bearing is rough it should be renewed.
5 Note that later models have a projecting sleeve on the thrust face of the bearing which locates inside the centre of the ends of the diaphragm spring blades. Earlier versions have a flush faced thrust bearing which bears on to a thrust ring fitted to the cover in the centre of the diaphragm spring and held by three straps.

7. Clutch pedal shaft and support bracket

1 Both brake and clutch pedal are supported on a common shaft which is simply a bolt with a sleeve and nylon bushes. In the event of the bushes becoming worn the nut can be taken off the shaft, the shaft withdrawn and new bushes fitted.
2 With a bit of care this can be done without having to disturb anything else although it is a good idea to unhook the clutch arm return spring so as to relieve any tension on the pedal - also the spring on the brake pedal for the same reason.
3 The pedal shaft is supported by a detachable bracket assembly which bolts to the bulkhead and dash panel.

8. Fault finding - symptom

Symptom	Reason/s	Remedy
Judder when taking up drive	Loose engine/gearbox mountings or over-flexible mountings	Check and tighten all mounting bolts and replace any 'soft' or broken mountings.
	Badly worn friction surfaces or friction plate contaminated with oil carbon deposit	Remove clutch assembly and replace parts as required. Rectify any oil leakage points which may have caused contamination.
	Worn splines in the friction plate hub or on the gearbox input shaft	Renew friction plate and/or input shaft.
	Badly worn bearing in flywheel centre for input shaft spigot	Renew bearing in flywheel.
	Propeller shaft or rear axle mounting faults	Examine propeller shaft, universal joints and rear axle to suspension arm attachment points.
Clutch spin (or failure to disengage) so that gears cannot be meshed	Clutch actuating cable clearance from fork too great	Adjust clearance.
	Clutch friction disc sticking to pressure surface or on the splines because of rust (usually apparent after standing idle for some length of time)	As temporary remedy engage top gear, apply handbrake, depress clutch and start engine. (If very badly stuck engine will not turn). When running rev up engine and slip clutch until disengagement is normally possible. Renew friction plate at earliest opportunity.
	Damaged or misaligned pressure plate assembly	Replace pressure plate assembly.
Clutch slip — (increase in engine speed does not result in increase in car speed - especially on hills)	Clutch actuating cable clearance from fork too small resulting in partially disengaged clutch at all times	Adjust clearance.
	Clutch friction surfaces worn out (beyond further adjustment of operating cable) or clutch surfaces oil soaked	Replace friction plate and remedy source of oil leakage.
Screeching noises when operating clutch	Worn out thrust release bearing	Renew.
	Worn out friction plate	Renew.

4.7. Comparison between new and old clutch friction plates

5.3. The clutch friction plate hub has the long boss (arrowed) towards the clutch cover

5.4. Centering the clutch friction plate

5.5. Tightening the cover retaining screw

6.2. The clutch release arm detached from the pivot pin (arrowed)

6.3. Removing the release arm and thrust release bearing from the gearbox input shaft. Note the retaining clip (arrowed) prevents the arm from coming off the pivot pin

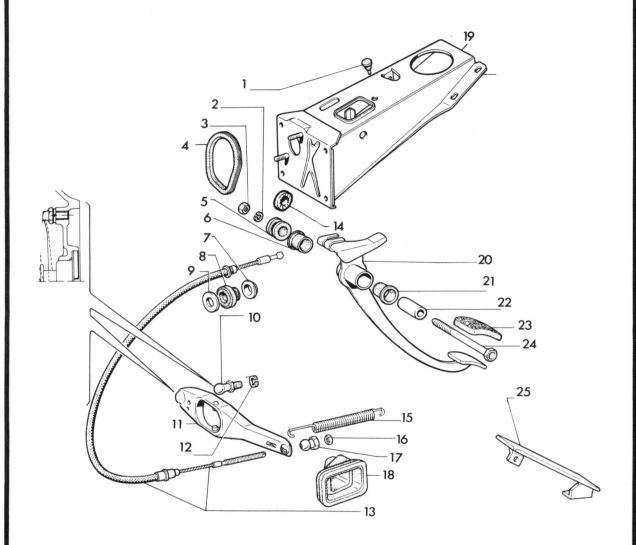

Fig.5.3. Clutch pedal and operating mechanism

1	Buffer	8	Grommet	14	Lockwasher	20	Clutch pedal
2	Spring washer	9	Thrust washer	15	Clutch release arm	21	Bush
3	Pedal shaft nut	10	Clutch release arm		return spring	22	Spacer sleeve
4	Insulator		pivot pin	16	Locknut	23	Pedal rubber
5	Grommet	11	Clutch release arm	17	Clutch adjustment	24	Pedal pivot shaft
6	Bush	12	Spring washer		nut	25	Foot rest
7	Cable bulkhead grommet	13	Clutch release cable	18	Dust cover		
	retainer		assembly	19	Pedal support bracket		

Chapter 6 Gearbox

Contents

Specifications

General

Number of gears	Four forward, one reverse
Type...	Constant mesh, helical spur gears with sliding baulk ring synchromesh on all forward speeds
Oil capacity...	2.3 pints/1.32 litres

Ratios

	124	124S
First	3.75 : 1	3.80 : 1
Second	2.30 : 1	3.17 : 1
Third..	1.49 : 1	1.41 : 1
Fourth	1 : 1	1 : 1
Reverse	3.87 : 1	3.65 : 1

Tolerances

Gear backlash	0.1 mm/.004 ins
Main gears to shafts	0.05 — 0.10 mm/.002 — .004 ins Limit 0.15 mm/.006 ins
Reverse gear to shaft	0.05 — 0.10 mm/.002 — .004 ins Limit 0.15 mm/.006 ins
Sleeve to hub spline flanks	0.07 — 0.16 mm/.003 — .006 ins Limit 0.25 mm/.010 ins
Radial clearance on bearings..	0.05 mm/.002 ins max
Axial clearance on bearings	0.50 mm/.020 ins
Maximum permissible shaft run-out	.025 mm/.001 ins

Torque wrench settings

Gearbox to engine mounting screws	62 ft lbs/8.5 kgm
Casing stud nuts M10...	36 ft lbs/5 kgm
Casing stud nuts M8	18 ft lbs/2.5 kgm
Layshaft front bearing screw	69 ft lbs/9.5 kgm
Propeller shaft sleeve nut..	58 ft lbs/8 kgm
Detent spring cover retaining nuts...	18 ft lbs/2.5 kgm
Gear lever support stud nuts..	7 ft lbs/1 kgm

1. General description

The gearbox is a four speed unit with synchromesh on all four forward speeds. A feature of the later type of gearboxes is the speed with which the synchromesh permits gear changes to be made. This is due to a redesigned system where the floating type of baulk ring (fitted on earlier models) is replaced by a spring loaded cone splined to the gear wheel itself which mates directly with the sliding sleeve of the hub prior to engagement.

The input shaft, mainshaft and lay gear are more or less conventional. The gearbox cover is at the bottom of the box and the selector mechanism consists of forks held to rails by lock bolts. The ends of the rails protrude from the rear of the main casing and the gear lever, which is mounted in the rear extension housing, engages directly with the rails. There is therefore, a very positive gearchange action.

The selector rails are controlled and located by conventional detent balls and springs with transverse interlock plungers.

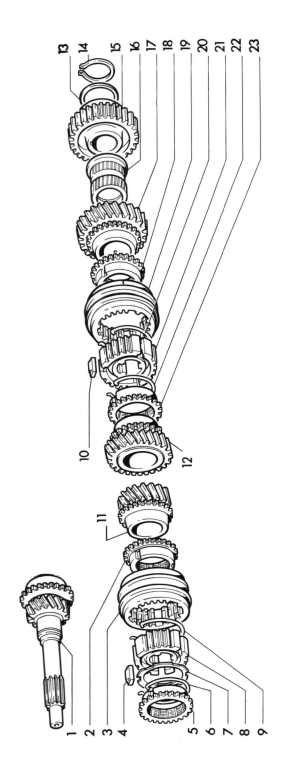

Fig.6.1. Gearbox input shaft, gears and baulk ring synchromesh assemblies (early type)

1 Input shaft
2 Baulk ring - 3rd gear
3 3rd/4th synchro unit
   outer sleeve
4 Sliding key

5 Baulk ring - 4th gear
6 Sliding keys retainer clip
7 Toothed washer
8 3rd/4th synchro unit hub
9 Sliding keys retainer clip

10 Sliding key
11 3rd gear
12 2nd gear
13 Convex washer
14 Circlip

15 Reverse mainshaft
    gear
16 1st gear hub
17 1st gear
18 Baulk ring - 1st gear

19 1st/2nd synchro unit
    outer sleeve
20 Sliding keys retaining
    clip
21 1st/2nd synchro unit

22 hub
    Sliding keys retaining
    clip
23 Baulk ring - 2nd
    gear

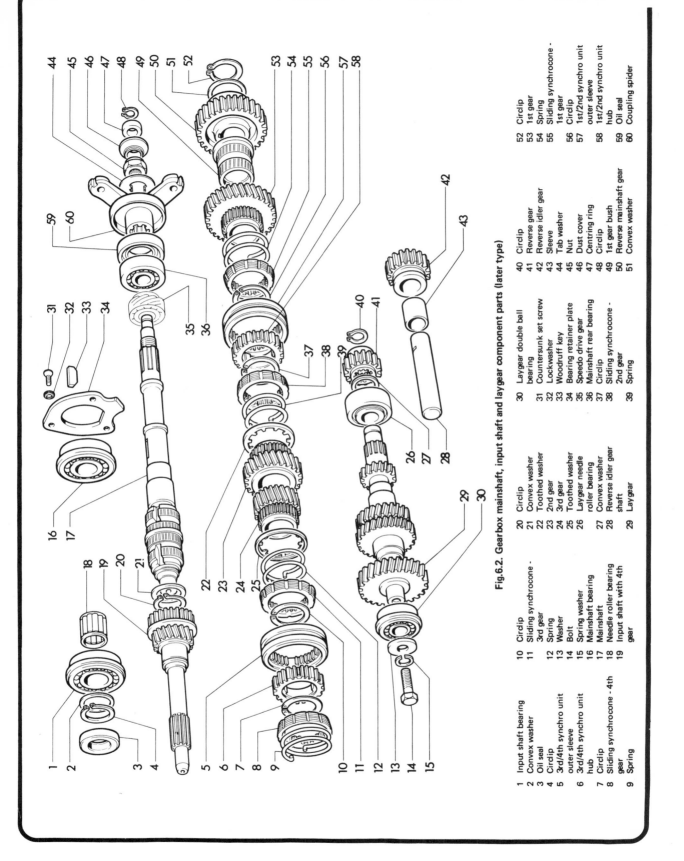

Fig.6.2. Gearbox mainshaft, input shaft and laygear component parts (later type)

1 Input shaft bearing
2 Convex washer
3 Oil seal
4 Circlip
5 3rd/4th synchro unit outer sleeve
6 3rd/4th synchro unit hub
7 Circlip
8 Sliding synchrocone - 4th gear
9 Spring
10 Circlip
11 Sliding synchrocone - 3rd gear
12 Spring
13 Washer
14 Bolt
15 Spring washer
16 Mainshaft
17 Mainshaft
18 Needle roller bearing
19 Input shaft with 4th gear
20 Circlip
21 Convex washer
22 Toothed washer
23 2nd gear
24 3rd gear
25 Toothed washer
26 Laygear needle roller bearing
27 Convex washer
28 Reverse idler gear shaft
29 Laygear
30 Laygear double ball bearing
31 Countersunk set screw
32 Lockwasher
33 Woodruff key
34 Bearing retainer plate
35 Speedo drive gear
36 Mainshaft rear bearing
37 Circlip
38 Sliding synchrocone - 2nd gear
39 Spring
40 Circlip
41 Reverse gear
42 Reverse idler gear
43 Sleeve
44 Tab washer
45 Nut
46 Dust cover
47 Centring ring
48 Circlip
49 1st gear bush
50 Reverse mainshaft gear
51 Convex washer
52 Circlip
53 1st gear
54 Spring
55 Sliding synchrocone - 1st gear
56 Circlip
57 1st/2nd synchro unit outer sleeve
58 1st/2nd synchro unit hub
59 Oil seal
60 Coupling spider

2. Gearbox - removal and replacement

1 Raise the front of the car on axle stands or ramps.

2 From inside the car remove the retaining plate and boot from around the root of the gear lever (photo).

3 The top section of the lever is held to the lower section by a nylon snap ring which can be prised out of the lower end of the tube with a screwdriver (photo).

4 The lever top section may then be lifted off.

5 Drain the gearbox oil.

6 Unhook the clutch arm return spring and remove the locknut and adjusting nut from the end of the clutch cable (details in Chapter 5).

7 Unscrew the knurled nut holding the speedometer drive cable.

8 Remove the lower sheet steel flywheel cover plate.

9 Remove the bolt securing the exhaust pipe clip to the bracket on the gearbox rear cover.

10 Remove the heat shield, from above the starter motor, held by two nuts to the exhaust manifold. Then undo and remove the three starter motor securing bolts. The starter stays where it is.

11 Disconnect the propeller shaft. This means undoing three of the six bolts holding the propeller shaft spider to the flexible front coupling. Then remove the cross piece under the front section of shaft followed by the centre section mounting. The shaft may then be moved to one side well out of the way.

12 Remove the four bolts holding the bellhousing section to the cylinder block. A long extension and universal joint will be needed for the socket to undo the top bolts.

13 Support the weight of gearbox on a suitable jack and undo the bolts securing the supporting crossmember to the bodywork. Draw the gearbox back off the engine until the input shaft is clear of the clutch and then lower it out of the car. Be sure to keep the weight supported fully until it is clear. On no account should it be allowed to 'hang' on the input shaft otherwise severe strain and possible damage could occur.

14 Replacement of the gearbox is a reversal of the removal procedure taking note of the following points:

a) Depending on what has been removed other than the gearbox, remember that the starter motor cannot be put in position with both the gearbox and engine manifolds attached. Do not forget the rear engine plate either (photo).

b) Having removed the gearbox it is worthwhile examining the amount of wear left in the clutch friction disc whilst the opportunity arises (see Chapter 5).

c) When refitting the gearbox on to the engine the clutch friction plate must be centred if it has been disturbed. When juggling the gearbox into position do not let any strain be imposed on the input shaft.

d) If the support crossmember has been detached from the gearbox refit it before getting the gearbox up into position on the engine.

e) Bolt the bellhousing to the engine before refitting the support crossmember back up to the bodywork (photo).

f) When refitting the flywheel lower cover plate do not forget the earth strap bolted on the left side (photo).

g) When refitting the gear lever upper section, make sure that the nylon snap ring is pushed securely home inside the housing.

h) Do not forget to adjust the clutch pedal travel.

i) Fill the gearbox with oil.

3. Gearbox - dismantling

1 Before taking the gearbox apart remember that individual parts are expensive and may take time to acquire. If the gearbox is in very bad condition the economies of fitting a new gearbox must be considered. If the problem is bearing failure early action in replacing them will be worthwhile. If, however, the gearbox has been used for sometime with failed bearings the wear patterns of the gears will have altered (and increased). The fitting of new bearings will not then necessarily cure all the noise that may have developed. If the

problem is one of jumping out of gear or a very sloppy feel to the gearchange it is possible that the detent springs may be the cause. These can be renewed without taking the gearbox from the car. Simply remove the detent balls and springs cover from the front right hand edge of the main casing when access to the springs (which can break) and balls (which can wear) is possible.

2 Preparation for dismantling should ensure that a good firm flat clean working space is available. Unless there are adequate facilities for laying parts out when removed the job will be many times more difficult.

3 Thoroughly clean off the exterior with paraffin and hose it down with water.

4 Remove the seven nuts holding the bellhousing to the front of the main casing and take it off complete with clutch operating arm and thrust bearing. Retrieve the convex washer from between the housing and input shaft bearing.

5 Stand the gearbox upside down and remove the bottom cover plate screws and gasket. From now on all dismantling and assembly work is carried out with the gearbox inverted so when references are made to the top or bottom of the box it means when the box is in position in the car. So remember, the cover plate is on the bottom of the box!

6 Remove the circlip from the rear end of the mainshaft and then take off the sleeve and rubber ring. Undo the lockwasher tab and take of the nut followed by the universal joint spider. In order to lock the mainshaft when doing this it will be necessary to lock the spider with a rod through one of the bolt holes.

7 Remove the speedometer cable drive unit after removing the securing nut.

8 Undo the two nuts holding the detent ball and spring retaining plate on the right rear of the main casing. Take care not to lose the three springs and balls which will fall out from the holes. Note that the one for the reverse rail is different from the others (the one nearest the bottom).

9 To take off the rear extension cover and gear lever assembly first remove the stop screw on the right hand side which restricts the sideways movement of the lever. Then unscrew the six nuts holding the extension to the main casing.

10 Move the gear lever over to the left and the cover can be drawn off.

11 From the rear end of the mainshaft draw off and collect the locating ball speedometer drive gear. Do not lose the locking ball in the shaft.

12 Reverse gear selector fork and rail (the bottom one) can now be drawn out of the casing, at the same time drawing the gear off the spindle with it.

13 With expanding circlip pliers remove the circlip holding reverse driving gear on the end of the layshaft. Remove the dished washer and gear and the washer behind the gear.

14 Undo the circlip holding the reverse gear on to the main shaft and remove the dished washer and gear.

15 Take the large Woodruff key out of its groove in the shaft.

16 Lock the shafts by engaging two gears simultaneously and from the front of the layshaft remove the front bearing retaining bolt and flat washer.

17 The front and rear layshaft bearings can be tapped out of the casing from the inside. Tilt the layshaft to lift it up and out.

18 Draw the centre selector rail (3rd/4th gears) out of the casing, releasing the fork from the end while doing so. Do not lose the small interlock plunger from the rail itself or the larger one which will be seen in the bore in the corner of the casing inside.

19 Remove 1st/2nd gear selector fork locking bolt and draw out the rail in the same way as before. Lift out the two forks.

20 The third interlock plunger can be retrieved now from the bottom of the bore in the casing.

21 The input shaft which has been left in position till now can be taken out complete with bearing from the front of the casing. The needle rollers which carry the mainshaft in the counterbore of the shaft may or may not be in a cage. If they are loose and fall out recover them without delay. There should be 23.

2.2. Removing the gearchange lever surround

2.3. Separating the upper and lower gear lever sections

2.4. Lifting off the upper lever section

2.13A. Refitting the plate behind the flywheel

2.13B. Raising the gearbox and mounting into position

2.13C. Using a universal joint on the socket to get at the top gearbox mounting bolts

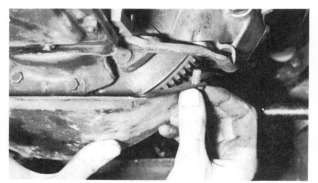

2.13D. Fitting the lower flywheel cover

2.13E. Securing the engine to chassis earth strap

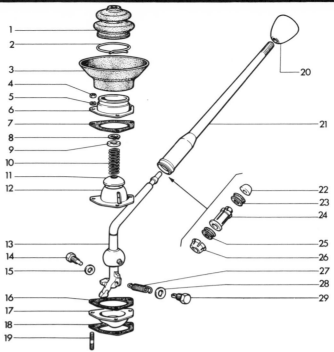

Fig.6.3. Gearchange lever assembly

1	Rubber boot	9	Washer	17	Plate	24	Spacer
2	Clip	10	Spring	18	Gasket	25	Rubber bush
3	Draught excluder	11	Cap	19	Stud	26	Nylon securing
4	Nut	12	Ball socket	20	Grip		collar
5	Spring washer	13	Change lever	21	Change lever	27	Spring
6	Mounting flange	14	Stop screw		extension	28	Washer
7	Gasket	15	Copper washer	22	Pad	29	Spring retainer
8	Circlip	16	Gasket	23	Rubber bush		screw

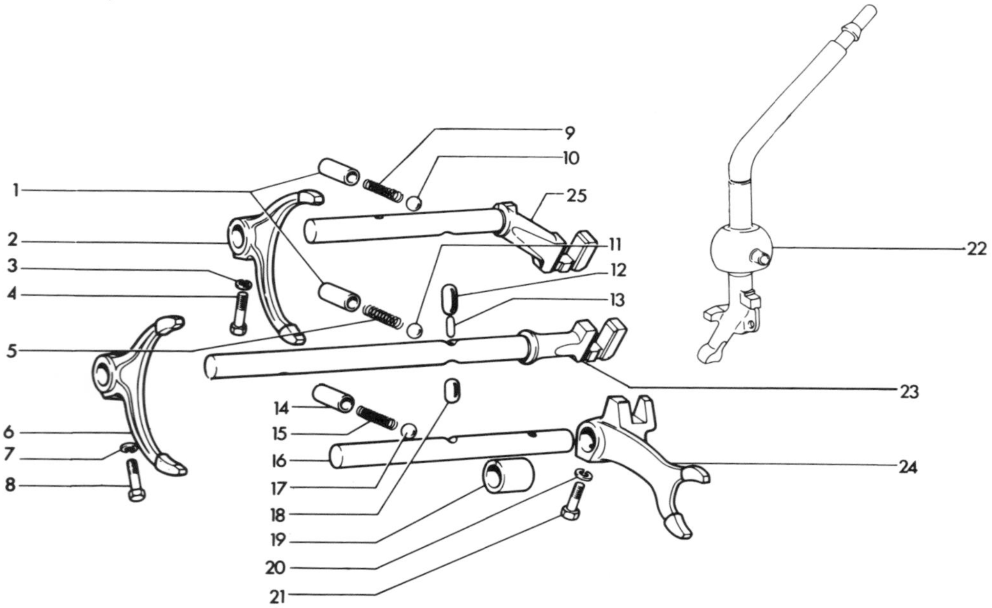

Fig.6.4. Gearbox - Selector forks and rails

1	Bushings (in casing)	8	Fork locking bolt	15	Detent spring	22	Gear lever
2	1st/2nd selector fork	9	Detent spring	16	Reverse selector fork rail		assembly
3	Spring washer	10	Detent ball	17	Detent ball	23	3rd/4th selector fork
4	Fork locking bolt	11	Detent ball	18	Interlock plunger		rail
5	Detent spring	12	Interlock plunger	19	Sleeve	24	Reverse selector fork
6	3rd/4th selector fork	13	Interlock plunger	20	Spring washer	25	1st/2nd selector fork
7	Spring washer	14	Bushing	21	Fork locking bolt		rail

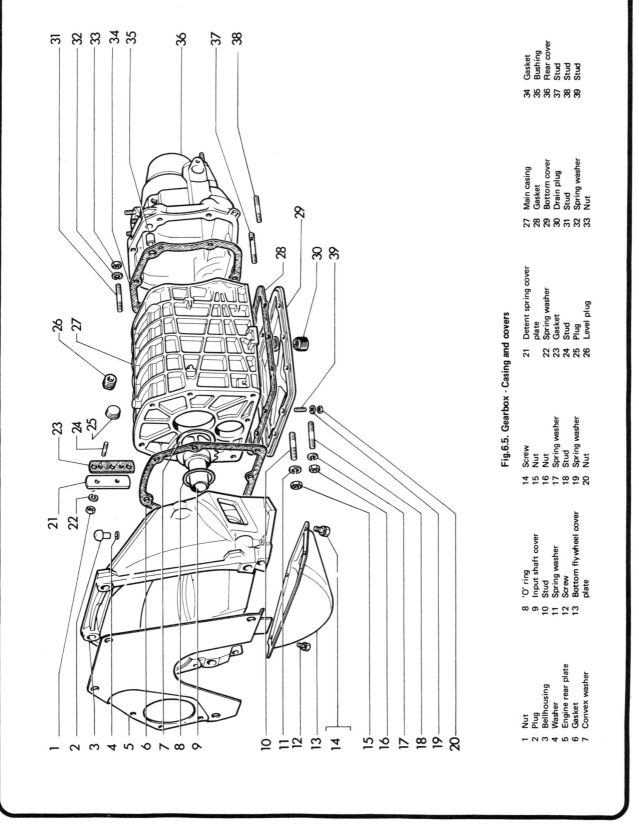

Fig.6.5. Gearbox - Casing and covers

1 Nut	21 Detent spring cover
2 Plug	plate
3 Bellhousing	22 Spring washer
4 Washer	23 Gasket
5 Engine rear plate	24 Stud
6 Gasket	25 Plug
7 Convex washer	26 Level plug
8 'O' ring	27 Main casing
9 Input shaft cover	28 Gasket
10 Stud	29 Bottom cover
11 Spring washer	30 Drain plug
12 Screw	31 Stud
13 Bottom flywheel cover	32 Spring washer
plate	33 Nut
14 Screw	34 Gasket
15 Nut	35 Bushing
16 Nut	36 Rear cover
17 Spring washer	37 Stud
18 Stud	38 Stud
19 Spring washer	39 Stud
20 Nut	

83

22 Undo the three countersunk cross head screws securing the mainshaft bearing retaining plate and the rear of the casing. The bearing can then be taken out. It is not a tight fit. The bearing retainer plate also locks into a slot in the reverse idler gear shaft which can now also be withdrawn.

23 Tilt the mainshaft inside the casing and carefully withdraw it complete with gears and hubs.

4. Mainshaft - dismantling

1 The mainshaft will have to be dismantled in order to renew any of the gears, baulk rings or synchro hubs fitted to it. Early versions had the floating type of baulk ring between the synchro hubs and the gear cones whereas later models had a complete design change and the gear cones became separate splined units on the gear and no separate baulk ring or sliding keys were required between the gear and the synchro hub. This manual details the procedure for the later type but reference to the exploded drawing will show that the principles of dismantling are not greatly affected. Items in the next paragraphs, which are in brackets, refer to the early type only.

2 From the rear end of the shaft take off in order:—
1st gear wheel and bush assembly (baulk ring)
1st/2nd gear synchro hub assembly (baulk ring)
2nd gear

From the front end of the shaft take off in order:—
(Baulk ring - may be with input shaft)
Circlip
Convex washer
3rd/4th gear synchro hub assembly (baulk ring)
3rd gear

3 To separate the cone from the gear wheel on later models all that is necessary is to remove the retaining circlip. Then draw off the cone, spring and the toothed washer behind the spring.

4 On early models the inner and outer sleeves of the synchro hubs incorporate three sliding keys between them which engage the cutouts in the baulk rings. If the synchro hubs are dismantled, see that the circular spring wire key retaining clips are so fitted (one on each side) that the hooked ends engage in two separate keys — not both in the same one (see Fig.6.6).

5 Bearings should run smoothly and with no radial play or chatter. The input shaft bearing may be removed from the shaft after releasing the circlip on the shaft and the convex washer.

5. Gearbox - inspection and renewal of components

Thoroughly wash all parts in paraffin to remove oil residue and lay them out to drain and dry on sheets of clean paper.

Examine the casing and covers for any signs of cracks and see that the mating faces are free from scratches and burrs. The lip type oil seals in the bellhousing and rear covers must be renewed if there is any sign of chipping or cracking on the sealing lip.

The seal can be levered out with a screwdriver and a new one tapped in square. The condition of the shafts, gears and synchro hubs is a question of degree. The mating of the cones in the synchro-mesh should be such that no rock is present. On the early models renewal of the baulk rings and sliding keys and springs from the hubs is a straightforward and relatively inexpensive operation. Similarly renewal of the gear cones on later versions should be made if there is any significant backlash in the splines or wear on the cone face. Serious backlash (more than .25 mm/.010 ins) in the hubs between the inner and outer sleeves means that the whole unit should be renewed and this can be expensive.

The gears themselves should not have chipped or excessively worn teeth. Backlash between gear teeth should not exceed .20 mm/.008 inches.

The clearance between the gears and mainshaft or bush should not exceed .15 mm/.006 inches.

The selector rails should slide easily in the transmission casing but without play which might cause jamming tendencies. The detent springs should not be weak and the balls not worn or pitted. The selector forks must be at right angles to the rails when fitted and the tongues which engage in the synchro sleeve grooves must not be worn on either face which would give rise to excessive clearance and consequent lost motion in gear engagement. This fault can cause gears to jump out of engagement.

6. Mainshaft - reassembly

1 If the synchro cones have been removed from the gears refit these first and ensure that the circlip is fully engaged in the groove (photo).

2 Starting at the front of the shaft, fit 3rd gear (the smallest of the 3 loose gears) over the shaft, gear teeth first (photo).

3 Fit the hub of 3rd/4th synchro unit, engaging the dogs into the shaft cutouts. It may go on either way round (photo).

4 Put the convex washer over the end of the shaft - convex side towards the shaft end (photo).

5 Put the circlip into position as near as possible. To get it into the groove a piece of pipe of suitable diameter (1.1/8") will be needed to drive the circlip down so it will engage in the groove (photo).

6 Turn to the other end of the shaft and place 2nd gear (the middle size one) over the shaft, gear teeth first (photo).

7 Replace the hub section of the 1st/2nd gear synchro unit - it can go on either way round (photo).

8 Fit the outer sleeves of both synchro hub units noting that they have special master locating splines with a flat section which must engage together (photo).

6.1. Removing the circlip holding a gearwheel synchro cone

6.2. Putting 3rd gear on the front of the mainshaft

6.3. Putting 3rd/4th synchro unit hub in position

6.4. Replacing the convex washer

6.5. Driving the circlip into its groove

6.6. Putting 2nd gear in position from the rear of the mainshaft

6.7. Putting 1st/2nd synchro unit hub in position

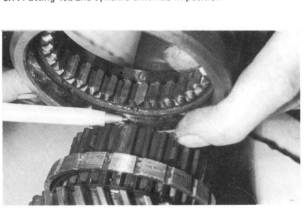

6.8. Lining up the master splines for the synchro hub and outer sleeve

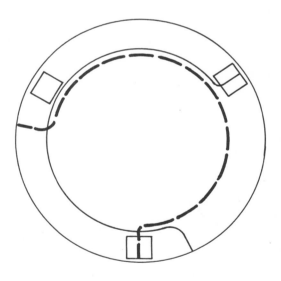

Fig.6.6. Baulk ring synchromesh - Arrangement of sliding key retaining clips

9 Put the bush into 1st gear from the gear teeth side (photo).
10 Place 1st gear together with its bush on the shaft with the synchro cone leading (photo).
11 The mainshaft is now ready for reassembly into the gearbox.

7. Gearbox - reassembly

1 Replace the mainshaft carefully into the casing making sure you get it the proper way round (photo).
2 Fit the rear bearing over the tail end of the shaft and into its recess in the casing. If a new bearing is fitted remember to replace the circlip in the outer annular groove. The circlip is towards the rear (photo).
3 Put the reverse idler gear shaft spindle into its hole in the casing and engage the bearing retaining plate in the slot, and push it fully home (photo).
4 Replace the screws and use an impact screwdriver to tighten them. Alternatively use a pair of self-grips on a screwdriver to obtain extra leverage (photo). It is a good idea to stake them when tight.
5 Take up the input shaft and place the needle rollers in the counter-bore (photo). If the rollers are not caged note that there is a spacer ring in front of and behind them. Hold them in position with grease and make sure that all 23 are fitted.
6 Put the input shaft into the casing engaging the needle bearings over the front of the mainshaft (photo). On early gearboxes with baulk rings do not forget the toothed washer and baulk ring that go between the fourth gear cone on the input shaft and the synchro hub on the mainshaft.
7 With the input shaft and bearing fully home the two shafts should rotate independently and together smoothly (photo).
8 Take up the shorter of the two selector rails (which have integral lugs at one end) and put it into the top hole of the three at the rear of the casing. The single transverse cutout in the rail faces the bottom of the box and the other three cutouts face the side.
9 When partly through fit 1st/2nd gear selector fork into the groove of the synchro hub sleeve and pass the rail through the fork boss (photo).
10 Replace and tighten the fork securing bolt.
11 Place one of the two large interlock plungers into the drilling in the casing (photo). If the selector is at the neutral position the end of the plunger will fit the transverse recess in the rail.

6.9. Putting the bush into 1st gear

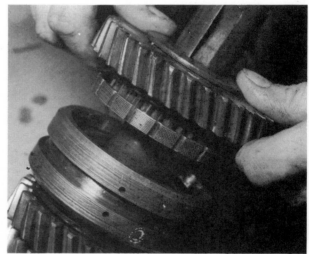

6.10. Putting 1st and bush onto the shaft

7.1. Mainshaft assembly going into the casing

7.2. Fitting the mainshaft rear casing bearing

7.3. Positioning the bearing retainer plate and reverse idler gear shaft. Note the shaft locking slot (arrowed)

7.4. Tightening the retainer plate screws

7.5. Putting the needle roller bearing into the input shaft counter bore

7.6. Replacing the input shaft in the casing

7.7. Mainshaft and input shaft assembled in the casing

7.8. Refitting 1st/2nd selector rail

7.9. 1st/2nd selector fork in the synchro sleeve groove and positioned on the rail

7.11. Dropping in the first of the interlock plungers

12 Fit the second selector rail into the centre hole and fit the 3rd/4th selector fork in the same manner as for the other one. Before pushing the rail right in put the small interlock plunger through the hole in the shaft and then trap it by pushing the rail into the casing (photo). Make sure the rear end of the rail lines up alongside the other with the gear lever cutouts together.

13 Tighten the selector fork locking screw (photo).

14 Place the laygear into the box with the larger gear towards the front (photo).

15 Fit the double ball bearing into the front of the casing over the nose of the laygear (photo), and tap it home.

16 Replace the securing bolt into the laygear with the spacer and lockwasher (photo).

17 Place the needle roller bearing into the casing at the rear, over the laygear (photo).

18 After tapping the laygear home fit the spacer ring (photo).

19 Replace the convex washer, convex side out (photo).

20 Replace the reverse gear onto the splines of the layshaft (photo) and then fit the circlip as near as possible to the groove in which it goes (photo).

21 To fit the circlip it has to be driven down against the pressure of the convex washer. Fit a socket on the bolt at the other end of the laygear and then stand the casing up on end on it (photo).

22 Using another tube or socket of suitable diameter drive the circlip down into position (photo). It may be necessary to finally tap the circlip ends in with a centre punch (photo).

23 Fit the large woodruff key into the mainshaft (photo).

7.12. Fitting the interlock plunger in 3rd/4th selector rail

7.13. Tightening 3rd/4th selector fork lock bolt

7.14. Placing the laygear in the casing

7.15. Fitting the laygear double ball bearing in the front of the casing

7.16. Replacing the bearing retainer bolt

7.17. Fitting the laygear rear needle roller bearing

7.18. Replacing the laygear roller bearing spacer collar ....

7.19.......... followed by the convex washer

7.20A.......... Reverse gear ....

7.20B .... and circlip

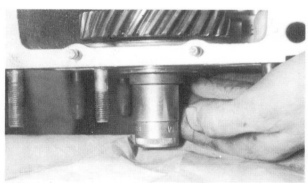
7.21. Supporting the laygear front end ....

7.22A .... in order to drive on the circlip at the rear

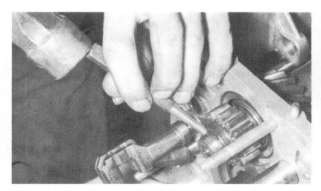
7.22B. A final tap to secure the circlip

7.23. The woodruff key fitted in the mainshaft

24 Fit the reverse gear on to the mainshaft with the hub extension rearwards and slide it over the key (photo).

25 Fit the convex washer over the shaft followed by the circlip. The convex side faces the circlip (photo).

26 To fit the circlip into the groove a suitable tube is once again needed and in the instance illustrated we used a piece of water pipe slotted across the end and tapped inwards to the correct diameter (photo).

27 The bolt on the front of the layshaft should be tightened next to a torque of 68 ft lbs/9.5 kgm (photo). The shaft can be locked by engaging two gears together.

28 With the two forward selector rails at neutral once more replace the last of the interlock plungers (photo).

29 Fit the sleeve over the reverse gear selector rail and replace the fork also if it has been taken off. Fit the rail a little way into the hole in the casing (photo).

30 Fit the reverse sliding gear onto the shaft together with the selector fork (photo).

31 Push the selector rail right home until the fork lug lines up with the other two. Secure the fork retaining bolt.

32 Turn the casing on its side and replace the detent balls and springs (photos).

33 Fit a new gasket and replace the cover (photo).

34 Fit the locking ball in the tail end of the mainshaft and refit the speedo drive gear so that the cutout engages the ball (photo).

35 Using a suitable tube drive on the mainshaft rear bearing behind the speedo gear (photo).

36 With the gear lever sideways stop pin moved out to permit sideways movement, and having checked that the lever return spring is intact, prepare to replace the rear cover (photo).

37 Offer up the rear cover having put a new gasket over the rear casing studs (photo).

7.24. Fitting the mainshaft reverse gear

7.25. The convex washer and circlip on the rear of the mainshaft

7.26. Driving on the mainshaft rear circlip

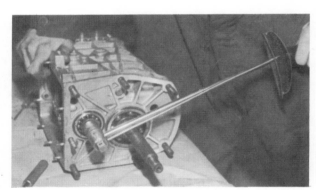

7.27. Tightening the laygear front bearing bolt

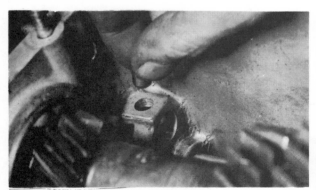

7.28. Dropping in the last interlock plunger

7.29. Fitting the reverse selector rail with sleeve and fork (arrowed)

7.30. Fitting reverse idler gear together with the selector fork and rail

7.32A. Replacing the detent balls

7.32B. Replacing the detent springs

7.33. Fitting the cover and gasket detent balls and springs

7.34. The speedometer drive gear and locking ball

7.35. Driving on the mainshaft rear bearing after the speedometer drive gear

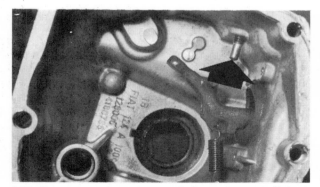

7.36. Rear cover and gear lever ready for replacement. Note stop screw which needs backing off (arrowed)

7.37. Fitting the rear cover

38 Make sure that the selector rails are all lined up in the neutral position (photo).

39 Fit the nuts to the studs not forgetting the exhaust pipe anchor bracket on the lower right hand corner (photos). There is a special square headed bolt for this - also one nut and washer goes on the stud before the bracket.

40 Fit the bottom cover plate using a new gasket (photo).

41 The bellhousing gasket is fitted over the studs on the front of the casing (photo).

42 Place the convex washer in position in the front of the housing using grease to hold it in position (photo).

43 Offer up the bellhousing to the casing (photo) and replace the securing nuts.

44 Replace the speedometer cable drive unit (photo).

45 Fit the flexible coupling spider on to the rear of the mainshaft (photo) followed by the tab washer and nut. Tighten the nut to 58 ft lbs/8 kgm and bend over the lockwasher (photo).

46 Refit the rubber dust cover followed by the coupling centring ring and circlip (photo).

47 Fit the flexible coupling to the spider with the three bolts in readiness for replacement (photo).

8. Speedometer drive gear

1 The speedometer drive gear unit may be removed without disturbing the gearbox. Its internal spindles and gears may be renewed or altered as required.

2 Having disconnected the knurled cable retaining collar, remove the nut from the single securing stud and draw the unit out of the casing. If the car is jacked up at the front there is every likelihood that some oil will come from the hole in the casing. Be ready to collect it.

3 If only the speedometer drive cable is to be removed it is simpler to take it out from the speedo head end after removing the instrument cluster (see Chapter 10), although if broken it may be necessary to undo the bottom end also in order to retrieve the lower broken part.

4 When refitting the drive gear unit make sure the gasket is in good condition. Top up the gearbox oil level if necessary.

7.38. Selector rails properly lined up prior to replacing the rear cover

7.39A. Fitting the exhaust pipe mounting bracket with the special bolt

7.39B. Do not forget the cover nut (arrowed) before fitting the bracket

7.40. Fitting the bottom cover plate

7.41. Positioning the bellhousing gasket

7.42. Placing the concave washer in the front of the bellhousing

7.43. Fitting the bellhousing

7.44. Replacing the speedometer drive gear assembly

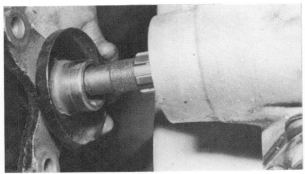

7.45A. Putting the flexible coupling spider on the mainshaft

7.45B. Bending over the lock tab after tightening the spider nut

7.46. After the dust cover and centering collar the circlip is replaced

7.47. Locating the flexible coupling to the spider on the gearbox

94

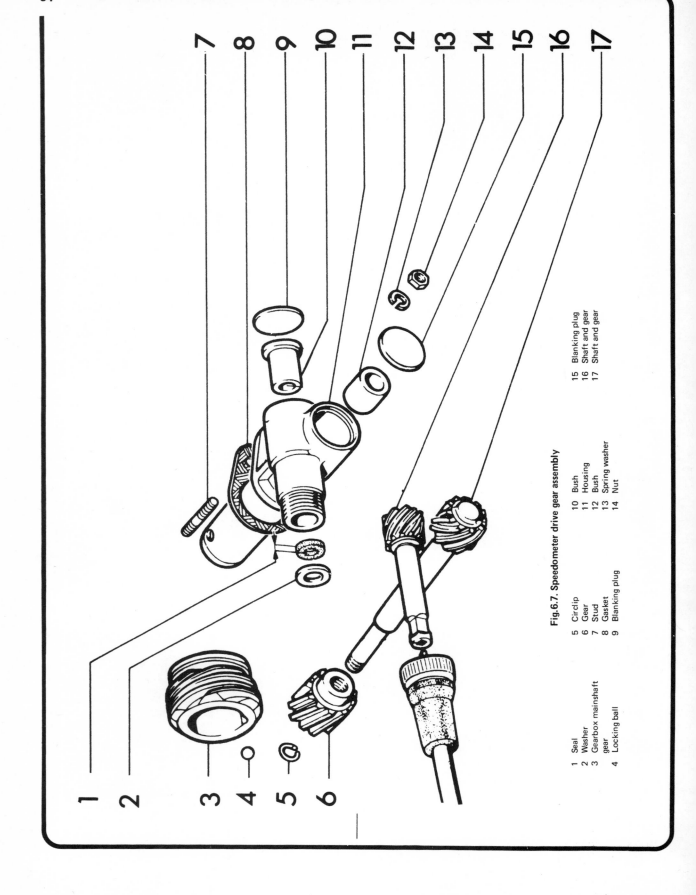

Fig.6.7. Speedometer drive gear assembly

1 Seal
2 Washer
3 Gearbox mainshaft
   gear
4 Locking ball

5 Circlip
6 Gear
7 Stud
8 Gasket
9 Blanking plug

10 Bush
11 Housing
12 Bush
13 Spring washer
14 Nut

15 Blanking plug
16 Shaft and gear
17 Shaft and gear

Chapter 7 Propeller shaft

Contents

Specifications

Type

Early models	2 sections with central support bearing and rigid rear section with torque tube
Later models	2 sections with central support bearing and tubular rear section connected to rear axle by universal joint

Torque wrench settings

Front flexible joint nuts for screws.	72 ft lbs/10 mkg
Nut for universal joint on front of rear shaft (early type)...	87 ft lbs/12 mkg
Bolts for torque tube to differential casing	50 ft lbs/7 mkg
Nut for universal joint on rear of front shaft (later type)	70 ft lbs/9.5 mkg
Nut for pillow block to chassis mounting..	14 ft lbs/2 mkg
Screw, pillow block to crossmember	18 ft lbs/2.5 mkg
Nut, rear universal joint flanges..	25 ft lbs/3.5 mkg

1. General description

The Fiat 124 has a split propeller shaft. This means that instead of one long tubular shaft with a universal joint at each end there are two short shafts with a universal joint in the middle as well. Advantages of this are the shallower angles at the joints, the reduced intrusion of a tunnel for the rear end of the shaft into the body floor and the greater rigidity obtained from 2 shorter shafts.

Earlier models are fitted with a torque tube enclosing the rear solid propeller shaft in order to absorb the torque reaction on to the rear axle. These models are easily identified because there is no universal joint at the rear. Later on this design was modified.

To explain in more detail; the front section of the early type is a tubular shaft with a sliding splined end shaft which fits into the sleeve of the flexible coupling. At the rear of the front section is a yoke which forms part of the universal joint which is bolted to the front of the rear shaft.

The rear section of the early type consists of a solid shaft. The front end is secured in a bearing and held by the nut which retains the universal joint. This bearing is mounted in the front end of a tube which in turn is mounted in a flexible mounting or pillow block on an intermediate crossmember. The rear end of the shaft connects to the rear axle pinion shaft by a splined sleeve and the surrounding tube is flanged so that it can be bolted to the differential casing.

The 124S and later 124 models have a modified arrangement. The front end of the front shaft is basically similar but the rear end of the front section is now supported in the pillow block bearing and the yoke of the universal joint is secured to it by a central nut. The rear section consists of a conventional tubular type shaft with the universal joint yokes welded at each end. The rear end now has a universal joint coupling to the final drive pinion in place of the splined sleeve as before. There is no torque tube.

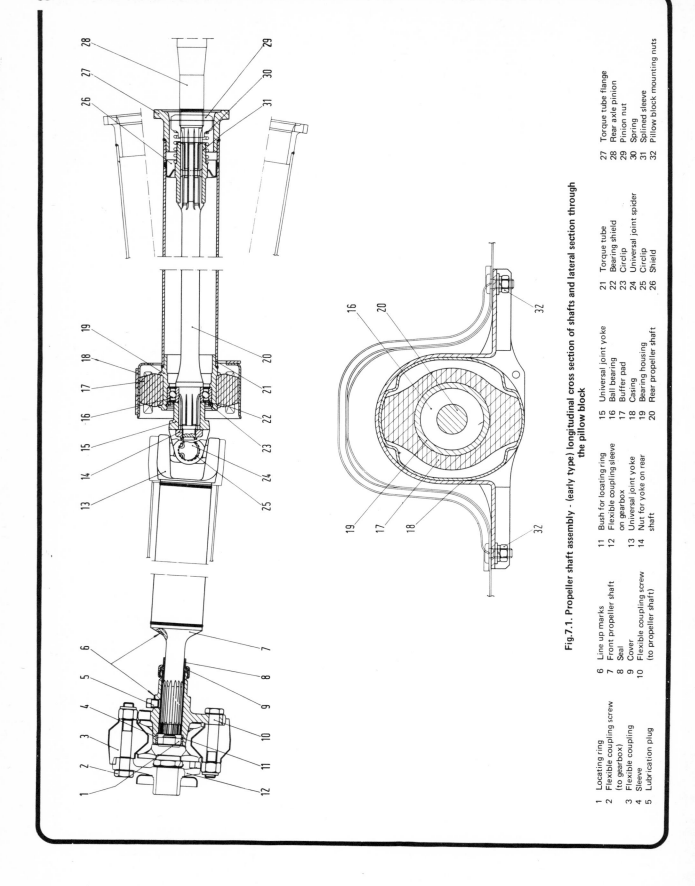

Fig.7.1. Propeller shaft assembly - (early type) longitudinal cross section of shafts and lateral section through the pillow block

1 Locating ring
2 Flexible coupling screw (to gearbox)
3 Flexible coupling
4 Sleeve
5 Lubrication plug

6 Line up marks
7 Front propeller shaft
8 Seal
9 Cover
10 Flexible coupling screw (to propeller shaft)

11 Bush for locating ring
12 Flexible coupling sleeve on gearbox
13 Universal joint yoke
14 Nut for yoke on rear shaft

15 Universal joint yoke
16 Ball bearing
17 Buffer pad
18 Casing
19 Bearing housing
20 Rear propeller shaft

21 Torque tube
22 Bearing shield
23 Circlip
24 Universal joint spider
25 Circlip
26 Shield

27 Torque tube flange
28 Rear axle pinion
29 Pinion nut
30 Spring
31 Splined sleeve
32 Pillow block mounting nuts

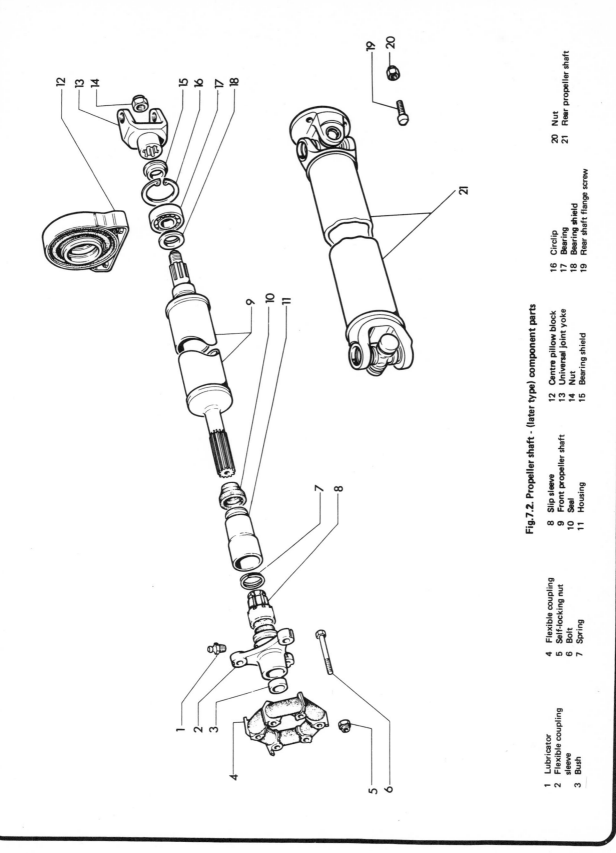

Fig.7.2. Propeller shaft - (later type) component parts

1	Lubricator	4	Flexible coupling	8	Slip sleeve	12	Centre pillow block
2	Flexible coupling	5	Self-locking nut	9	Front propeller shaft	13	Universal joint yoke
	sleeve	6	Bolt	10	Seal	14	Nut
3	Bush	7	Spring	11	Housing	15	Bearing shield

16	Circlip	20	Nut
17	Bearing	21	Rear propeller shaft
18	Bearing shield		
19	Rear shaft flange screw		

2. Propeller shaft - removal and replacement

1   If the propeller shaft is merely being disconnected so as to move the gearbox then first remove the three bolts holding it to the flexible coupling at the front. If possible put a large hose clip round the flexible coupling to compress it before removing the bolts. It makes assembly much easier. On early models the front shaft can then be swung aside on the universal joint. On later models, where the universal joint is behind the pillow block bearing it will be necessary also to undo the nuts securing the pillow block bearing crossmember to the underside and also the safety crossmember just in front of it. This will enable the front shaft to be moved to one side.

2   To remove an early type propeller shaft assembly completely, next disconnect the rear brake hose and pipe from the torque tube on the rear section.

3   Undo the bolts holding the rear of the torque tube to the differential casing.

4   Disconnect the handbrake spring from the central bearing support crossmember and then the four nuts holding the crossmember to the body.

5   Draw the whole assembly forward a little way only so that the relative positions of the rear splines and sleeve can be marked. Then draw the whole assembly forward and off.

6   On later models, having proceeded as far as described in paragraph 1, all that remains is for the rear universal joint flange to be marked for realignment. The four nuts and bolts may then be removed and the shaft assembly withdrawn.

7   Replacement is a reversal of the removal procedure. However, on the earlier models the 4 central pillow block mounting nuts should not be tightened until the gaps between the torque tube and the pillow block housing are correct as shown in Fig.7.4. On later models this does not apply. These models have two securing nuts only.

2.1A. Separating the front propeller shaft from the universal joint

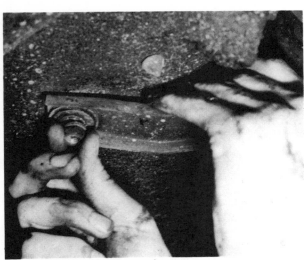

2.1B. Undoing the pillow block crossmember nuts (later models)

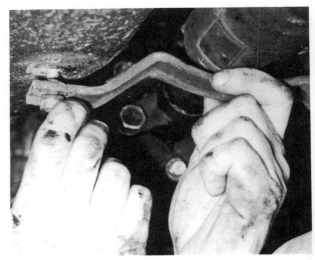

2.1C. Undoing the safety strap crossmember bolts (later models)

Fig.7.3. Propeller shaft - (early type). Central pillow block mounting

1 Body fixing nuts   2 Torque tube   3 Pillow block assembly   4 Front propeller shaft

SECTION A-A

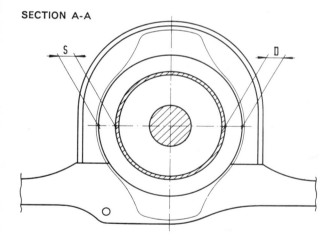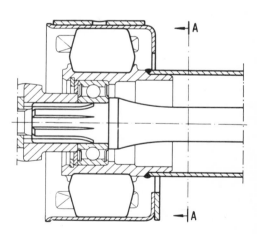

Fig.7.4. Pillow block - early type. Two cross section views

Gap 'D' should be equal to or no more than 1 mm greater than gap
'S' unloaded or 3—4 mm loaded

3. Propeller shaft - inspection and overhaul

1 Excessive vibration knocking noises on taking up the drive can often be attributed to a worn pillow block bearing, deteriorated pillow block pad or worn splines. Quite often it is a combination of all three.

2 To carry out any renovation successfully the shaft assembly should all be removed first. On early models trouble was often experienced with the splines wearing on the rear of the rear shaft. At the very least this meant renewing the shaft and sleeve and sometimes the final drive pinion as well, making the job a very expensive one.

3 To renew the pillow block bearing it is necessary first to separate the two shafts, be they late or early models, by dismantling the centre universal joint. This can be done by removing the circlips from the yokes which hold the needle roller bearings in place. By tapping the yokes the spider bearing can then be removed.

4 With the universal joint dismantled the yoke retaining nut must then be undone and the yoke drawn off. Behind this is a circlip holding the bearing shield in position. With these removed the shaft and bearing together will come out of the pillow block. The bearing may then be taken off the shaft.

5 If any play is detected in the needle roller bearings of the universal joints they must be renewed. New bearings will be supplied with the necessary seals and circlips. When fitting them put the spider in the yoke. Then fit the cup washers and seal washers on to the spider and press the bearing housings and needles on through the yoke until the circlips can be snapped back in place. Each bearing cup should be 1/3 filled with Castrol LM grease.

6 The flexible coupling sleeve can be drawn off the front end of the front shaft. On some models there is a knurled cover to be unscrewed first. When refitting the front sleeve see that the balancing marks on both the sleeve and the shaft are realigned correctly.

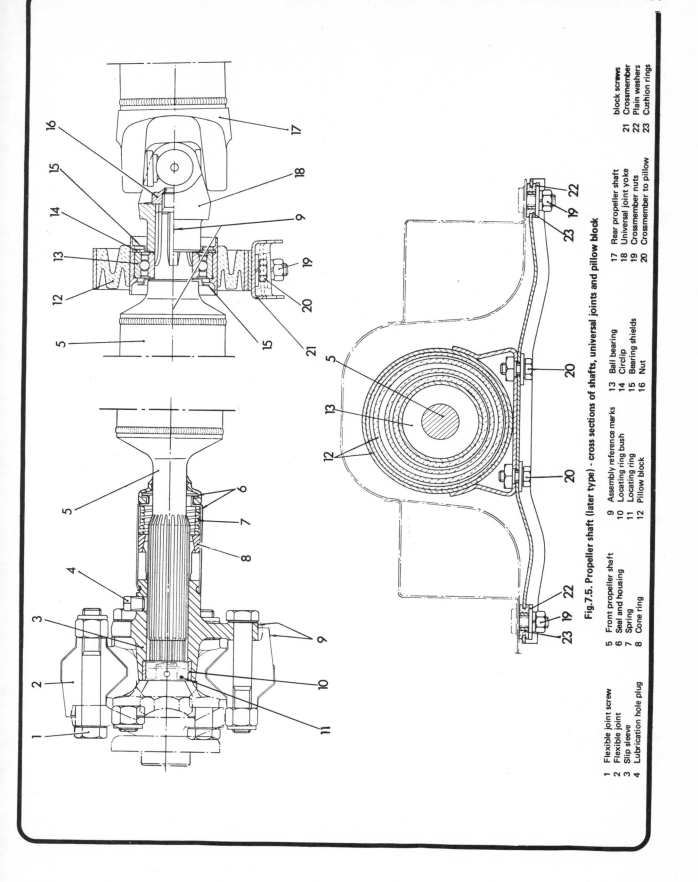

Fig.7.5. Propeller shaft (later type) - cross sections of shafts, universal joints and pillow block

1 Flexible joint screw
2 Flexible joint
3 Slip sleeve
4 Lubrication hole plug
5 Front propeller shaft
6 Seal and housing
7 Spring
8 Cone ring
9 Assembly reference marks
10 Locating ring bush
11 Locating ring
12 Pillow block
13 Ball bearing
14 Circlip
15 Bearing shields
16 Nut
17 Rear propeller shaft
18 Universal joint yoke
19 Crossmember nuts
20 Crossmember to pillow block
21 block screws
22 Crossmember
23 Plain washers
23 Cushion rings

Chapter 8 Rear axle

Contents

Specifications

Type...	Semi-floating - hypoid final drive
Ratio	
124	4.3 : 1
124S	4.1 : 1
124 Estate ... ...,...	4.4 : 1
Oil capacity	
124	0.7 litres/1.25 pts
124S	1.3 litres/2.3 pts
Pinion bearing pre-load	By compressible spacer and shaft nut
Differential bearing pre-load	0.20 — 0.25 mm/.008 — .010 in.
Crownwheel to pinion gear backlash	0.08 — 0.12 mm/.003 — .005 in.
Torque wrench settings	
Pinion bearing shaft nut for pre-load	108 — 166 ft lbs/15 — 23 kgm*
Crownwheel to differential case bolts...	72 ft lbs/10 kgm
*Dependent on pinion turning torque requirement *	1.2 — 1.4 ft lbs (16 — 20 kg cm)

1. General description

The live rear axle is conventional, with hypoid final drive gears and semi-floating axle shafts running on a single ball bearing at the outer end. The axle shaft inner ends are splined into the differential side gears.

The pinion runs in two taper roller bearings which are preloaded and also located by a compressible spacer between them. The crownwheel to pinion mesh is set by the lateral movement of the differential cage. This lateral position is controlled by screwed retaining rings which both position and pre-load the differential side bearings.

Axle shafts can be removed without difficulty and the differential casing and assembly can be removed from the rear axle as a unit once the propeller shaft has been detached and the axle shafts withdrawn a short distance.

2. Axle shafts and oil seals - removal and replacement

1 Loosen the wheel nuts of the wheel on the shaft to be removed and then jack up the car and support the axle casing on a stand. If both shafts are to be taken out it is important that the rear axle is supported firmly on two stands.
2 Remove the wheel and detach the brake caliper and disc from the shaft hub. Details for the caliper and disc removal are given in Chapter 9.

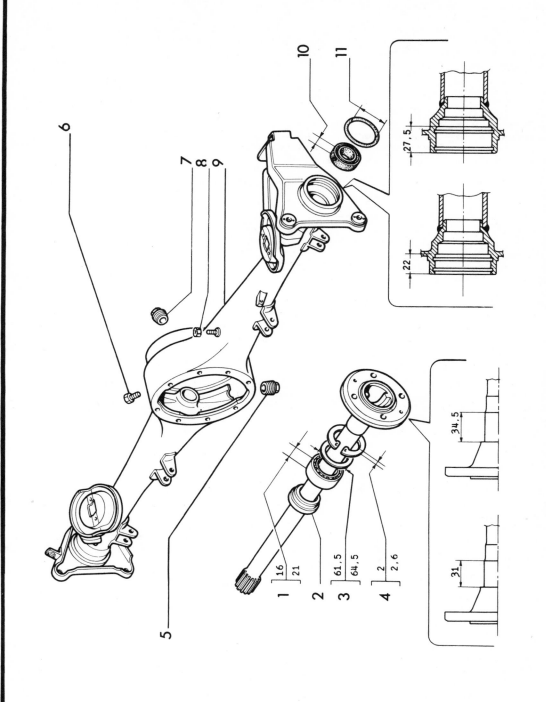

Fig.8.1. Rear axle and axle shafts. Dimensional variations, in bearings, bearing lands, housings, seals, spacers and circlips, dependent on chassis number, are all indicated. Measurements in millimetres.

| 1 Axle shaft bearing | 3 Bearing shield | 5 Oil drain plug | 7 Oil level plug | 9 Axle casing | 11 'O' ring |
| 2 Bearing retaining ring | 4 Circlip | 6 Vent plug | 8 Nut | 10 Oil seal | |

3 From behind the axle shaft flange remove the internal circlip holding the bearing into the housing with a suitable pair of circlip pliers (photo).

4 Behind the circlip there is also a dust shield over the bearing.

5 The shaft and bearing have to be drawn out together and this normally involves some percussion to force the bearing from the housing. If a slide hammer is available there is no problem. Otherwise an alternative is to refit a wheel (or if possible an old rim without a tyre) and strike it from the inside to draw the axle out. Do not under any circumstances strike the axle shaft flange directly. It can be distorted and damaged too easily.

6 With the axle removed the oil seal and 'O' ring behind the bearing may be taken out.

7 Replacement of the axle shaft is a straightforward reversal of the removal procedure. Do not forget the oil seal which should preferably be a new one, or the 'O' ring, which should certainly be new. Note that modifications on the bearings resulted in oil seals of different widths being used. Make sure you purchase the correct one. (Spares are supplied according to chassis number).

8 Check and top up the oil level if required.

3. Axle shaft bearings - renewal

1 If the ball bearing on the shaft is obviously worn and in need of renewal it is best done by someone with the proper equipment. The bearing is held on the shaft by a retaining ring which requires heating to 300°C and 5 tons weight under a press to get it on. Somewhat more than 5 tons is needed to get it off and the use of hammers, cold chisels, hacksaws and the like will probably have a net result of a ruined axle shaft. Take it along to a Fiat franchise garage who will have the part (note once again that more than one type of bearing may be fitted) and the appropriate tools and press to fit it without damage to either the axle or bearing.

4. Differential and final drive - removal and replacement

1 Removal of the final drive and differential is possible without disturbing the crownwheel to pinion setting or without removal of the axle assembly.

2 Jack up the car, support it on stands and draw out both axle shafts about 3 inches only to disengage them from the differential side gears.

3 Disconnect the propeller shaft from the drive pinion as described in Chapter 7.

4 Undo the drain plug in the bottom of the casing and let the oil out into a clean container. It may be re-used.

5 Support the differential casing and remove the eight bolts securing it to the front of the axle. The whole unit may then be withdrawn.

6 If the differential assembly or crownwheel and pinion are severely worn or damaged the average owner will be wise to get a professional opinion before attempting to repair it himself. If either the crownwheel or pinion is damaged both will have to be renewed as they are matched in pairs. When this is done the re-setting of the pinion and pinion bearings calls for a special dummy pinion gauge and a selection of special spacer shims to choose from. The pinion, crownwheel and bearings are very expensive parts and anything other than professional setting up would be folly. There is also no question of adjusting an axle in service. Once it becomes noisy or full of backlash the reason is wear. Repositioning of existing components may conceivably reduce backlash in certain circumstances but it will hardly ever reduce the noise, and wear will accelerate as non-aligned surfaces are presented to each other.

7 Replacement of the differential assembly into the rear axle casing is a reversal of the removal procedure. Use a new gasket between the carrier and casing and tighten the retaining bolts to a torque of 51 ft lbs/7 kgm.

8 Do not forget to refill the casing with oil.

5. Rear axle assembly - removal and replacement

1 Removal of the rear axle assembly is a rare enough job in view of the relative ease with which the sub-assemblies may be taken from it whilst in position. In certain circumstances however - such as external damage to the casing or rear suspension it may be necessary.

2 Slacken the wheel bolts and jack up the rear of the car. Support it on stands under the body jacking points at each side. Then securely chock the front wheels in front and behind.

3 Remove the wheels and disconnect the propeller shaft from the rear axle.

4 Inside the engine compartment remove the hydraulic fluid reservoir cap and seal the reservoir by putting plastic film under the cap before screwing it back on again. Then disconnect the flexible hose where it joins the brake pipe on top of the rear axle casing.

5 Disconnect the brake cables from each lever at the rear wheel and then disengage the cable outers from the adjacent anchorages.

6 Next disconnect the two links to the stabilizer bar from the brackets on the axle housing by removing the nut and bolt. On all 124S models and late model 124s there are two short longitudinal arms fitted instead of the stabilizer bar. Disconnect these at the axle end.

7 The brake regulator control rod is disconnected from the axle housing lug by removing the bolt and self-locking nut.

8 Support the axle housing with a suitable jack and from inside the boot disconnect the upper anchorages of the rear dampers. On estate cars the rear dampers are mounted outside the springs so that they can be disconnected at the lower end by removing the eye bolt and nut.

9 Finally remove the bolts securing the two main trailing arms and the transverse Panhard rod to their respective brackets on the axle. The axle may then be lowered and drawn back from the car.

10 Refitting the rear axle assembly is a reversal of the removal procedure. Make sure that the springs and their seats are properly located and the necessary bushes fitted to the upper ends of the dampers. Move the assembly into position under the rear of the car. Then lift the axle on the jack until the ends of the trailing arms and the Panhard rod can be reconnected to their brackets. Do not tighten the nuts and bolts more than finger tight.

11 Extend the dampers upwards as far as they will go and then jack up the axle until the top ends of the dampers can be secured in position.

12 Reconnect the tie rods of the brake regulator and the stabilizer bar but do not tighten up the bolts and nuts for the stabilizer at this stage.

13 Reconnect the handbrake cables and the hydraulic brake hose; Then bleed the hydraulics and adjust the handbrake as described in Chapter 9.

14 Refit the propeller shaft, replace the wheels and lower the car to the ground. Check the rear axle oil level.

15 Finally the suspension arm bolts must be correctly tightened. The car should be stood on a smooth level surface. Just forward of the rear wheel arch there is at each side an assembly line slinging bracket. The car must be loaded so that the bracket centre support is 211 mm/ 8.31 ins. above the ground at each side. The bolts should then be tightened to their specified torques (trailing arms and Panhard rod 72 ft lb/10 kgm and stabilizer bar links 25 ft lbs/3.5 kgm).

Fig.8.2. Rear axle bearing, housing and shaft — Cross section

1 Circlip   5 Axle shaft
2 'O' ring   6 Axle casing
3 Retaining ring   7 Ball bearing
4 Oil seal   8 Dust shield

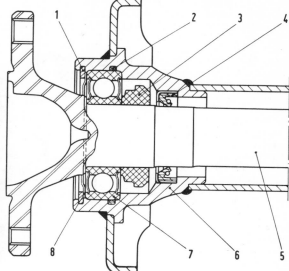

2.3. Using circlip pliers to remove the half shaft bearing retaining circlip

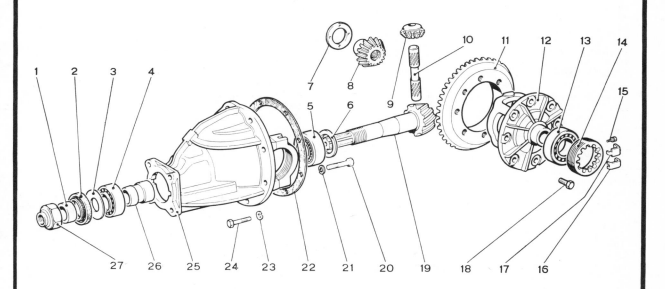

Fig.8.3. Final drive and differential

1 Spacer	washer	13 Differential side bearing
2 Oil seal	7 Side gear thrust washer	14 Bearing adjuster ring
3 Oil slinger	(selective)	15 Locking clip bolt
4 Pinion front roller	8 Side gear	16 Locking clip (alternative)
bearing	9 Differential pinion gear	17 Locking clip (alternative)
5 Pinion rear roller	10 Pinion gear shaft	18 Crownwheel screws
bearing	11 Crownwheel	19 Pinion
6 Rear bearing thrust	12 Differential casing	20 Side bearing carrier

cap bolt	
21 Spring washer	
22 Gasket	
23 Spring washer	
24 Differential carrier bolt	
25 Differential carrier	
26 Compressible spacer	
27 Pinion nut	

Chapter 9   Braking system

Contents

Specifications

Type ... ...   Hydraulically operated disc brakes on all 4 wheels with a
mechanical handbrake to the rear wheels only

Calipers ... ...   Single cylinder - floating

Discs diameter
Nominal disc thickness	227 mm/9 inch
Minimum thickness (reground)	10 mm/.39 inches
Minimum thickness (wear)	9.5 mm/.37 inches
Maximum permissible runout	9 mm/.35 inches
Friction pad material minimum thickness	2 mm/.079 inches
Master cylinder diameter	1.5 mm/.06 inches
Caliper cylinder diameter - front	19.05 mm/.75 inches
- rear	48 mm/1.875 inches
Brake servo cylinder bore	34 mm/1.375 inches
Servo piston pushrod to master cylinder piston gap	158.5 mm/6.24 inches
	1.05 − 1.25 mm/.04 − .05 inch

1. General description

The Fiat 124 is fitted with disc brakes on all four wheels. These are hydraulically operated from either a single or dual circuit system which may be servo assisted on the 124S.

The calipers are of the floating type with a cylinder in one side only. Incorporated in the hydraulic pressure line to the rear brakes only is a fluid pressure regulating valve which reduces the braking force on the rear wheels in certain light load applications.

The handbrake operates on the rear brakes only and a device incorporated in the piston automatically adjusts the actuating lever as the friction material wears down and the piston assumes a new static position.

The vacuum servo is fitted as standard on 124S models and this uses manifold depression from the engine intake manifold to boost hydraulic pressure with lower pedal pressures.

2. Brake adjustment and inspection

1   Disc brakes are self adjusting and under normal circumstances no attention is necessary until the friction material on the pads has reached its minimum permissible thickness.

2   With the handbrake also the action is self adjusting. It is important however, to make sure that the cable is not set too tight. If it is the auto adjusting device will over-adjust and cause binding. The brakes should not operate until the lever ratchet has passed at least 5 clicks, and no more than 7. The cable adjustment is under the car in the centre, at the stirrup round which the cable loops. The stirrup position can be altered by adjusting the nut on the threaded rod, (Fig.9.1).

3   Routine inspection of the brakes should be carried out so that possible deterioration in their efficiency can be foreseen and corrected before it is too late.

4   The discs themselves should have a smooth shiny bright surface on both sides where the pads rub. In time the outer edges of the discs particularly can get rusty and pitted despite the constant friction of the pads. When this occurs, or when the surface becomes significantly scored the discs will need refacing or even renewal. Sometimes the discs can warp so the run-out measurement must be checked. See Section 5 for details.

5   The other area for inspection is the hoses and pipes for the hydraulic fluid. These must be unchafed, unkinked and corrosion free, and no signs of fluid leakage must be visible. Fluid leakage is a danger signal.

Fig.9.1. Handbrake cable tension adjustment

1 Stretcher
2 Stretcher retainer spring
3 Adjusting nut
4 Locknut

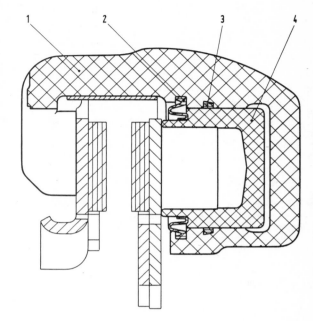

Fig.9.2. Front brake caliper - assembled cross section

1 Caliper body
2 Caliper piston dust seal
3 Hydraulic seal
4 Piston

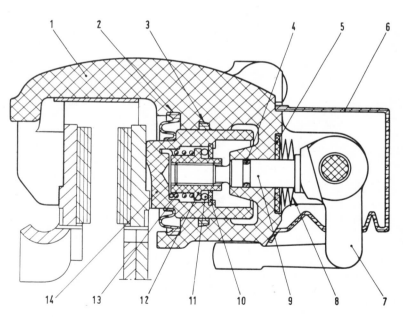

Fig.9.3. Rear wheel caliper - assembled cross section

1 Caliper body
2 Piston dust seal
3 Hydraulic seal
4 Seal ring
5 Spring backing washer
6 Rubber dust cover
7 Handbrake actuating lever
8 Spring
9 Actuating pin
10 Automatic adjuster retaining plate
11 Ball bearing
12 Automatic adjuster nut
13 Automatic adjuster spring
14 Hydraulic piston

3. Calipers and disc pads - removal, inspection and replacement

1 Before dismantling any parts of the brakes they should be thoroughly cleaned. The best cleaning agent is hot water and a mild detergent. Do not use petrol, paraffin or any other solvents which could cause deterioration to the friction pads or piston seals.

2 Jack up the car and remove the wheel.

3 Take out the two clips which hold the caliper locking blocks in place.

4 Hold the caliper and pull out the locking blocks, with a pair of pliers if necessary, and swing the caliper to one side out of the way. Take away the spring plate.

5 The pads may be taken out of the caliper support bracket. If they are not being renewed note which side they come from so they may be put back in the same place. The friction pad material should be no less than 2.0 mm (0.079 in). If the pads are not worn out but have a black and shiny surface it is helpful to roughen them up a little on some emery cloth before replacing them. Disc pads last normally about 12,000 miles, a little longer on the rear.

6 Behind the pads on the carrier bracket are two pad anchor springs (photo). Remove these and clean them up after ensuring that they are intact. Renew them otherwise.

7 Provided that discs, and pads are in good condition and the brake pedal pressure is firm, with no signs of fluid leakage, any inefficiency in the brakes is most likely to be in the operation of the caliper pistons. One or more may be partially or completely seized, so reducing the effective pressure at that particular wheel.

8 To check the pistons only one caliper should be detached at a time. The other three should be in position with their pads.

9 With the caliper detached from the carrier bracket but still attached to the hydraulic system get someone to depress the brake pedal — GENTLY and only a little way at a time under your direction. The piston should be seen to move out a little way and you should be able to press it back wtihout any undue pressure once the brake pedal has been released. Do this with each wheel in turn. Any piston which is reluctant to move will indicate that the caliper should be removed from the car and dealt with as described in Section 4.

10 On the rear brakes, after testing the pistons in the manner described check that the automatic brake adjuster is correctly set — if new pads were being fitted. Follow the procedure given later in this section. If, during examination of the caliper pistons there are any traces whatsoever of hydraulic fluid seepage then the pistons must be removed, examined and new seals fitted as described in Section 4.

11 The caliper is still attached to the hydraulic fluid hose. If it is to be taken off the car completely seal the hydraulic fluid reservoir cap with a piece of plastic film to prevent excess fluid loss, and unscrew the union from the caliper.

12 Replacement of the pads and calipers is a reversal of the removal procedure, but when fitting new pads certain additional matters must be attended to.

13 Make sure that the new pads have the same colour code stripe as the ones taken off. If there is some doubt about the pads taken off check that the pads on all four wheels have the same colour code on the front.

14 Push back the piston in the caliper with a suitable blunt instrument to provide the necessary clearance for the new, thicker pads.

15 On the back brake calipers the piston face has a slot in it and with a broad bladed driver it should be screwed in as far as it will go. It is a touch turn so a bar may be needed. Then turn it back in order that the reference line also cut in the face of the piston is upwards towards the bleed valve (photo). This ensures that the piston is in the correct position for complete venting when the brakes are bled.

16 Refit the pads into the carrier, replace the caliper with the retaining spring (photo), tap in the locking blocks (photo) and refit the clips (photo).

17 If the caliper has been detached from the hydraulic hose it will be necessary to bleed the system as described in Section 11.

18 On the rear brakes the handbrake should be operated several times to let the automatic adjusting device inside the caliper piston take up its proper position. If necessary adjust the handbrake cable after this has been done as described in Section 2.

4. Calipers - overhauling hydraulic pistons and seals

1 Remove the caliper from the car as described in Section 3.

2 With the front brake calipers, if the piston is only partially seized it should be possible to force it right out under pressure from an air line on the hydraulic fluid inlet. With an air line from a petrol station this should be fairly easy but on a foot pump it will be necessary to make up a suitable air tight adaptor.

3 With the rear brakes the piston may be screwed out using a suitable blade in the slot of the piston head. This will disengage it from the plunger on the handbrake mechanism.

4 If the pistons are seized solid it is more likely that you will be unable to get the piston out without damaging the caliper or piston. However it is worthwhile having a go. Pull out the rubber dust seal and leave the whole assembly to soak in methylated spirits for a time. If this does not soften things up then a new caliper assembly will have to be bought.

5 With the rear brake calipers the handbrake lever mechanism should be dismantled also so that the plunger seal may be renewed. Remove the rubber dust cover and take out the lever pivot pin. The plunger, disc spring and thrust washer can then be taken out. If the self adjusting mechanism inside the rear brake piston seems to be malfunctioning a new piston will be needed as they cannot be satisfactorily dismantled.

6 Assuming the pistons have been removed without difficulty, clean them thoroughly with methylated spirit and remove the seal from the annular groove in the cylinder bore. Any hard residue deposits may be removed with careful use of some 600 grit wet and dry paper. If there are any ridges or scores in the cylinder or on the piston the parts must be renewed.

7 Remove the seal from the rear brake plunger and then clean all parts thoroughly in meths or water and detergent and blow them dry.

8 Fit new seals in the cylinder groove and on rear piston plungers, lubricate the cylinders and pistons with hydraulic fluid and replace the pistons. Fit the dust seals so that they fit in the caliper groove and on to the piston.

9 Make sure the rear brake pistons are set as described in Section 3 (for fitting new pads).

10 When the calipers have been reassembled and fitted back to the car bleed the hydraulic system as described in Section 12.

5. Discs - inspection and renovation

1 Discs do not last forever. Under ideal conditions and with proper and regular maintenance of caliper pistons and brake pads they will last a long time. Under other circumstances they can warp, wear irregularly, get rusted and pitted, develop score lines and as a result provide poor braking and rapid consumption of pads. Remember, disc brakes are only better than drum brakes if they are in good condition.

2 A disc in good condition should have a smooth, shiny bright surface on the pad contact area. Do not hope to improve a deteriorated disc by the burnishing effect of new pads! Another fault which a disc may have, even though the surfaces are good, is a warp (or run-out). This means it does not run true. If bad it can be seen when the wheel is spun. However, to measure the run-out accurately a clock gauge pointer should be set against one face. The deviation should not exceed 0.15 mm/ .006 ins. If you do not possess a clock gauge it is worth holding a steel pointer firmly on a nearby support with the point on the disc face. Variations can be detected in this way also. Remember that the wheel bearings must be completely devoid of any end float in order to check disc run out. Worn or

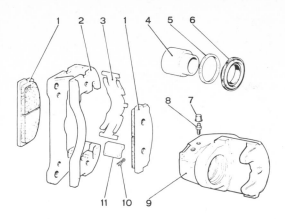

Fig.9.4. Front brake caliper - components

1	Friction pads	7	Dust cover
2	Caliper support bracket	8	Bleed nipple
3	Caliper spring	9	Caliper body
4	Hydraulic piston	10	Clip
5	Seal	11	Caliper retaining
6	Piston dust seal		block

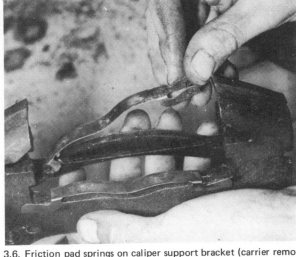

3.6. Friction pad springs on caliper support bracket (carrier removed from hub)

3.15. Rear caliper piston in correct position for bleeding in relation to bleed nipple (arrowed)

3.16A. Refitting a rear caliper. Note the pressure spring (arrowed)

3.16B. Replacing the caliper locking blocks

3.16C. Fitting the locking block clip

maladjusted bearings can be a contributory factor in disc deterioration.

3 To renovate a disc calls for either re-facing or renewal and for this they must be taken off as described in the next section. The cost of re-facing should be checked against the cost of a new disc. Remember also that the thickness of the disc should not be less than 10 mm/.39 inches. If it is very deeply scored or pitted, or the run out is excessive the only remedy may be a new one. If the disc is too thin it loses some of its capability to disperse heat and also its rigidity.

6. Discs - removal and replacement

1 Jack up the car and remove the wheel, caliper and disc pads as described in Section 3.
2 Remove the two screws which hold the support bracket to the steering knuckle on the front or to the axle tube flange on the rear. On rear wheels it is convenient to remove the front section of the shield plate first (photos).
3 Remove the two screws holding the retaining plate and disc to the hub and then pull off the disc (photos).
4 Replacement is a reversal of the removal procedure.

7. Hydraulic master cylinder

1 The hydraulic master cylinder pressurizes the hydraulic system under the action of the foot pedal which forces a piston along a cylinder.
2 Failure of the cylinder or the seals within is usually indicated by a lack of pedal pressure and the ability to move the pedal all the way to the floor without much or any stopping power.
3 Before assuming the master cylinder is defective check the whole hydraulic system, pipes, hoses and calipers to make sure that there are no leaks. If there are, they should be attended to first.
4 The master cylinder is in the engine compartment on the bulkhead. To remove it first disconnect the reservoir pipe and drain the reservoir or clamp the pipe.
5 Disconnect the three way adaptor from the top of the cylinder by undoing the single securing screw. It is not necessary to undo the three pipe unions.
6 Remove the two nuts and washers holding the cylinder to the bulkhead (or servo unit) and take the cylinder off.
7 To dismantle remove the rubber boot from the flange end of the cylinder and take out the circlip inside the cylinder bore.
8 Pull out the piston, valve ring carrier and the piston return spring.

6.2A. Removing a rear brake guard plate front section

6.2B. Removing a rear bracket caliper support bracket

6.3A. Taking off the disc retaining plate and screw

6.3B. Removing the disc

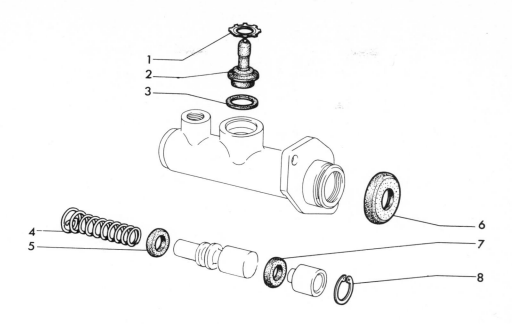

Fig.9.5. Hydraulic master cylinder — Components

1	Reservoir washer	3	Seal	5	Seal	7	Seal
2	Reservoir connector	4	Piston spring	6	Cylinder boot	8	Circlip

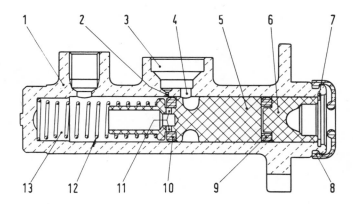

Fig.9.6. Hydraulic master cylinder - assembled cross section

1	Cylinder body	4	Fluid feed port	7	Circlip	11	Fluid ports
2	Compensating port	5	Piston and valve	8	Rubber boot	12	Return spring
3	Reservoir pipe union		carrier	9	Seal	13	Pressure chamber
	seating	6	Piston	10	Seal		

9 The piston and cylinder may be cleaned out with meths and should have a perfectly smooth unpitted unscored surface. If either is worn a new unit is needed.

10 Pull the rubber sealing rings from the piston and valve carrier and fit new ones. They are interchangeable.

11 Check that the compensating port in the cylinder body is clear. This will involve removing the union plug for the reservoir pipe.

12 With everything perfectly clean, lubricate the parts with hydraulic fluid - use nothing else - and replace the spring, wide end first, valve carrier and piston. Replace the circlip and fit a new boot over the cylinder end.

13 The cylinder is refitted in the reverse order of removal. Make sure that the pushrod from the brake pedal fits snugly through the rubber boot into the piston recess.

14 After the cylinder has been refitted the complete braking system must be bled as described in Section 12.

8. Hydraulic dual circuit master cylinder

1 The principle of the dual circuit cylinder is the same as the single one except that there are two pistons and two fluid outlets. These two are independent of each other as far as maintaining pressure is concerned and one outlet goes to the front and one to the rear brakes. It is removed from the car in the same way as the single circuit cylinder and the only thing to note before dismantling it is that there is a locating screw which must be removed from under the cylinder before the front piston can be drawn out.

2 When dismantling place each part down carefully in order as it comes out so that there is no confusion on replacement. Note the type of seals on each piston so that the correct new ones are fitted.

3 When reassembly is carried out it may be necessary to force the

front piston forward against the spring in order to line up the slot for the locating plug to be replaced underneath.

9. Rear brake pressure compensation

1 As mentioned in the introduction a special valve is incorporated in the hydraulic fluid line to the rear wheels. This is mounted on the underbody. It consists basically of a plunger in a housing which when released reduces the pressure on the outlet side of the valve. The plunger is held in the housing by a rod and link bar attached to the rear axle. When the distance between the body and axle increases, as it would under sharp braking causing a nose down tail up attitude, the link, rod lets the plunger out and the braking pressure to the rear wheels is reduced. This prevents the wheels from locking and consequent skidding.

2 If the pressure regulator is suspected of malfunction first check that the operating bar is correctly set. The end of the adjusting bar which connects to the top end of the link shackle should be set 147 mm/5¾ inches from the underside of the body. This will involve jacking up the body in relation to the axle and disconnecting it. In this position the other end of the operating bar should just touch the end of the plunger under the rubber dust cover.

3 The plunger position may be altered by slackening the two regulator mounting screws. One hole is slotted so the unit may be tilted as required and tightened in the correct position.

4 The unit itself may be removed from the car after undoing the two hydraulic pipe unions and removing the mounting bolts. It is difficult to test the working properties without proper equipment. Seals can be renewed if the cover plug is taken off but the usual practice is to replace the whole unit.

5 When refitting the brake lines note that the lower port on the regulator is for the line from the master cylinder.

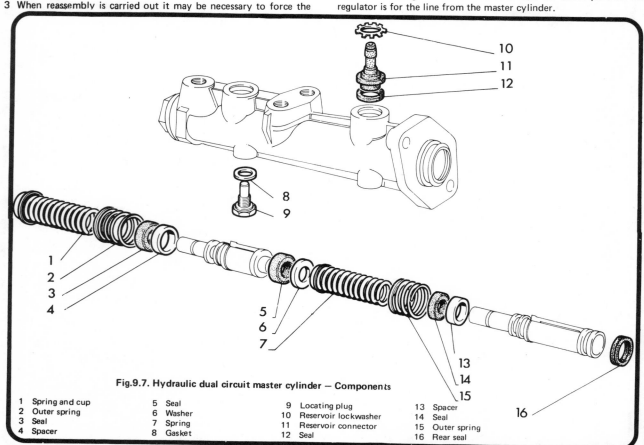

Fig.9.7. Hydraulic dual circuit master cylinder — Components

1	Spring and cup	5	Seal	9	Locating plug	13	Spacer
2	Outer spring	6	Washer	10	Reservoir lockwasher	14	Seal
3	Seal	7	Spring	11	Reservoir connector	15	Outer spring
4	Spacer	8	Gasket	12	Seal	16	Rear seal

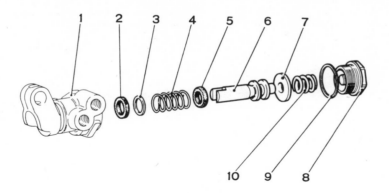

Fig.9.8. Rear wheel brake pressure regulator — Components

1 Regulator body	4 Spring	7 Washer	10 Spring
2 Seal	5 Seal	8 Plug	
3 Spring support washer	6 Valve piston	9 Plug seal ring	

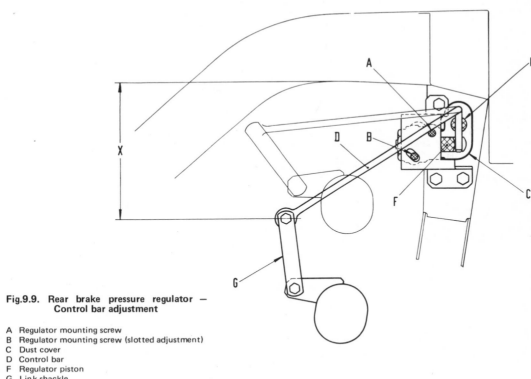

Fig.9.9. Rear brake pressure regulator — Control bar adjustment

A Regulator mounting screw
B Regulator mounting screw (slotted adjustment)
C Dust cover
D Control bar
F Regulator piston
G Link shackle
I Pin
X Setting distance — 147.5 mm/5.75 inches

10. Brake vacuum servo

1   The brake vacuum servo is incorporated between the brake pedal and the master cylinder. It uses inlet manifold vacuum to provide boosted pressure on the master cylinder piston.

2   Maintenance and adjustments to the servo unit are minimal. There is an air filter round the pushrod from the brake pedal.

3   The use of the servo piston rod which engages into the master cylinder should protrude 1.05–1.25 mm/.042–.050 inches beyond the front face of the cover. The end of the rod is threaded and has an adjustable nose piece.

4   If the servo unit malfunctions it is possible to dismantle it but normal procedure is to obtain a new unit. The main body cover is a bayonet fit on to the base. When released the main diaphragm return spring is released and the diaphragm and seals can all then be renewed. The piston rod is released from the diaphragm retainer by pulling out the locking plate.

11. Hydraulic pipes and hoses

1   Periodically all brake pipes, pipe connections and unions should be completely and carefully examined.

2   First examine for signs of leakage where the pipe unions occur. Then examine the flexible hoses for signs of chafing and fraying and, of course, leakage. This is only a preliminary part of the flexible hose inspection, as exterior condition does not necessarily indicate the interior condition, which will be considered later.

3   The steel pipes must be examined equally carefully. They must be cleaned off and examined for any signs of dents, or other percussive damage and rust and corrosion. Rust and corrosion should be scraped off and, if the depth of pitting in the pipes is significant, they will need replacement. This is particularly likely in those areas underneath the car body and along the rear axle where the pipes are exposed to full force of road and weather conditions.

4   If any section of pipe is to be taken off, first of all remove the fluid reservoir cap and line it with a piece of polythene film to make it air tight, and replace it. This will minimise the amount of fluid dripping out of the system, when pipes are removed.

5   Rigid pipe removal is usually quite straightforward. The unions at each end are undone, the pipe and union pulled out, and the centre sections of the pipe removed from the body clips where necessary. Underneath the car, exposed unions can sometimes be very tight. As one can use only an open ended spanner and the unions are not large burring of the flats is not uncommon when attempting to undo them. For this reason a self-locking grip wrench (Mole) is often the only way to remove a stubborn union.

6   Flexible hoses are always mounted at both ends in a rigid bracket attached to the body or a sub-assembly. To remove them it is necessary first of all to unscrew the pipe unions of the rigid pipes which go into them. The hose ends can then be unclipped from the brackets. The mounting brackets, particularly on the bodyframe, are not very heavy gauge and care must be taken not to wrench them off.

7   With the flexible hose removed, examine the internal bore. If it is blown through first, it should be possible to see through it. Any specks of rubber which come out, or signs of restriction in the bore, mean that the inner lining is breaking up and the pipe must be replaced.

8   Rigid pipes which need replacement can usually be purchased at any garage where they have the pipe, unions and special tools to make them up. All they need to know is the total length of the pipe, the type of flare used at each end with the union, and the length and thread of the union. Fiat is metric remember.

9   Replacement of pipes is a straightforward reversal of the removal procedure. If the rigid pipes have been made up it is best to get all the sets (bends) in them before trying to install them. Also if there are any acute bends, ask your supplier to put these in for you on a tube bender. Otherwise you may kink the pipe and thereby restrict the bore area and fluid flow.

10   With the pipes replaced, remove the polythene film from the reservoir cap and bleed the system as described in Section 12.

12. Hydraulic system - bleeding

1   Hydraulic brake systems need bleeding for the purpose of expelling air. Air gets into the system when any part is disconnected for any reason or if the car has been standing idle for a long time and the fluid has absorbed air (which it does). If bleeding is necessary at intervals even though nothing has been done to the system then a fault somewhere has let air in. For this to happen there must be a leak allowing fluid to come out so further bleeding is futile unless the fault is traced.

2   Localised work at each wheel end of the system only will not require bleeding of the whole system provided care is taken to keep the loss of fluid at the wheel to a minimum. This can be achieved if the master cylinder reservoir cap is sealed. Any work carried out at the master cylinder or the fluid lines leading from it will mean that the whole system will require bleeding at each wheel.

3   Before beginning to bleed the system make sure you have everything you need — A fresh unopened ½ pint tin of fluid, a suitable piece of neoprene pipe that will fit snugly on the bleed nipple - and about 18 ins/40 cms long, a clean jar and finally, and most important two spanners, one open ended and one ring that are the correct size for the nipple. The bleed nipples can be a very tight fit and a ring spanner is essential sometimes. If you have none of the equipment to hand it is worthwhile buying the Castrol kit which will supply the fluid and pipe you need. It also enables you to fit the fluid container to the reservoir in such a way that there will be no danger of the fluid level going down too low. If the whole system is to be bled you will need at least 1 pint of fluid.

4   A second person is needed to depress the brake pedal whilst bleeding is being done.

5   Where a servo unit is fitted the engine must not be running and the brake pedal should be depressed a few times to make sure all residual vacuum is gone from the unit.

6   If all four wheels need bleeding it is best to jack up the car and support it on stands so that all four wheels may be removed together.

7   Remove the wheel and thoroughly clean the area round the bleed nipple on top of the caliper, removing the dust cap if fitted.

8   Check that the fluid reservoir is full and put some fluid in the bottom of the jar so that the end of the pipe can be immersed in it. If you are using a tube with a non-return valve fitted this is not necessary. Where all four brakes have to be bled it is a good idea first of all to open all four bleed nipples at once and pump the brake pedal until some fluid escapes from all of them. This moves any air at the centre of the distribution system towards the extremities and there is less likelihood of air getting back from another part to a line that has already been bled.

9   Fit the tube over the bleed nipple and undo the nipple ½—1 turn only.

10   With the end of the tube in the jar depress the brake pedal slowly to the floor and let it return. Then give two or three sharp stabs on the pedal - about ½ stroke only - followed by another steady stroke to the floor. The short stabs force any air bubbles trapped in corners to come out rather than sending the fluid past them. Check the reservoir level. Continue like this, including the short stabs until fluid with no bubbles in it emerges from the bleed nipple.

11   Repeat this procedure at each wheel in turn; remember to keep the reservoir topped up. Do not re-use fluid bled from the system.

12   If work has been carried out on the rear brake calipers make sure before bleeding that the piston is correctly positioned as described in Section 3.

13   Having bled the brake tighten the bleed nipple whilst the foot pedal is depressed.

14   After bleeding has been carried out the car should be tested on the road without delay.

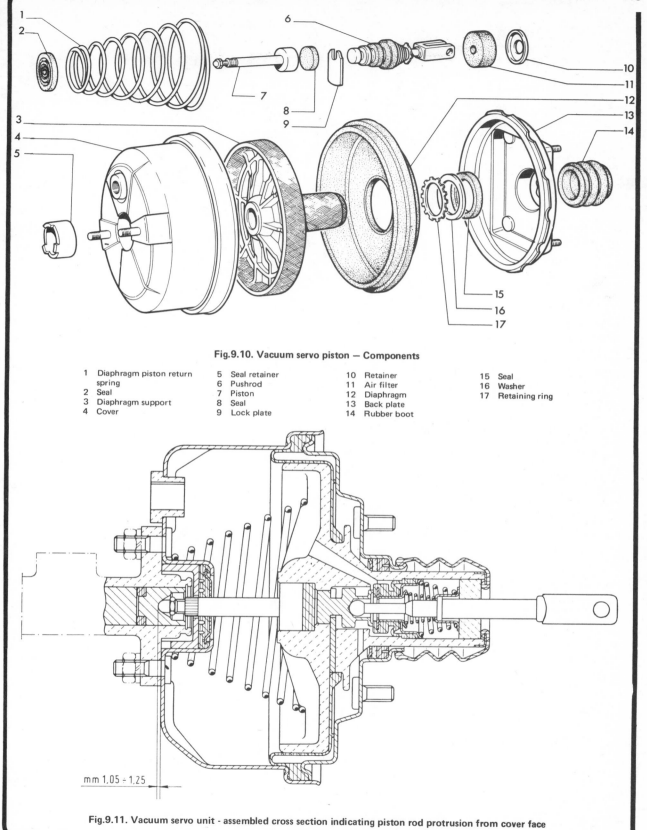

Fig.9.10. Vacuum servo piston — Components

1	Diaphragm piston return spring	5	Seal retainer	10	Retainer	15	Seal
2	Seal	6	Pushrod	11	Air filter	16	Washer
3	Diaphragm support	7	Piston	12	Diaphragm	17	Retaining ring
4	Cover	8	Seal	13	Back plate		
		9	Lock plate	14	Rubber boot		

mm 1,05 - 1,25

Fig.9.11. Vacuum servo unit - assembled cross section indicating piston rod protrusion from cover face

13. Brake pedal and mounting bracket

1 If any serious wear develops in the pedal cross-shaft it can affect the proper operation of the master cylinder. Also the master cylinder pushrod pivots on a bush on the side of the brake pedal and this should not be worn.

2 To remove the pedal shaft and renew the bushes is a relatively easy matter and details are given in Chapter 5.

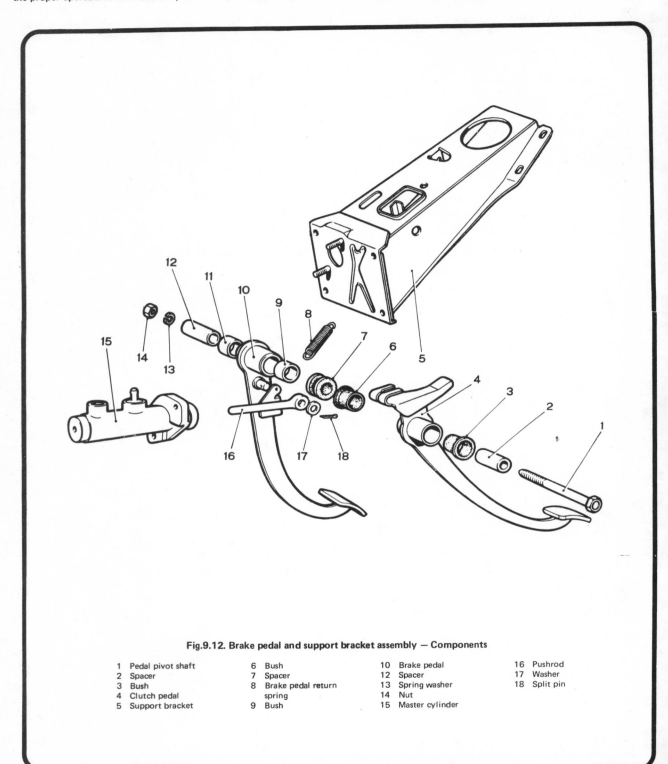

Fig.9.12. Brake pedal and support bracket assembly — Components

1	Pedal pivot shaft	6	Bush	10	Brake pedal	16	Pushrod
2	Spacer	7	Spacer	12	Spacer	17	Washer
3	Bush	8	Brake pedal return	13	Spring washer	18	Split pin
4	Clutch pedal		spring	14	Nut		
5	Support bracket	9	Bush	15	Master cylinder		

14. Fault finding

Before deciding that there are any faults in the braking system make sure that the following points are correct first:—

1 Types are of the correct 'mix' on the axles and the pressures are correct.
2 The steering geometry is correct.
3 The springs and dampers are all functioning properly.
4 The bodyframe is aligned correctly,

Symptom	Reason/s	Remedy
Foot pedal moves a long way before the brakes operate	Rear brake automatic adjuster not working properly	Overhaul rear calipers.
	Master cylinder mounting bolts loose	Tighten mounting bolts.
Stopping ability poor, even though pedal pressure is firm	1 Worn out brake pads	Renew pads.
	2 Seized caliper hydraulic piston(s)	Overhaul caliper.
	3 Scored or warped discs	Recondition or renew discs.
	4 Oil contaminated pads	Renew pads.
	5 Wrong type of pads fitted	Renew pads.
	6 Caliper assembly(ies) seized in the carrier preventing correct float	Check all calipers and carriers.
	7 Servo unit not working	Check and renew if necessary.
Car veers to one side when brakes are applied	As for 1—5 above, occuring particularly on one or other of the front brakes	Check front brakes completely.
Pedal feels spongy when brakes are applied	Air in the hydraulic system	Bleed the system and check throughout for leaks.
Pedal feels springy when brakes are applied	Loose master cylinder mounting	Tighten up the nuts.
	Carrier bracket mounting bolts loose	Check and tighten.
Foot pedal travels to the floor with little or no resistance and brakes are inoperative (N.B. On dual brake systems this possibility is highly unlikely)	Leak in hydraulic system resulting in lack of pressure	Examine whole system and repair and test each leak source.
	Master cylinder seals failing to sustain pressure	Remove master cylinder and overhaul.
Binding, juddering and overheating	One or a combination of the causes already given	Complete check of whole system.

Chapter 10 Electrical system

Contents

Specifications

Battery

Voltage	12 D.C.
Capacity (20 hr. rate)...	48 ampere/hours
Polarity	Negative earth

Starter motor

Type...	Pre-engaged with solenoid engagement control
Voltage	12 D.C.
Power (nominal) ... ...:	0.8 KW
No load running characteristics at 20°C	
- current...	25 amps max.
- voltage...	11.9
- speed	8000 rpm
Normal operation characteristics	
- current...	170 amps
- speed	2000 rpm
- voltage...	9.5
Commutator segment insulator undercut	1 mm/.04 ins.
Spring loading on new carbon brushes..	1.15—1.3 kg/2.5—2.8 lbs

Generator (dynamo)

Type...	12v D.C. Fiat D90/12/16/3E
Maximum steady output	16 amps
Intermittent peak output	22 amps
Cut in speed (12 volts)	1700—1800 rpm
Speed for maximum steady output	2500—2700 rpm
Peak current speed..	3000—3200 rpm
Drive ratio - engine to generator	1 : 1.86
Armature resistances (20°C)..	0.145 ohms
Field winding resistance (20°C)..	8 ohms
Spring loading on new brushes	.6 — .7 kg/21 — 25 ozs
Commutator segment insulation undercut	1 mm/.04 ins.
Voltage regulator type	Fiat GN2/12/16
Cut-out closes at	12.6 volts
Cut-out air gap - contacts closed	0.35 mm/.013 ins.
Cut-out points gap..	.45 — .06 mm/.017 — .002 ins.
Voltage regulator air gap)..	.99 — 1.11 mm/.038 — .043 ins.
Current regulator air gap)..	ditto

(Alternator)

Type...	Fiat A12 M124/12/42M

Voltage	12v AC (rectified)
Cut in speed (12 volts)	1000 rpm
Current output at 14 volts at 5000 rpm	42 amps
Maximum current output	53 amps
Rectifier diode type	4AF2
Voltage regulator type	RC1/12 B

Windscreen wiper motor

Speed (warm)	52—68 rpm
Current consumption (warm)	2.4 amps

Fuses..	Block of mounted to left of steering column under the instrument panel

Model 124

No 1 (left end of block) 8 amps	Oil pressure indicator light
	Engine temperature warning light
	Fuel gauge and reserve light
	Windscreen wiper
	Instrument lights
	Glove box light
	Heater fan motor
	Direction indicator lights
	Stop lights
No 2. 8 amps or 16 amps on later models	Interior lights
	Horns
No 3. 8 amps	L.H. headlamp low beam
No 4. 8 amps	R.H. headlamp low beam
No 5. 8 amps	L.H. headlamp high beam
	High beam indicator light
No 6. 8 amps	R.H. headlamp high beam
No 7...	Parking light L.H. front
	Parking light R.H. rear
	Parking light indicator
	Registration plate light - left bulb
	Engine compartment light
	Luggage compartment light
No 8...	Parking light R.H. front
	Parking light L.H. rear
	Registration plate lamp - right bulb 1 and 2

NOTE With the exception of No 2 all fused circuits are controlled by the ignition switch in positions 1 or 3

Fuses 124S

A. 26 amp	Courtesy light
	Horn relay and horns
	Cigarette lighter
B. 8 amp..	Windscreen wiper motor
	Heater fan motor
	Rear window heater
C. 8 amp..	Headlamps high beam, left, and indicator
D. 8 amp..	Headlamps high beam - right
E. 8 amp..	Headlamp low beam - left
F. 8 amp..	Headlamp low beam - right
G. 8 amp..	Parking light front - left
	Parking light indicator
	Parking light rear - right
	Licence plate light (1 bulb)
	Instrument light
	Luggage compartment light
	Cigarette lighter light
H. 8 amp..	Parking light front - right
	Parking light rear - left
	Licence plate light (1 bulb)
	Reverse light
	Engine compartment light
I. 8 amp...	Oil pressure indicator
	Water temperature gauge
	Fuel gauge and reserve indicator
	Glove compartment light
	Direction signals and indicator
	Stop lights

L. 8 amp.. ... .   Voltage regulator (alternator)
                                                                                             Alternator field winding

Bulbs

Headlamps	45/40W double filament
Front parking and flashers	5/20W double filament
Side indicator repeaters	3W
Rear flashers	20W
Rear parking and stop lights..	5/20W double filament
Rear number plate..	5W (two)
Interior light	5W
Instrument illumination	3W
Engine compartment...	5W
Luggage compartment	3W
Glove compartment	3W
Warning and indicator lights (7)..	3W
Reverse lamp	21W
Cigarette lighter light...	4W

On 124S with dual headlamps the two inboard lights are single filament high beam only, which go out on dip.

1. General description

The electrical system operates at 12 volts D.C. and the major components, excluding the ignition circuits are:—

Battery, 12 volt negative earth
Generator, dynamo or alternator, driven by a V belt from the crankshaft
Voltage and current regulator
Starter motor, pre-engaged, mounted at the right rear of the engine under the manifolds.

The battery supplies current for the ignition, lighting and other circuits and provides a reserve of power when the current consumed by the equipment exceeds the production of the generator.

The starter motor places very heavy demands on the power reserve. The generator uses engine power to produce electricity to re-charge the battery and the rate of charge is automatically controlled by a regulator. This regulator keeps the power output of the generator within its capacity (an uncontrolled generator can burn itself out) and also adjusts the voltage and current output depending on the state of the battery charge and the electrical demands being made on the system at any one time.

2. Battery - maintenance, removal and replacement

1 Any new battery, if properly looked after, will last for two years at least (provided also that the generator and regulator are in correct order).
2 The principal maintenance requirements are cleanliness and regular topping up of the electrolyte level with distilled water. Each week the battery cell cover or caps should be removed and just enough water added, if needed, to cover the tops of the separators. Do not overfill with the idea of the topping up lasting longer - it will only dilute the electrolyte and with the level high the likelihood of it 'gassing' out is increased. This is the moisture one can see on the top of a battery. 'Little and often is the rule'.
3 Wipe the top of the battery carefully at the same time removing all traces of moisture. Paper handkerchiefs are ideal for the job.
4 Every three months disconnect the battery terminals and wash

both the posts and lead connectors with a washing soda solution. This will remove any corrosion deposits. Dry them off and smear liberally with petroleum jelly - not grease, before re-connection.
5 Battery removal is simply a matter of disconnecting the lead terminal clamps, slackening the battery retaining clamp and lifting it out. Always undo the earth terminal clamp first and when re-connecting replace it last. In this way there is no danger of short circuiting the other terminal to earth. Always carry and place the battery in an upright position so as to prevent spillage of the electrolyte.
6 If a significant quantity of electrolyte is lost through spillage it will not suffice to merely re-fill with distilled water. Empty out all the electrolyte into a glass container and measure the specific gravity. Electrolyte is a mixture of sulphuric acid and water in the ratio of 2 parts acid to 5 parts water and the ready made solution should be obtainable from battery specialists or large garages. The 'normal' solution can be added if the battery is in a fully charged state. If the battery is in a low state of charge, use the normal solution, then charge the battery, empty out the electrolyte, swill the battery out with clean water and then refill with a new charge of normal electrolyte.

3. Battery - charging

1 In winter certain conditions may result in the battery being used in excess of the generators ability to recharge it in the running time available. This situation does not occur however on cars fitted with alternators which have a much higher rate of output at low revolutions.
2 Where necessary therefore, an external charging source is needed to keep the battery power reserve at the proper level. If batteries are being charged from an external source a hydrometer is used to check the electrolyte specific gravity. Once the fully charged reading is obtained charging should not continue for a period in excess of four hours. Most battery chargers are set to charge at 3—4 amps initially and as the battery charge builds up this reduces automatically to 1—2 amps. The table below gives details of the specific gravity readings, at 21°C/70°F. Do not take readings just after topping up, just after using the starter motor, or when the electrolyte is too cold or too warm. The variation is S.G. readings is .004 for every 6°C/10°F charge - the higher readings being for the higher temperatures.

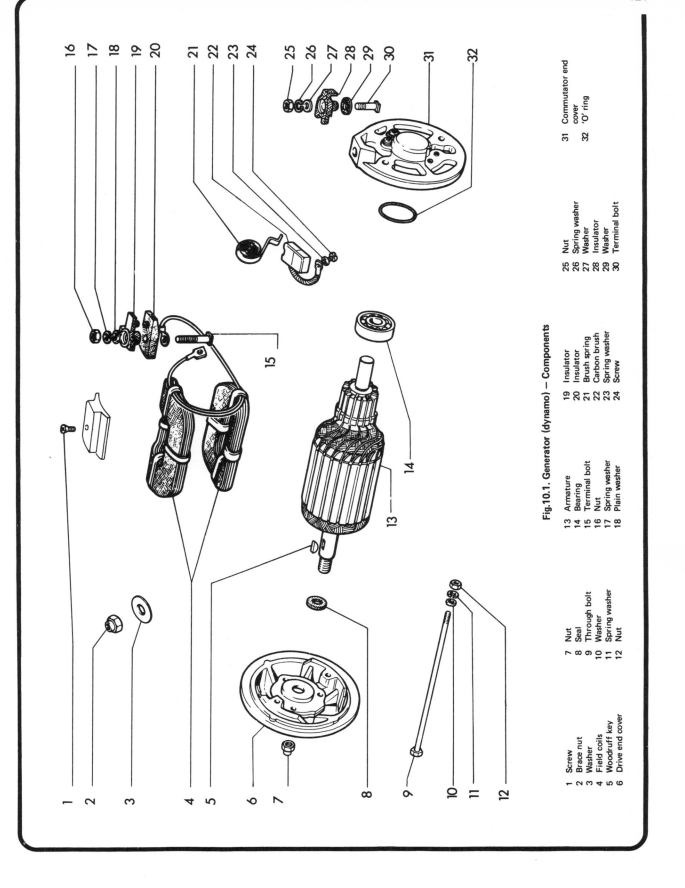

Fig.10.1. Generator (dynamo) – Components

1	Screw	7	Nut	13	Armature	19	Insulator	25	Nut	31	Commutator end
2	Brace nut	8	Seal	14	Bearing	20	Insulator	26	Spring washer		cover
3	Washer	9	Through bolt	15	Terminal bolt	21	Brush spring	27	Washer	32	'O' ring
4	Field coils	10	Washer	16	Nut	22	Carbon brush	28	Insulator		
5	Woodruff key	11	Spring washer	17	Spring washer	23	Spring washer	29	Washer		
6	Drive end cover	12	Nut	18	Plain washer	24	Screw	30	Terminal bolt		

Specific gravity	Battery state of charge
1.28	100%
1.25	75%
1.22	50%
1.19	25%
1.16	Very low
1.11	Discharged completely

4. Generator (dynamo) - description, maintenance and testing

1 The D.C. generator or dynamo consists of an armature running in bearings. It is surrounded by field coils bolted to the outer casing or yoke. At one end of the armature is the commutator consisting of copper segments. Two carbon brushes, spring loaded and in holders run on the commutator.

2 The only maintenance required is to check that the fan belt is correctly tensioned. The armature runs in ball bearings with sealed in lubrication. Some owners may wish to check the carbon brush length and this can be done by seeing that the ends are not below the ends of the brush holders. If they are new brushes should be fitted.

3 A generator normally works properly or not at all. There are few instances of poor performance. A quick check can be made if a voltmeter is available. Disconnect both leads from the dynamo and join the two terminals together with a piece of bare wire. From the centre of the wire run a lead via the voltmeter to earth. With the engine running at a fast tickover there should be a reading of about 15 volts. If there is no voltage then suspect the carbon brushes. If the voltage is low — 2—8 volts then suspect the field windings or armature. Either of the latter will require renewal or a re-build by specialists.

5. Generator (dynamo) - control box

1 The regulator box regulates the voltage and current, according to the demands of the system. It also prevents feed back from the battery when the generator is producing voltage less than battery voltage. The unit is not designed for adjustment or repair and under normal circumstances it will function perfectly and last indefinitely.

2 If the charging system is not working correctly, indicated by the warning lamp not going out when the engine speed increases the generator should first be checked as this is the most usual cause of the trouble.

3 If the generator is found to be satisfactory make a careful check of the connections on the control box to make sure they are tight and corrosion free. If the vehicle has been standing unused for a long time in a damp climate the control box will probably be defective.

4 Where a control box is defective the whole unit must be renewed.

6. Generator (dynamo) - dismantling and fitting new carbon brushes

1 Remove the generator from the car. (See Section 9).

2 Remove the two long bolts and nuts which run right through the generator and mark both the end frames of the assembly in relation to the yoke.

3 Ease off the end frame from the end opposite the drive pulley. It cannot be separated completely because of the lead from the field coil.

4 The brush holders are now accessible. Lift up the springs and push them to one side so that they hold in position against the brush holders.

5 Lift out the brushes from the holders and undo the terminal tag screws.

6 If the commutator surface is black it can be cleaned with petrol. If it is badly scored or grooved it should be sent to a specialist for skimming. Between each segment of the commutator is insulating material and this should be cut back below the commutator surface at least 1 mm/.040 inches.

7 On early generators the bearing in the commutator end cap is a plain bronze bush. Later models are fitted with ball bearings at both ends. The bearing at the commutator end can be renewed but if it is very badly worn it is likely that the armature has been running off centre so that replacement of the bearing should always be accompanied by a check for correct centring of the commutator. It may require skimming on a lathe. The bearing in the drive end frame cannot be separated from it so the whole end frame must be obtained if necessary.

8 To remove the drive end frame the drive pulley must be removed from the keyed shaft first.

9 When fitting new brushes make certain they are a snug slide fit in the holders. If they are tight carefully rub down the sides on fine abrasive paper until they just slide easily. Brushes which slop about in the holders will soon wear out and may damage the armature due to excessive arcing.

10 When refitting the commutator end frame to the armature shaft the brushes will need to be held up in their holders until the end frame is in position. This can be done by jamming the springs against their sides. Make sure you put the springs on the side nearest the end frame apertures. Otherwise you will not be able to unhook them and place them in position on top of the carbon brushes.

7. Alternators - description and precautions

The 124S and some later versions of the 124 are fitted with alternators in place of the more generally wellknown D.C. 'dynamos'. The alternator generates alternating current (A.C.) which is rectified by diodes into D.C. and is the current needed for battery storage.

The regulator is a transistorized unit which is permanently sealed and requires no attention. It will last indefinitely provided no mistakes are made in wiring connections.

Apart from the renewal of the rotor slip ring brushes and rotor shaft bearings, there are no other parts which need periodic inspection. All other items are sealed assemblies and must be replaced if indications are that they are faulty.

If there are indications that the charging system is malfunctioning in any way, care must be taken to diagnose faults properly, otherwise damage of a serious and expensive nature may occur to parts which are in fact quite serviceable.

The following basic requirements must be observed at all times, therefore, if damage is to be prevented:

1 ALL alternator systems use a NEGATIVE earth. Even the simple mistake of connecting a battery the wrong way round could burn out the alternator diodes in a few seconds.

2 Before disconnecting any wires in the system the engine and ignition circuits should be switched off. This will minimise accidental short circuits.

3 The alternator must NEVER be run with the output wire disconnected.

4 Always disconnect the battery from the car's electrical system if an outside charging source is being used.

5 Do not use test wire connections that could move accidentally and short circuit against nearby terminals. Short circuits will not blow fuses - they will blow diodes or transistors.

6 Always disconnect the battery cables and alternator output wires before any electric welding work is done on the car body.

Fault diagnosis on alternator charging systems requires sophisticated test equipment and even with this the action required to rectify any fault is limited to the renewal of one or two components. Knowing what the fault is is only of academic interest in these circumstances.

8. Generators - removal and replacement

1 The generator is held by two pivot bolts on the lower front side of the crankcase and an upper slotted brace which allows it to be

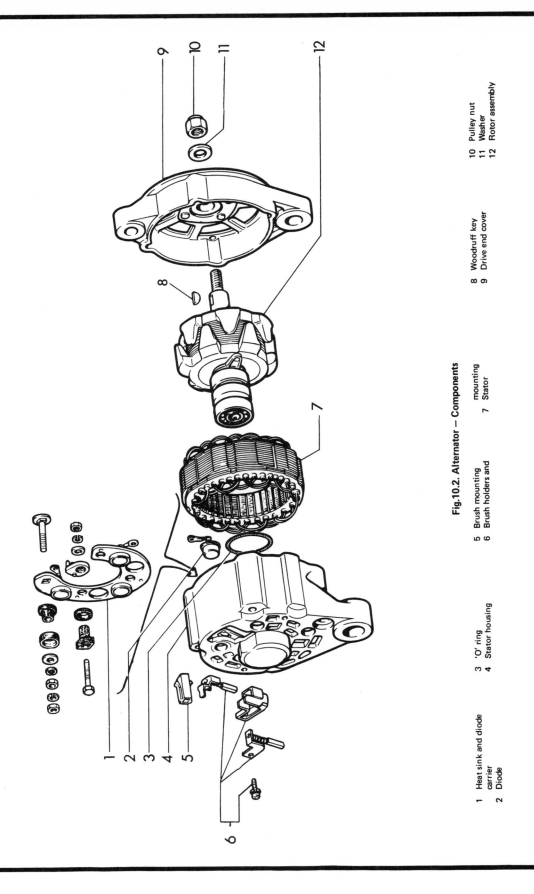

Fig.10.2. Alternator – Components

1	Heat sink and diode carrier	3	'O' ring
2	Diode	4	Stator housing
		5	Brush mounting
		6	Brush holders and mounting
		7	Stator
		8	Woodruff key
		9	Drive end cover
		10	Pulley nut
		11	Washer
		12	Rotor assembly

positioned in order to adjust the fan belt tension.

2 Remove the nuts holding the two leads (photo) or withdraw the plug connections on an alternator.

3 Slacken the nut on the slotted brace and the two lower pivot bolts, move the generator inwards and disengage the fan belt.

4 Remove the slotted brace securing bolt (photo).

5 Remove the two pivot bolts completely and lift the generator away (photo).

6 Replacement is a reversal of this procedure. Tension the fan belt by pulling the generator away from the crankcase. A lever may be used for a dynamo but with an alternator the case is more fragile so leverage should not be used. Then tighten the locknut on the brace followed by the two pivot bolts.

9. Starter motor - removal and replacement

1 Removal of the starter motor is a lousy job and takes a lot of time because of all the other things that have to be taken away first. If you are removing it because it does not work (and if it does not work you can do nothing except remove it first) make quite sure first that it is not just a disconnected lead. One of the leads to the starter is a straight bullet connector and it may be loose or dirty. You will have to feel round behind the exhaust shield plate to get to it. It cannot be seen.

2 Having decided to remove the starter first remove the carburettor air cleaner if a side draught carburettor is fitted.

3 Remove the two bolts holding the heat shield over the starter motor (photo). Then disconnect the leads from the starter solenoid.

4 There are two alternatives at this point one is to separate the exhaust pipe from the manifold. This will also require the disconnection of the exhaust pipe underneath the car. A new exhaust pipe to manifold flange gasket should also be obtained. The other alternative is to take the generator off, permitting the starter to be drawn straight out forward. This is the least difficult method.

5 Whichever method is used the three starter mounting bolts have to be undone. The upper two are not too inaccessible. The lower one needs a long socket extension and a universal joint adaptor. It must be got at from underneath.

6 The starter motor can be drawn back and out from the side with the exhaust pipe out of the way.

7 The starter is replaced in the same way. In the photo showing the starter being replaced the exhaust pipe had not yet been reconnected after putting the engine back in the car. We were able to fit it in the manner shown. It can be seen from the photograph that if the exhaust was connected and the generator removed the starter could be drawn out straight forward.

10. Starter motor - testing, dismantling and fitting new solenoid and carbon brushes

1 With the starter removed clamp it in a vice and connect up to it two wires of heavy capacity. They need not be like the wires on the car because it is going to be run without a load on. One of the wires should be connected to the large terminal from which the battery lead was disconnected and the other to the small bullet connection terminal. If battery power is applied and the solenoid does not throw the drive pinion forward then the solenoid at least is faulty.

2 Next connect the wires so that one is to the other large terminal on the solenoid and the other to the body of the starter motor. If the motor turns you may have reasonable assurance that it will work in the car. It it does not dismantling may reveal the need for new carbon brushes or skimming of the commutator in a similar manner to the dynamo.

3 A faulty solenoid must be renewed complete. Undo the nut securing the lead from the starter and the three through bolts holding it to the pinion end frame. After unhooking it from the pinion lever it can be removed. A new one may be fitted in the reverse order.

4 To examine the brushes and commutator remove the steel cover band round the starter body.

5 The commutator end bracket with the brush holders can be removed after undoing the nuts on the through bolts. Do not lose the fibre and steel thrust washers between the bracket and the shaft.

6 If the brushes are renewed only, make sure that the starter is tested again after reassembly as described earlier. If it still does not turn then there must be something wrong with either the armature or the field coils and it should be checked and repaired by specialists.

11. Fuses

1 All circuits are fused with the exception of the charging circuit, ignition circuit and starter motor circuits. The fuses are the weakest link in the circuit and any fault causing a short circuit will therefore blow the fuse rather than cause burning and a possible fire at the fault point.

2 The fuses are mounted under the instrument panel to the right of the steering column (photo).

3 No.1 fuse is at the left and each one protects the circuits as listed in the Specifications at the beginning of the Chapter.

4 If any item of electrical equipment fails to operate first check the appropriate fuse. If the fuse has blown the first thing to do is to find out why, otherwise it will merely blow again - (fuses can fail with old age but this is the exception rather than the rule). Having found the faulty fuse, switch off all electrical equipment and then fit a new fuse. From the Specifications note which circuits are served by the blown fuse and then start to switch each one on separately in turn. (It may be necessary for the ignition circuit to be turned on at the same time). The fuse should blow again when the faulty item is switched on. If the fuse does not blow immediately, start again only this time leave the circuits switched on and build up the cumulative total on the fuse. If and when it blows you will have an indication of which circuits may be causing the problem. It may take a little longer to isolate the fault which may not be serious at this stage. If the new fuse does not blow until the car is moving then look for a loose piece of wire which only causes a short circuit when moved.

12. Direction indicators

1 The direction indicators at the front are linked with the parking lamps and therefore have double filament bulbs with offset bayonet caps. To change a bulb on a front lamp remove the screws securing the lens and take off the lens and sealing gasket to get access to the bulb. At the rear the indicator bulb is a single filament and is housed in the outer reflector. To replace the rear bulb remove the lens securing screw, remove all the lenses and then gain access to the bulb. The bulbs for the repeater light on the side of the front wings are accessible from inside the wing. Remove the bulb holder and then take the bulb from the holder.

2 Failure of one or more of the indicator lights may be caused by a blown bulb. If the bulb is good the most likely reason otherwise is a bad earth connection from either the bulb to the bulb holder (corrosion caused by damp is a common cause) or from the bulb holder to the body frame. Check all these before assuming the flasher unit or switch is at fault. If each pair of terminals on the flasher unit is bridged then it can be seen whether the lamps light. It is then best to try and borrow a flasher unit known to be good to check whether the fault lies there. If the switch is suspect it will be necessary to remove the steering wheel in order to bridge the switch terminals for testing or to remove the switch for renewal. The switch has two half collars which must first be removed. Then slacken the clamp securing it to the column bracket and slide it off the column.

13. Windscreen wipers

1 Failure or malfunction will be due to a blown fuse, burnt out motor, or wear in the mechanical linkage causing stiffness or

8.2 Disconnection of the generator leads

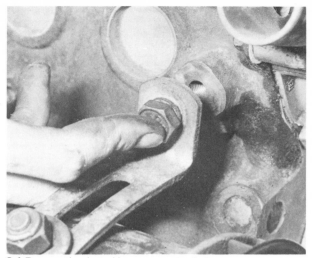

8.4 Remove the slotted brace mounting bolt

8.5 Taking the generator away

9.3 Undoing the bolts securing the starter motor heat shield (arrowed)

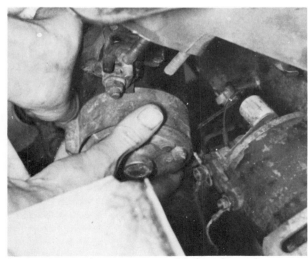

9.7 Drawing out the starter motor with the exhaust pipe front section removed

11.2 View of fuse board. Number 6 fuse is removed

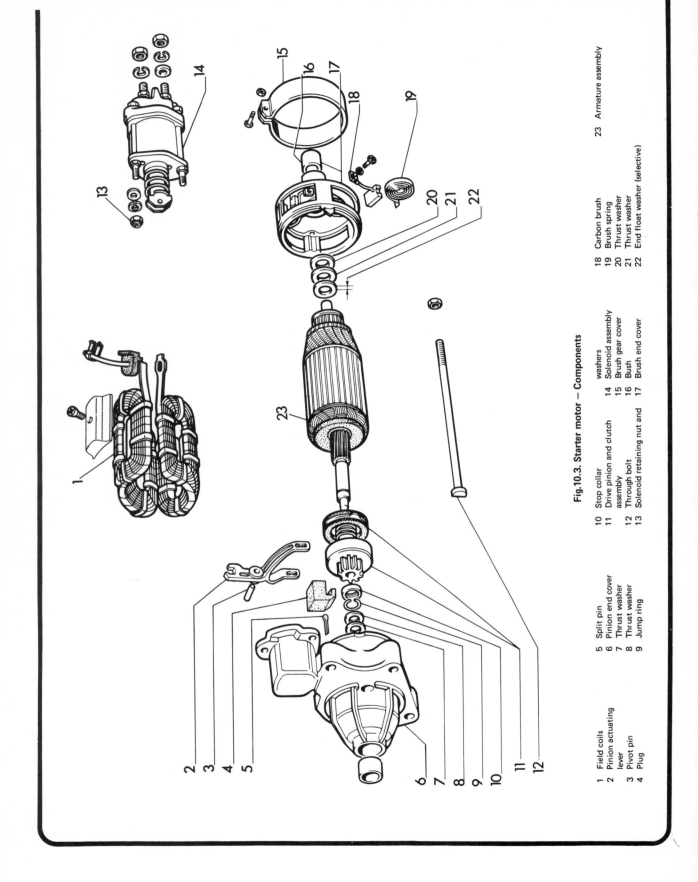

Fig.10.3. Starter motor – Components

1 Field coils
2 Pinion actuating lever
3 Pivot pin
4 Plug

5 Split pin
6 Pinion end cover
7 Thrust washer
8 Thrust washer
9 Jump ring

10 Stop collar
11 Drive pinion and clutch assembly
12 Through bolt
13 Solenoid retaining nut and washers

14 Solenoid assembly
15 Brush gear cover
16 Bush
17 Brush end cover

18 Carbon brush
19 Brush spring
20 Thrust washer
21 Thrust washer
22 End float washer (selective)

23 Armature assembly

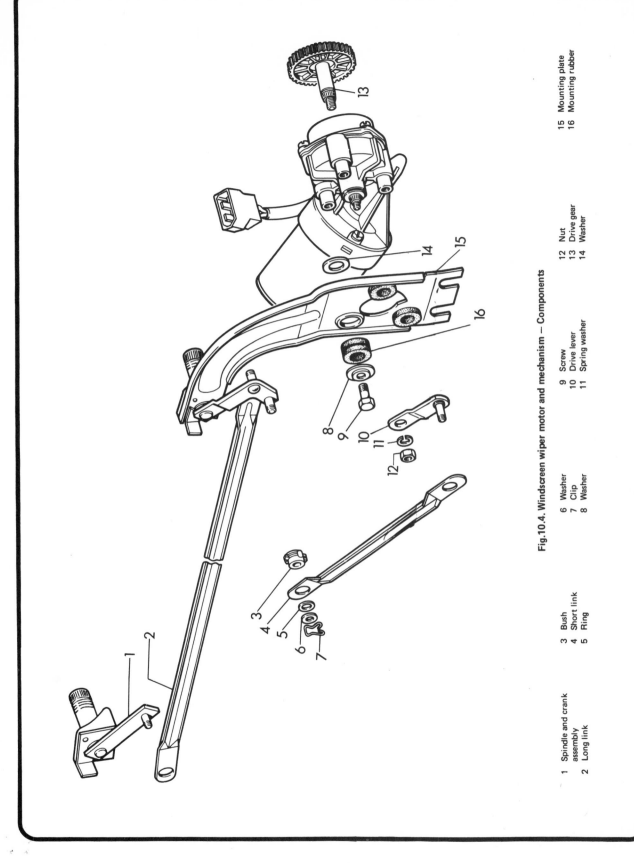

Fig.10.4. Windscreen wiper motor and mechanism — Components

1 Spindle and crank assembly
2 Long link
3 Bush
4 Short link
5 Ring
6 Washer
7 Clip
8 Washer
9 Screw
10 Drive lever
11 Spring washer
12 Nut
13 Drive gear
14 Washer
15 Mounting plate
16 Mounting rubber

jamming. The latter fault could also be caused by incorrect mounting or a distorted support bracket.

2 To remove the whole unit from the car simply take off the blades, unplug the connector for the motor and slacken the two mounting bracket units.

3 Disconnect the link arm from the motor to facilitate taking the assembly out.

4 The various bushes in the mechanical linkages can be renewed as can the main drive spindle from the wheel box. If the motor is out of order it will be necessary to renew it completely as spares are not available.

14. Windscreen washer

1 The screen washer is a manually operated pump mounted on the dashboard with a flexible pressure bulb. The unit contains two one-way valves so that when the bulb is pressed water is forced out to the screen through one valve and when it is released more liquid is drawn through the other valve from the reservoir bag hanging on the side of the engine compartment.

2 Malfunction is usually due to blocked jets on the screen delivery nozzles. These can be cleared with fine wire. Other causes of failure are usually due to blocked pipes, kinked pipes or disconnected pipes. The latter is usually apparent when the pump is operated.

3 If the pump is proved unserviceable it must be renewed.

15. Lights (front) and main light switch

1 The headlamp assemblies must be removed to change the bulbs. First undo the screw holding the bezel at the top. On twin headlamp models there are two screws. Draw the bezel forward at the top a little and unhook it at the bottom.

2 On single lamp versions a single wire spring clip is unhooked and

the lug on the opposite side of the unit can then be released from the retaining pin and the unit lifted out. On twin lamp models the head-lamp lens is secured by a retaining ring. Slacken the three screws on each lamp which hold the ring. Then turn the ring clockwise so that it can be detached together with the lamp. Do not confuse the three clamp screws with the two beam adjusting screws on each lamp.

3 To remove the bulb on single lamp versions first unclip the wire springs holding the bulb and connector into the lamp unit. On twins, first disconnect the terminal block from the bulb and then twist out the springs to release the bulb.

4 Replacement is a reversal of the removal procedure. Do not use bulbs of different wattage values from those specified or the balance of the system will be upset.

5 Headlamp beam alignment is best carried out at a garage with the proper equipment needed. However, the owner is able to do reasonably accurate setting himself provided he can arrange to line up the car on level ground facing a suitably surfaced vertical flat plane at a distance of 5 m/16½ ft. The car should be unladen and the tyre pressures and suspension standing heights correct.

6 On the vertical surface mark crosses in line with each headlamp centre. Taking single headlamp models first of all, mark a point 12 cm/4¾ in below each cross. With the headlamps switched on low beam the light zone should correspond with this point as shown in Fig.10.8.

7 Dual headlamps are arranged so that only the outer pair illuminate on dip. Having marked the four crosses on the wall mark the outer lamp reference points 10 cm below the crosses and the inner lamp reference points 5 cm below the crosses. With the lamps on dip the outer lamp light zones should line up as indicated in Fig.10.9. With all four lamps on the centre point of the inner lamp pool of light must correspond with the reference point.

8 There are two lamp adjusting screws to each unit, one altering the vertical and the other the horizontal settings.

9 The beam setting charts show the light zones for cars where traffic goes on the left. For right side traffic countries the angled

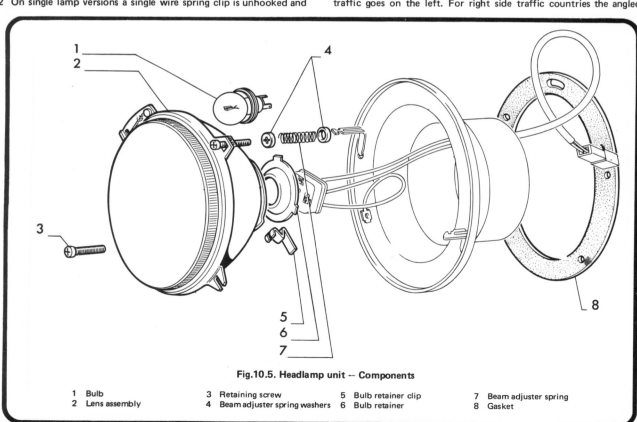

Fig.10.5. Headlamp unit -- Components

1	Bulb	3	Retaining screw	5	Bulb retainer clip
2	Lens assembly	4	Beam adjuster spring washers	6	Bulb retainer
				7	Beam adjuster spring
				8	Gasket

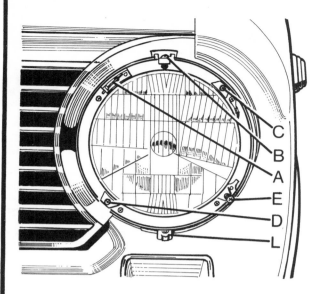

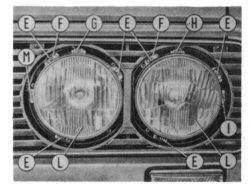

Fig.10.6. Single headlamp unit mounting (bezel removed)

A   Unit retaining spring hook   D   Vertical beam adjuster screw
B   Bezel screw location thread   E   Lock screw
C   Horizontal beam adjuster screw   L   Bezel lower retaining lug

Fig.10.7. Dual headlamps — mountings (bezel removed)

E   Lamp unit mounting screws   I   Horizontal beam adjuster
F   Lamp retaining rings   M   Horizontal beam adjuster
G   Vertical beam adjuster   L   Lamp units
H   Vertical beam adjuster

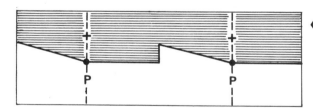

Fig.10.8. Headlamp beam alignment (R.H.D. single units)

P. Reference point for light zone on dipped beams
For L.H.D. vehicles the light zones slant away the other side of
the reference points

Fig.10.9. Headlamp beam alignment (R.H.D. dual head-lamps)

Pe. Reference point for exterior lamps on dipped beams
Pi. Centre of light zone for inner lamps on high beam
For L.H.D. vehicles the light zones slant away the other side of
the reference points

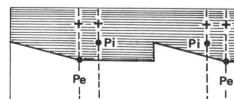

lines from the reference points run to the right instead of the left.

10 Front parking light bulbs are accessible after removing the two lens mounting screws. These bulbs are double filament incorporating the flasher as well. The bayonet fitting is offset so that the bulb only goes in one way. This ensures that the 5 watt filament is used for the parking light circuit and the 20 watt filament for the flasher.

11 There are three separate switches which affect the lights. First is the ignition key switch which must be in the 'ignition on' or 'auxiliary' positions; second the circuit switch on the dash panel; and third the dip switch stalk on the steering column. In case of faults or failure each of these three switches will need to be checked. The connections at each switch should be bridged to ascertain whether or not the switch is faulty. If any of the switches is faulty it must be replaced completely. The dip switch on the steering column is integral with the flasher switch unit and how to remove it is described in Section 12. The dashboard switch is incorporated in a cluster of 3 which can be pushed out from behind (photo). The ignition switch assembly can be removed after taking off the surrounding canopy. However, the switch is held in position with special 'break head' bolts for security reasons. These must be drilled out using a drill capable of getting through specially hardened steel. Alternatively it may be possible to unscrew the bolt shanks with a centre punch and hammer.

16. Lights - rear

1 The direction indicator bulb and the stop tail light bulb are housed in a common cluster. The two separate lenses are interlocked and secured by a single central screw. When the screw is removed the lenses may be drawn out from the locating slots at each end. The bulbs can then be removed. The stop/tail lamp bulb is a double filament one with offset bayonet pins. It is the same as the side/flasher bulb used at the front. The registration plate lamp is mounted in the rear bumper. The bulb holder snaps in and can be pulled out from underneath.

17. Interior lights (boot, glove compartment, engine compartment, passenger compartment)

1 The boot light operates when the parking lights are switched on and the lid is opened. The switch and bulb are held to the body by a screw. The bulb may be simply eased out of the clip on the bracket for renewal purposes.

2 The glove compartment switch and bulb are similar and work

15.11. Switch block removed from facia panel

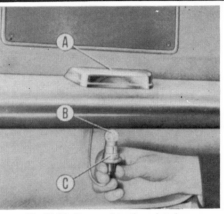

Fig.10.10. Rear registration plate lamp

A Lens unit
B Bulb
C Snap in bulb holder

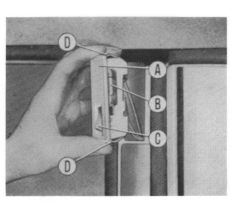

Fig.10.11. Passenger compartment lamps

A Lens   C Switch
B Bulb   D Spring clips

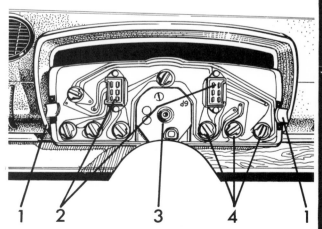

Fig.10.12. Instrument cluster - rear view

1 Spring retainer clips   3 Speedometer head
2 Multi-socket connection points   4 Bulb holders

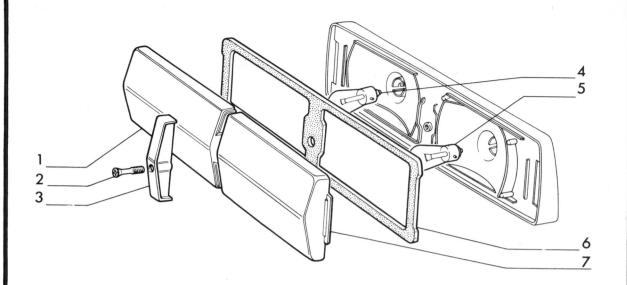

Fig.10.13. Rear lamp cluster -- Components

1 Rear stop lamp lens   3 Lens securing fillet   5 Flasher bulb   7 Flasher lens
2 Lens securing screw   4 Double filament bulb   6 Gasket

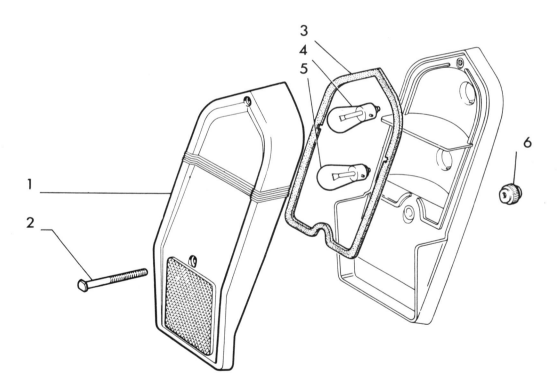

Fig.10.14. Rear lamp cluster - estate car - components

1 Lens   3 Gasket   5 Bulb
2 Lens securing screw   4 Bulb   6 Lens screw nut

independently of the other lights.

3 The engine compartment bulb has a bayonet fitting.

4 The passenger compartment lamps are housed in the door pillars, one on each side of the car. The units are held in the recesses by spring leaf clips and can be removed by carefully easing them out with a flat blade. The festoon bulb can then be taken out.

18. Instrument cluster

1 The instruments are housed in a single unit which is easily removed. Reach round behind the dashboard and press inwards the leaf spring at each side so releasing the unit which can then be pushed out a little way. On 124S models there is a single spring only on the lower edge. When it is pushed forward far enough reach in and undo the knurled collar securing the speedometer cable. Pull out the two multi-socket connectors and the whole panel is then free.

2 Individual bulbs for warning and illumination lamps are held into the rear by small bayonet holders which can be taken out after twisting them a ½ turn anticlockwise.

3 The circuits to the warning lamps and instruments are on a printed circuit sheet which can only develop a fault if it is physically damaged or over-fusing in a circuit has caused it to burn out. Once all the lamps and the multi socket connectors have been removed the printed circuit can be taken off and renewed if necessary. Individual instruments may also be detached from the cluster and renewed as required. If any instrument or the printed circuit show signs of over heating or burning out it is essential to check the fuses, equipment and wiring of the circuit in question before renewing anything on the panel. Otherwise it is almost certain that the overheating or burn out will recur.

19. Speedometer and cable

1 The speedometer cable may break or cause erratic operation of the speedometer. To investigate first pull out the instrument cluster as described in the previous chapter. Then undo the cable securing collar and draw out the inner cable. If the cable is not broken wash it with petrol and with some fine emery smooth it down throughout its length to take off any high spots which may be causing it to 'twitch' in the outer cable. Re-grease it and replace it. If the cable is broken it will be necessary to undo the lower end where it connects to the gearbox in order to remove the other piece of cable.

2 Although it is not essential always to renew the cable outer when the drive cable breaks, it is conceivable that the outer cable could have been snagged by the broken ends of the inner cable. This may cause erratic running or even failure of a new cable fitted into it.

3 When fitting a new cable outer section take care that when passing it through the bulkhead and securing it that no severe bending occurs - otherwise it will be irredeemably kinked - and that it is secured by its clips so that all the curves are not too acute.

20. Horns and horn switch

1 Two horns are fitted, one giving a high and the other a low note. The switch is operated by a ring on the steering column and is accessible after the ring has been removed.

2 Both horns have adjusting screws in the back and the volume can be adjusted with these.

3 Horn failure is usually due to a fault in the spring loaded contact ring on the switch - or corrosion on the switch contact surfaces.

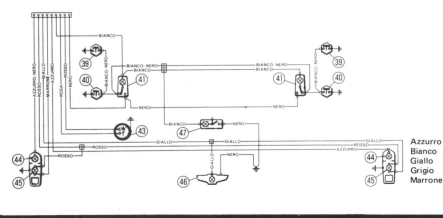

Wiring Diagram 124 saloon and estate. (Estate variations shown below)

1 Front parking and direction indicator lamps	14 Engine compartment lamp with switch
2 Headlamps (high and low beams)	15 Fuses
3 Horns	16 Flasher unit, direction signals
4 Ignition distributor	17 Stop lights jam switch
5 Spark plugs	18 Wiper motor
6 Generator	19 Electrofan
7 Direction signal side repeaters	20 Generator regulator
8 Horns, remote control	21 Fuel gauge
9 Ignition coil	22 Outer lighting master switch
10 Sending unit, for low oil pressure indicator	23 Instrument cluster light switch
11 Battery	24 Windshield wiper switch
12 Thermal sending unit for head indicator	25 Key-type ignition switch, also energizing warning lights & starting circuits
13 Starter	
26 Direction signal switch	37 Electrofan switch
27 Horn ring	38 Glove compartment light, with jam switch built-in
28 Change-over switch for outer lighting and low beam flashes	39 Jam switches, between front doors and pillars for lamps 41
29 Fuel reserve supply indicator (red)	40 Jam switches, between rear doors and pillars, for lamps 41
30 Low engine oil pressure indicator (red)	41 Pillar lamps with switch built-in
31 Generator charge indicator (red)	42 Luggage compartment light
32 Instrument cluster light	43 Fuel gauge sending unit
33 Direction signal tell-tale light (green)	44 Rear direction signal lights
34 Parking lights indicator (green)	45 Rear parking and stop lights
35 High beam indicator (blue)	46 License plate lights
36 Heat indicator (red)	47 Rear door interior light and switch

CABLE COLOUR CODE

Azzurro	= Blue	Nero	= Black
Bianco	= White	Rosa	= Pink
Giallo	= Yellow	Rosso	= Red
Grigio	= Grey	Verde	= Green
Marrone	= Brown	INT	= Switch

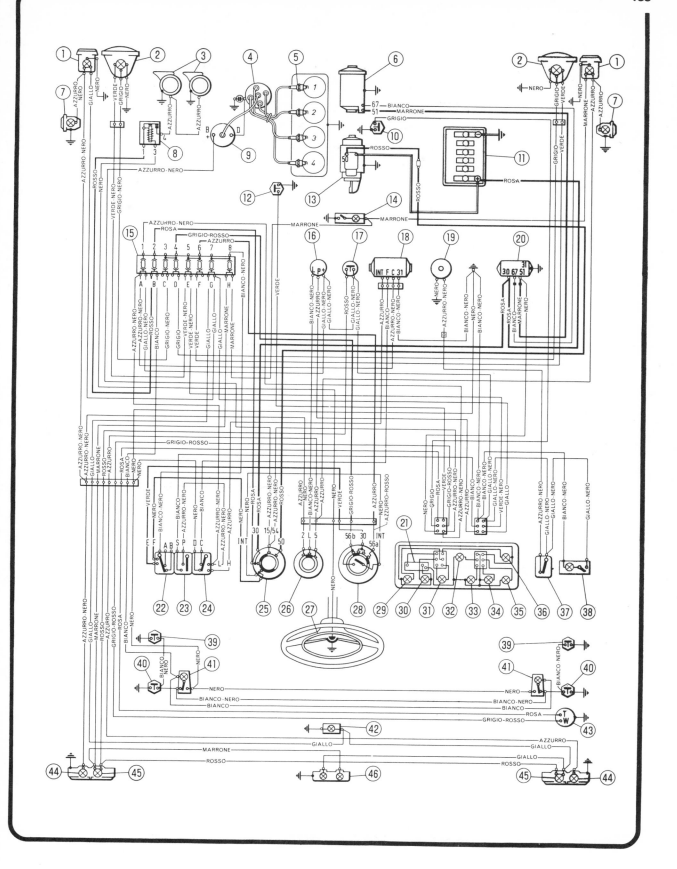

LIGHT BLUE — FROM MOTOR TO CONTROL

LIGHT BLUE+ WHITE ,, ,, ,, ,,

LIGHT BLUE + BLACK FROM MOTOR TO FUSE

BLACK TO EARTH

(SWITCH) YELLOW + BLACK
WHITE + BLACK

Wiring Diagram 124 Special

1 Front parking and direction indicators
2 Outer headlamps (high and low beams)
3 Inner headlamps (high beams)
4 Horn control relay switch
5 Horns
6 Ignition distributor
7 Spark plugs
8 Alternator
9 Ignition coil
10 Insufficient oil pressure indicator sending unit
11 Water heat gauge sending unit
12 Direction indicator side repeaters
13 Battery
14 Battery charge indicator relay
15 Voltage regulator
16 High beam headlamps relay switch
17 Starter
18 Fuses
19 Flasher, direction indicators
20 Engine compartment lamps with incorporated jam switch
21 Stop lights pressure-switch
22 Back window demister fuse, in separate holder (optional)
23 Relay switch for optional back window demister
24 Switch for wiper intermittent operation
25 Windshield wiper motor
26 Electrofan motor, two-speed
27 Electrofan motor additional resistor
28 Instrument cluster lights
29 Connectors
30 Directional signal arrow tell-tale (green)

31 Engine water heat gauge
32 Insufficient oil pressure indicator (red)
33 Parking lights indicator (green)
34 Fuel gauge
35 Fuel reserve indicator (red)
36 Headlamp high beam indicator (blue)
37 Battery charge indicator (red)
38 Back window demister indicator (optional)
39 Back window demister switch (optional)
40 Outer light switch
41 Electrofan 3–position switch
42 Instrument cluster light switch
43 Electric cigarette lighter (with housing indicator)
44 Glove compartment light, with incorporated jam switch
45 Windshield wiper 3–position lever switch
46 Lock switch
47 Headlamp change-over and flashes switch
48 Direction indicators switch
49 Horn control sector
50 Pillar light (courtesy) jam switches on front doors
51 Pillar light (courtesy) jam switches on rear doors
52 Pillar lights with incorporated switch
53 Back-up lamp jam switch
54 Back window demister (optional)
55 Fuel gauge sending unit
56 Luggage compartment lamp
57 Rear direction indicators
58 Rear parking and stop lights
59 Number plate lights
60 Reverse lamp

CABLE COLOUR CODE

Arancio = **Orange**   Bianco = **White**   Giallo = **Yellow**   Marrone = **Brown**   Rosa = **Pink**   Verde = **Green**
Azzuro = **Light blue**   Blu = **Dark blue**   Grigio = **Grey**   Nero = **Black**   Rosso = **Red**   Viola = **Violet**

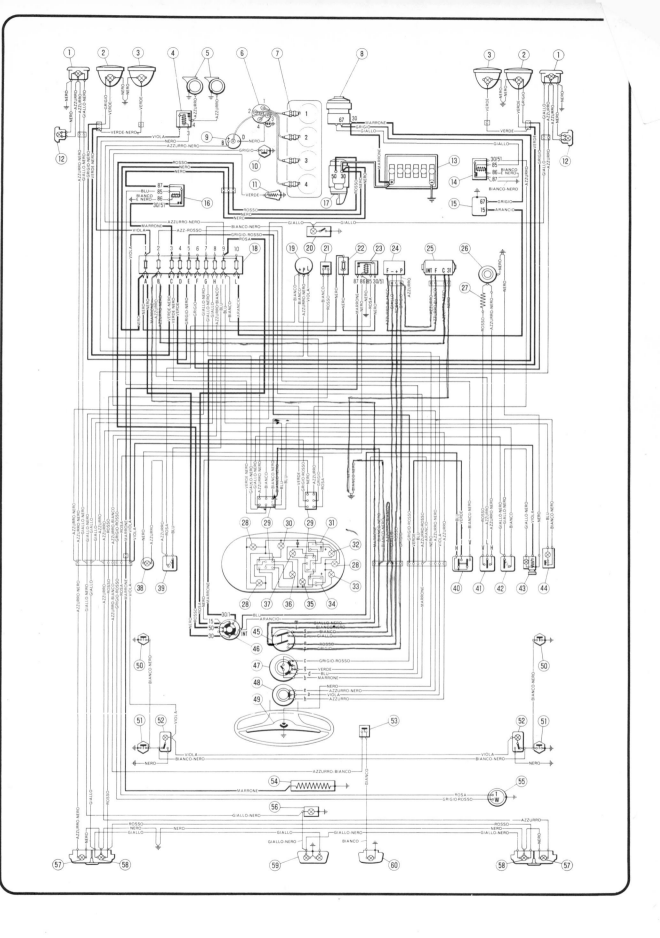

Chapter 11 Suspension, dampers and steering

Contents

Specifications

Front suspension

Type... ... ...   Independent, coil spring with upper wishbones and lower control arms.
Track 1330 mm/52.36 inches

Front springs

Number of active coils	(Saloon)	7.75
	(Estate)..	7.5
Free length	124	366 mm/14.4 inches
	124 Estate..	335 mm/13.81 inches
	124S	358 mm/13.1 inches

Rear suspension

Type... ... ...   Live axle mounted on coil springs and located by four longitudinal radius arms and a transverse Panhard rod
Track 1300 mm/51.18 inches

Rear springs

Number of active coils	... ...	8.25 (Saloon)
		8 (Estate)
Free length	124	492 mm/19.4 inches
	124 Estate..	441 mm/17.36 inches
	124S	366 mm/14.4 inches

Steering

Type...	Worm and roller
Ratio..	16.4 : 1
Turning circle	10.7 mm/35.1 ft
Linkage	Two independent tie rods with intermediate rod and idler arm
Steering box oil capacity	0.215 litres/.38 pts

Steering geometry

Toe-in	7 mm/.275 inches
Toe-in (laden)	3 mm
Camber angle	0° 05' (positive)
Camber angle (laden)...	0° 30' (positive)
Castor angle..	2° 15'
Castor angle (laden)	3° 30'
Steering pivot inclination (k.p.i)	6°

Laden means with 4 occupants and 50 kgs/110 lbs of luggage.

Dampers

Type... ... ...   Direct acting, double acting telescopic hydraulic front

Wheels and tyres

Type...	Steel disc - bolt fixing
Rim size	13 in x 4½J
Tyres (Saloons)	155S — 13 in/6.15S — 13 in radials
(Estates)	560S — 13 in crossply

Tyre pressures (Saloon)

Average load	20 p.s.i/ 1.4 kg/cm^2 front
	23 p.s.i/ 1.6 kg/cm^2 rear
Maximum load	21½ p.s.i /1.5 kg/cm^2 front
	26 p.s.i /1.8 kg/cm^2 rear

Tyre pressures (Estate)

Front..	20 p.s.i/1.4 kg/cm^2
Rear (average load)	24½ p.s.i./1.7 kg/cm^2
(5 people + 80 kg)	31½ p.s.i/2.2 kg/cm^2
(1 person + 360 kg)..	35½ p.s.i/2.5 kg/cm^2

Torque wrench settings

Front axle beam centre bolt nut	25 ft lbs/3.5 kg cm
Front axle beam to body bolts...	25 ft lbs/3.5 kg cm
Upper wishbone pivot nut	72 ft lbs/10 kg cm
Lower wishbone pivot nut	72 ft lbs/10 kg cm
Lower pivot to crossmember nuts...	43 ft lbs/6 kg cm
Steering knuckle to ball joint nuts	72 ft lbs/10 kg cm
Steering arm and caliper bracket nut	43 ft lbs/6 kg cm
Front damper top mounting nut	11 ft lbs/1.5 kg cm
Front damper lower mounting nut..	36 ft lbs/5 kg cm
Anti-roll bar anchorage nuts..	11 ft lbs/1.5 kg cm
Rear suspension lower longitudinal and transverse arm nuts	72 ft lbs/10 kg cm
Rear damper mounting nuts..	11 ft lbs/1.5 kg cm
Upper longitudinal stabilizer bar nuts - on body	11 ft lbs/1.5 kg cm
- on axle	25 ft lbs/3.5 kg cm
Steering wheel nut..	36 ft lbs/5 kg cm
Steering box mounting nut	29 ft lbs/4 kg cm
Idler arm bracket nut	29 ft lbs/4 kg cm
Drop arm to roller spindle nut	174 ft lbs/24 kg cm
Steering tie rod ball joint nuts	25 ft lbs/3.5 kg cm

1. General description

The front suspension comprises double wishbones and coil springs with a telescopic hydraulic damper attached to the lower wishbone and passing through the spring to a mounting on a bracket on the body side frame. The lower suspension arms pivot on a detachable crossmember which also supports the engine. The upper wishbones pivot on a bracket forming part of the body side frame. The wishbones are sufficiently broad to obviate the need for brake reaction rods to counteract the torque effect when brakes are applied.

A stabilizer anti-roll bar passes across between the lower wishbones. It is clamped to them at each end on a special bracket and is fixed to the body frame by rubber bushed brackets.

Coil springs are also used for the rear suspension. The rear axle is located by two long longitudinal radius arms and a transverse Panhard rod. Early models of the 124 had a transverse reaction bar linked to the axle. The 124S and later models of the 124 had short radius reaction arms fitted in place of it. The telescopic hydraulic dampers are mounted within the coil springs on saloons and outside them on estate models.

The steering gear is worm and roller linked by a drop arm to a track rod the other end of which is supported by an idler arm. From the drop arm and the idler arm a short tie rod runs to the steering arm and knuckle of each front wheel. On early models the steering column shaft was one piece but later models incorporated an articulated section in a different alignment. This section is a safety feature designed to collapse on impact.

2. Suspension - inspection

1 With the tyre pressures correct, fuel tank full and the car standing on level smooth ground, bounce it up and down a few times and let it settle. The height of the centre of the front crossmember should not be less than 164 mm ($\pm$ 3 mm). The height of the body at the rear in the centre (behind the rear axle) should be no less than 400 mm ($\pm$ 3 mm). The car should also rest quite level on its springs. The vehicle standing height is dependent particularly on the condition and tightening positions of the rubber bushes in the suspension arms at front and rear. If the ground clearance is obviously too low it will mean examination and resetting of all the suspension bolts through

the pivot bushes and possible renewal of some or all of the bushes. Broken or weakened springs are normally obvious due to sagging at the particular corner of the car.

Bouncing the car will indicate the state of the dampers. Normally the car will return to its position and stop when bounced. If it should return and then dip again it is an indication that the damper is partly or wholly ineffective and should be changed.

3. Front dampers - removal and replacement

1 Jack up the car and support it under the body side frame so that the suspension hangs down. Remove the wheels.
2 From inside the engine compartment grip the square end of the protruding shank of the piston rod with a suitable grip and undo the nut.
3 Remove the through bolt attaching the lower end of the damper to the lower wishbone, the damper may then be drawn out from underneath.
4 The dampers fitted to the Fiat 124 (if they are the originals) are capable of being overhauled - see Section 10.
5 Replacement of the dampers is a reversal of the removal procedure. Fit the lower end first having extended the piston to its limit. Do not forget the rubber ring on the upper shank before putting it up in position. Then jack up the lower wishbone so that the shank re-enters the upper mounting hole. Replace the second rubber ring, flat washer, spring washer and nut and tighten the nut right up as far as it will go.

4. Front springs - removal and replacement

1 Although it is possible to remove a spring without using a spring clamp it is dangerous and liable to cause accidents so the method given here requires a suitable spring clamp to be available. It should be of the type which does not protrude beyond the length of the spring. (The Sykes-Pickavant model is eminently suitable).
2 Jack up the car and remove the wheels. With the car supported on stands then remove the damper as described in Section 3. This will be made a little easier if the spring is first compressed.
3 With the spring compressed sufficiently to take the pressure off the lower wishbone remove the nuts which hold the pivot pin onto the studs of the axle beam. Pull the wishbone away from the axle far enough to lower it at the same time taking great care to note that there will be some shims on the studs between the pin and the axle. These shims control the camber angle of the wheels and must be replaced exactly as they came off.
4 The transverse stabilizer bar must also be detached from the wishbone so that it can be lowered.
5 Remove the spring together with the compressor tool.
6 When replacing the spring make sure that the upper end fits snugly into the specially shaped spring seat.
7 New springs are supplied in two classes - Class A marked with yellow paint and Class B with green. The same class should be used on all four wheels although in exceptional cases Class B can be fitted at the rear when Class A are on the front. No other mixture is suitable.

5. Front suspension arm ball joints - removal and replacement

1 The ball joints on the wishbones which carry the steering knuckle are not normally supplied separately and it is necessary to replace the complete wishbone when one is worn. To remove either or both of the arms follow the procedure as given in Section 6.
2 It is a good idea to check with a Fiat agency whether or not they can fit a new ball joint for you before buying a complete new wishbone. Service procedures change all the time and it is possible that they may be able to do it. The part is listed as a spare. Much depends on its availability.

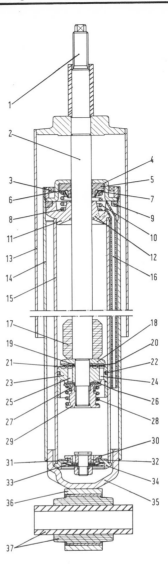

Fig.11.1. Front damper — Cross section

1 Threaded shank, upper mounting	washer
2 Rod	20 Valve star-shaped spring
3 Cylinder upper blanking threaded ring	21 Inlet valve
	22 Piston
4 Seal housing	23 Compression ring
5 Rod seal	24 Inlet valve holes in piston
6 Tab spring	
7 Spring cup	25 Rebound valve holes in piston
8 Gasket packing spring	
9 Casing gasket	26 Rebound valve
10 Vapour pocket drain chamber	27 Valve guide cup
	28 Rebound valve spring
11 Rod guide bushing	29 Piston mounting plug
12 Vapour pocket drain capillary hole	30 Compensating valve
	31 Compensating valve annular passage
13 Dust shield	
14 Casing	32 Compensating-and-compression valve carrier plug
15 Working cylinder	
16 Vapour pocket drain passage	33 Compression valve
	34 Compression valve orifices
17 Rubber buffer	35 Lower plug
18 Valve lifting limiting disc	36 Lower mounting eye
	37 Pin and bushing, lower mounting eye
19 Valve lift adjustment	

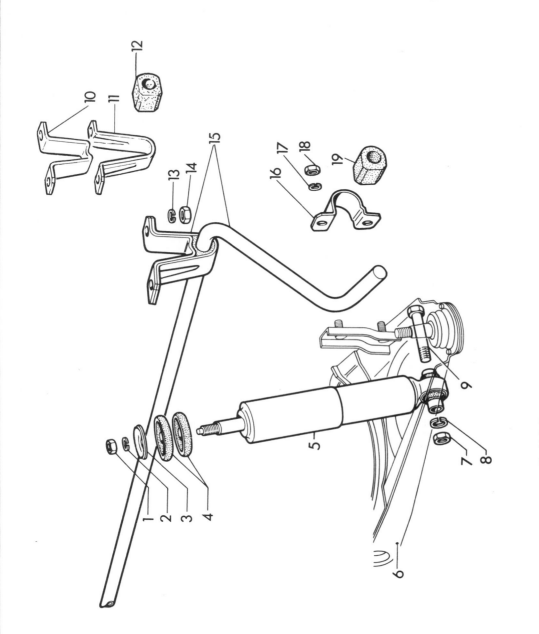

Fig.11.2. Front suspension – Damper and anti-roll bar mountings

1	Nut	5	Damper	8	Lockwasher	11	Outer clamp
2	Spring washer	6	Lower wishbone	9	Bolt	12	Mounting pad
3	Washer	7	Nut	10	Inner clamp	13	Lockwasher
4	Rubber mounting bushes						

14	Nut	16	Clamp
15	Stabilizer bar and clamp assembly	17	Lockwasher
		18	Nut
		19	Mounting pad

6. Front suspension arms - removal and replacement

1 Remove the damper and spring as described in Sections 3 and 4.
2 Disconnect the brake pipe to the caliper, having sealed the fluid reservoir cap with a piece of plastic film.
3 Disconnect the steering tie rod from the steering arm, using a suitable extractor, wedges or by tapping the eye of the arm on both sides with hammers to 'squeeze' the pin out.
4 Slacken and remove the pivot pin nut on the upper wishbone and then draw the pin out. The whole hub and two wishbones can then be removed. Do not forget to keep careful track of the shims which go between the lower wishbone pivot pin and the front axle cross-member.
5 To separate the ball joints of the wishbones from the steering knuckle remove the nuts and with a suitable extractor or wedges draw the pins out.
6 The rubber pivot bushes of the wishbones should be firm yet flexible. Those of the upper wishbone are steel bushed and the pivot pin should be a snug fit in these bushes. On the lower arm the pin is clamped with the compressed bushes by nuts. With the nuts removed check that the bushes are firm yet flexible and that the pin is not sloppy inside them.
7 The bushes can be pressed out with a suitable long bolt and nut in conjunction with large washers and tubular spacers. On the lower arm the bushes are fitted from the outside and the pivot pin itself has to be used to force the first bush out. As it is easy to damage the pin or distort the wishbone using makeshift methods it is best to get the services of a press to do this. The same goes for putting the new bushes in.
8 Reassembly is a reversal of the removal procedures. Do not tighten up the pivot pin nuts until the whole assembly is replaced and the car on the ground. If necessary - and it should be - the car must be loaded so that the standing height dimensions given in Section 2 are achieved before all the wishbone nuts are tightened to the specified torques.
9 If the bushes are renewed on the wishbones of one side it is normal practice to renew those on the other side at the same time. This ensures that the suspension characteristics do not vary from side to side.

7. Front suspension anti-roll bar - removal and replacement

1 The stabilizer bar will be stressed when in position so care should be taken to avoid accidents from it springing down.
2 First remove the two centre brackets and bushes holding the bar to the body frame and then undo the clamp brackets securing the bar at each end to the lower wishbone.
3 Renew any rubber mounting bushes as required.
4 When replacing the bar fix the ends first and if necessary use a jack to raise it in the centre so that the body mountings can be secured. Take care not to bend it whilst doing so.

8. Front axle - removal, checking and replacement

1 As the front axle does not support the whole of the front suspension assembly (the top wishbone is fixed to the body frame) there is no opportunity for the whole of the front suspension to be taken off as a complete assembly. Consequently there will be few reasons for taking off the crossmember - damage being the principal one.
2 To remove the axle first remove the front dampers and springs as described in Sections 2 and 3.
3 The engine must be supported so that the engine mountings may be released. This support can be from either above or below. Support from above can be a hoist or a suitable beam placed across the engine compartment. From below, position a jack as far forward under the engine as possible so that it will not interfere with the lowering of the crossmember.
4 With the engine weight supported release the engine mountings (see Chapter 1).
5 Undo the two nuts and the horizontal bolt at each side which hold the axle to the body frame. There may be slotted shims under the head of the horizontal bolt to take up dimensional variations. Make sure that these shims are kept safe for replacement otherwise stresses and distortion will occur when the bolt is re-tightened.
6 The axle can then be removed. If it is suspected of being distorted take it to a Fiat agent who has the necessary jig to check the alignment. There is no other accurate way of doing it.
7 Replacement is a reversal of the removal sequence, remembering to put any shims in their correct position and ensuring that the studs of the engine mounting pads are properly located in the slotted holes on the crossmember.

9. Rear dampers - removal and replacement

1 Removal of the rear dampers on the saloon is a somewhat tedious operation because the rear axle has to be unshipped from the suspension arms. On the estate car the dampers are mounted outside the springs so removal is straightforward.
2 Raise the rear of the car and support it on stands under the side frame members. Remove the wheels.
3 Undo the four nuts which hold the central bearing support flange of the propeller shaft to the body.
4 From inside the boot unscrew the four nuts holding the upper mounting. Then remove those holding the lower mounting.
5 Disconnect the axle ends of the two stabilizer bar links (or upper radius reaction rods on later models and the 124S).
6 Disconnect the brake regulator link from the lug on the axle.
7 Support the axle with a jack and then disconnect the two main radius arms at the attachments to the body and also the transverse Panhard rod from the body bracket.

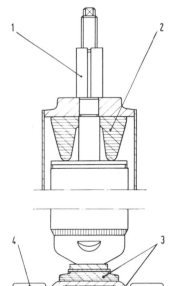

Fig.11.3. Rear damper upper and lower mountings — Cross section

1 Mounting shank	3 Lower bracket and bush
2 Buffer pad	4 Mounting screw

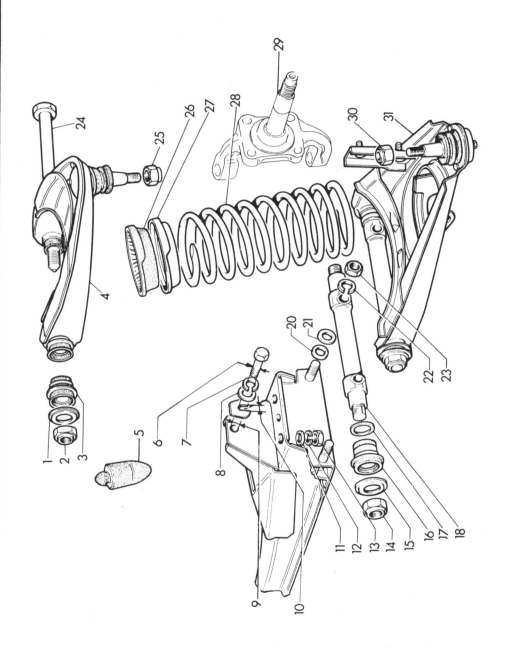

Fig.11.4. Front suspension — Wishbones, axle and springs

1 Washer
2 Self-locking nut
3 Bush
4 Upper wishbone
5 Buffer
6 Axle mounting bolt

7 Lockwasher
8 Washer
9 Axle (different hole sizes on some models)
10 Shim (to suit bolt)
11 Washer

12 Lockwasher
13 Nut
14 Self-locking nut
15 Washer
16 Bush
17 Washer

18 Lower wishbone pivot pin
20 Shim (selective)
21 Washer
22 Lockwasher
23 Nut

24 Upper wishbone pivot pin
25 Self-locking nut
26 Rubber insulator
27 Spring seat
28 Spring

29 Steering knuckle and stub axle
30 Self locking nut
31 Lower wishbone

8 Lower the rear axle on the jack until the springs are clear sufficiently to enable the dampers to be taken out.

9 Replacement is a reversal of the removal procedure. Take care to reseat the springs correctly and do not tighten the nuts on the radius arm and Panhard rod fixing points until the whole assembly is replaced and the vehicle lowered to the ground. The vehicle should then be loaded so that the specified standing height is reached, (Section 2). The suspension arm nuts should then be tightened to the specified torques.

10. Dampers - dismantling and reassembly

1 It is somewhat unusual to come across dampers that can be dismantled nowadays but this is the case on the Fiat 124 although the economics and availability of parts should be worked out before spending too much time on them.

2 The cross section drawing shows the component parts and the double action operation.

3 With the piston rod fully extended the threaded ring is undone from the top of the outer reservoir tube and this allows the piston and inner working cylinder to be drawn out together. The compression valve assembly may then be prised out of the lower end of the working cylinder with a screwdriver. This gives access to the plug inside on the end of the piston rod and the plug is unscrewed whilst holding the piston rod in a vice.

4 This releases the suction and rebound valves and the buffer and the piston rod can be drawn out of the inner working cylinder.

5 All valves, discs, springs and seals should be renewed and the internal bore of the cylinder checked to ensure it is not scored or damaged in any way.

6 Front and rear shock absorbers are of the same construction, the only differences being the mounting lugs and the oil capacity. The front dampers contain .120 litres each and the rear .215 litres. All the oil cannot be put in at once. Some goes into the inner working cylinder first - not more than can be put in without overflowing - and the rest is put into the outer reservoir cylinder prior to replacing the threaded ring.

7 When reassembled, the damper should be held vertically the right way up and pumped steadily. A built-in bleed device ensures that air from the inner cylinder is vented out to the air space in the reservoir cylinder. Keep dampers the right way up before and during replacement.

11. Rear springs - removal and replacement

1 The procedure for removing the springs is exactly the same as for removal of the dampers. The same procedure is followed for the estate car also. The method is given in Section 9.

12. Rear suspension arms and Panhard rod - removal and replacement

1 If all suspension arms are to be removed it is best to first of all remove the back axle from the car as described in Chapter 8. The only thing to remember is to disconnect the arms from the body and leave them attached to the axle. Then remove them from the axle after it has been taken out.

2 To remove any single suspension arm jack up the car and support the body and then support the axle independently on a jack near to the arm that is to be removed. Undo the nuts and bolt from each end and remove the arm.

3 When replacing a suspension arm it is quite likely that the mounting holes do not line up exactly. Use a tapered drift or an old bolt of the same diameter with the head cut off and a taper ground on it. Drive this in first and follow it through with the mounting bolt. Otherwise you will damage the mounting bolt threads and even if it is possible to replace the nut the tightening torques will be inaccurate. The suspension tightening torques are important if the mounting bushes

are to be properly stressed.

4 The suspension arm securing bolts should be tightened only when the vehicle is standing on the ground and loaded to give the ground clearance as indicated in Section 2.

13. Front wheel hub bearings - inspection and adjustment

1 Early models had trouble with front wheel bearings which tended to wear out rather quickly. When deciding that adjustment is necessary make sure that the bearings are in fact in good condition.

2 Before making any adjustments, obtain two new wheel nuts. They are locked into position by being staked into a groove in the stub axle and when they are disturbed this staking is broken and the nut cannot be re-used satisfactorily.

3 The free play in the bearings should be from .025—.10 mm/ .001—.004 ins. This end float can be measured accurately only with a dial micrometer so the alternative is to jack the wheel off the ground and grip the tyre at the top and bottom. Then try to rock it. It should be possible to feel a fractional amount of play in the bearing. Spin the wheel and if the bearing 'rumbles' or feels rough when you move the wheel with your hands placed on the tyre then it is most likely that new bearings will need fitting.

4 To adjust the bearing tap out the bearing hub cover and after tapping out the nut staking with a punch take the nut right off. Note that the right wheel nut has a left hand thread. Clean the spindle threads and check that they are not damaged. Then fit the new nut and tighten it to a torque of 14½ ft lbs/2 kgm. Keep spinning the wheel whilst doing this to ensure the bearing is settled. Then back the nut right off and re-tighten it to 5 ft lbs/0.7 kgm. Then back the nut off 30° (which is equivalent to 1/12 revolution or ½ a flat). At this position the play should be as specified and no bearing roughness apparent. Stake the nut into the groove using a round nosed punch.

14. Front wheel hub bearings - removal, inspection and replacement

1 If checking and adjustment indicate that new bearings are needed first obtain both roller bearings needed for the wheel. It is not good practice to replace just one of the pair.

2 Remove the wheel after jacking the car up and then unbolt the brake caliper from the mounting bracket and put it to one side. It is not necessary to disconnect the hydraulic fluid lines.

3 Remove the hub cap and take off the bearing adjusting nut. It should be possible to then pull off the hub and disc together. If not take the disc off the hub and then use a suitable puller to draw the hub off the spindle.

4 The inner race of the inside bearing will be left on the spindle and this will have to be drawn off with a suitable puller also.

5 The outside race of the outer bearing will also need drifting out of the hub.

6 When fitting new bearings first fit the inner race of the inside bearing to the spindle and the outer race of the outer bearing to the hub. Make sure all traces of old grease are first thoroughly cleaned off. Remember too that the smaller diameter of the roller bearing cone faces the centre of the hub.

7 Each hub should be greased with 2 ozs/60 grams of suitable bearing grease (Castrol LM). This should be thoroughly worked into the roller races and the balance of the grease spread on the inside of the hub adjacent to the bearings. After this the spacer and grease seal should be fitted against the inner bearing. (Prior to May 1966 no spacer was fitted).

8 Replace the hub onto the spindle and with a new nut adjust the bearing as described in the previous section.

9 The bearing hub cover should be cleaned out and 20 grams/¾ oz of grease placed in it before refitting. Do not put more grease than specified into either the hub or cap.

10 Refit the brake caliper and wheel.

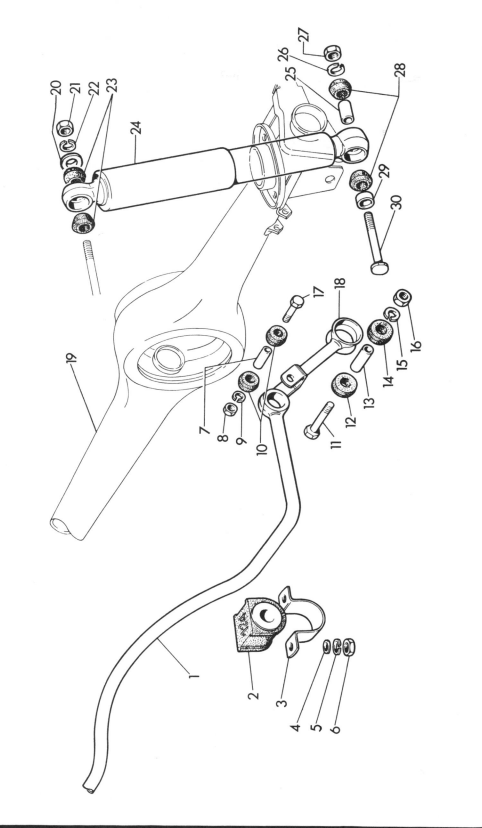

Fig.11.5. Rear suspension - early version. Dampers and stabilizer bar mountings

1	Stabilizer bar	6	Nut	11	Bolt
2	Rubber mounting	7	Sleeve	12	Bush
3	Securing clip	8	Nut	13	Sleeve
4	Washer	9	Spring washer	14	Bush
5	Spring washer	10	Rubber bushes	15	Spring washer

16	Nut	21	Nut	26	Spring washer
17	Bolt	22	Spring washer	27	Nut
18	Stabilizer link	23	Rubber bushes	28	Rubber bushes
19	Rear axle	24	Rear damper	29	Spacer
20	Washer	25	Sleeve	30	Bolt

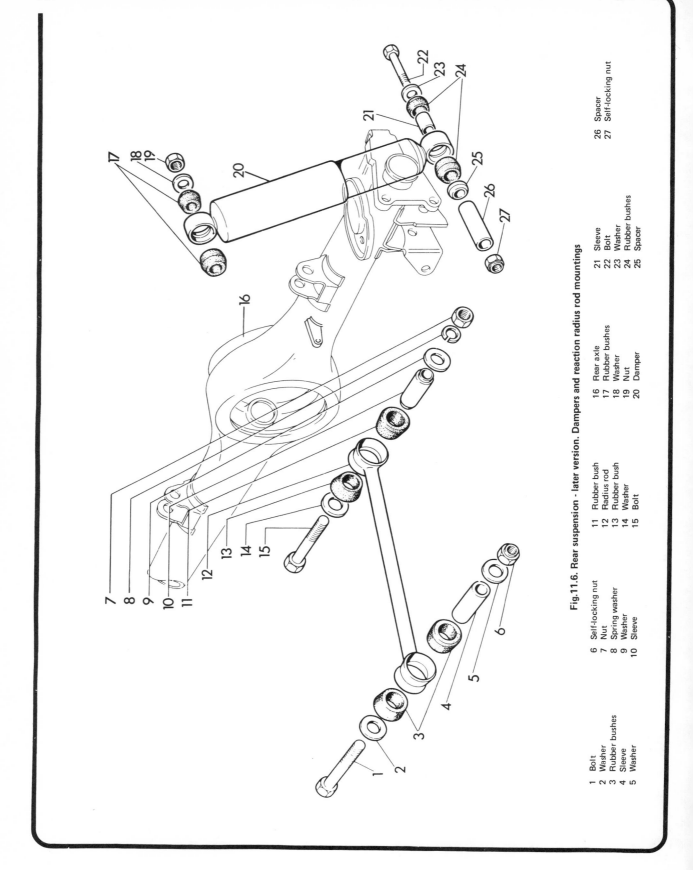

Fig.11.6. Rear suspension - later version. Dampers and reaction radius rod mountings

1	Bolt	6	Self-locking nut	11	Rubber bush	16	Rear axle	21	Sleeve	26	Spacer
2	Washer	7	Nut	12	Radius rod	17	Rubber bushes	22	Bolt	27	Self-locking nut
3	Rubber bushes	8	Spring washer	13	Rubber bush	18	Washer	23	Washer		
4	Sleeve	9	Washer	14	Washer	19	Nut	24	Rubber bushes		
5	Washer	10	Sleeve	15	Bolt	20	Damper	25	Spacer		

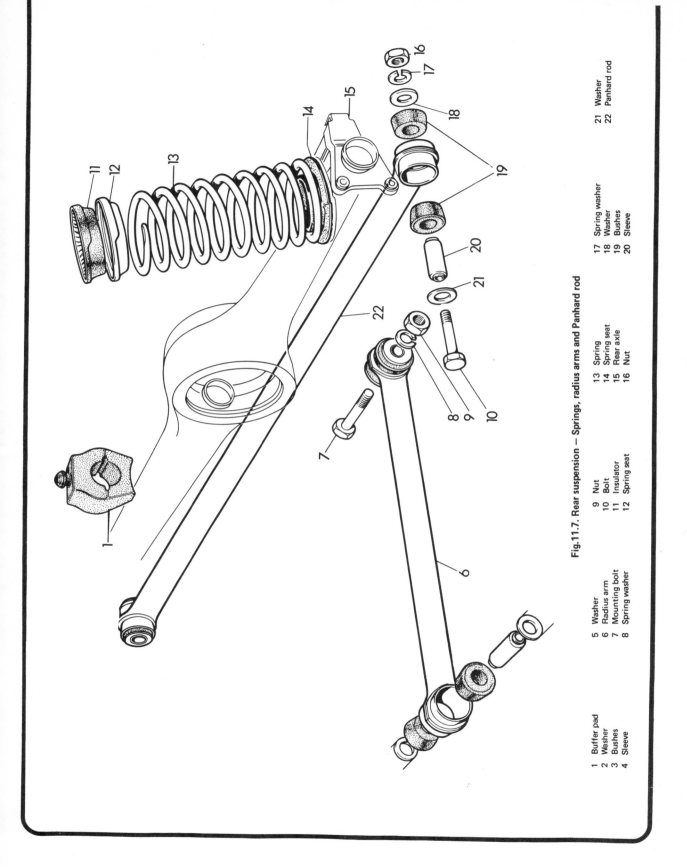

Fig.11.7. Rear suspension — Springs, radius arms and Panhard rod

1 Buffer pad
2 Washer
3 Bushes
4 Sleeve

5 Washer
6 Radius arm
7 Mounting bolt
8 Spring washer

9 Nut
10 Bolt
11 Insulator
12 Spring seat

13 Spring
14 Spring seat
15 Rear axle
16 Nut

17 Spring washer
18 Washer
19 Bushes
20 Sleeve

21 Washer
22 Panhard rod

15. Steering mechanism - inspection

1 The steering is one of the most neglected parts of the car and yet is the most important from the safety point of view. Any turning of the steering wheel which does not move the front wheels indicates that movement is being 'lost' somewhere in the linkage between the two. It is normal to start checking at the wheels and work back.

2 First ensure that the wheel bearings are correctly adjusted as described in Section 13. Then examine the wheel ends of the tie rods where they join the steering arm by means of ball joints. The outer ball joints are the most common point of wear in the steering mechanism. If the steering wheel is moved from side to side it will be possible to see if the joint is in good condition or not. Any movement of the tie rod which does not move the steering arm on the wheel means that the joint is worn and must be renewed.

3 Next check the joints at the inner ends of the tie rods in the same way.

4 Between the tie rods is a track rod which runs from the drop arm of the steering box to the idler arm on the other side. The ball joints at each end of this track rod should next be checked in a similar manner. If either end is worn the whole rod should be renewed.

5 Next check the idler arm support pivot. This is a shaft running in bushes and if the bushes wear the shaft can rock and cause lost motion. When the steering wheel is rocked it is possible to detect any lost motion. If there is the bushes need renewal.

6 Finally the steering box should be examined. The surest way to detect the degree of wear in the steering box is to disconnect the track rod and tie rod from the drop arm and then grip and move the drop arm to feel the play. Depending on the amount it may be possible to improve the situation by adjustment. Otherwise the steering box will need overhaul or renewal.

16. Steering tie rod ball joints - removal and replacement

1 The renewal of a steering rod joint is easy once the taper pin has been extracted from the arm into which it fits. There are various methods of removing stubborn pins after having first taken off the retaining nut. Special claw clamp extractors are available and also slotted steel wedges which may be forced in between the rod and arm. If none of these is to hand then use two hammers, one held against the side of the arm where the taper pin goes through whilst the other is used to strike the opposite side. This, in effect, squeezes the pin out of the arm.

2 The ball joints on the short tie rods are screwed on and held by a clamp. Slacken the clamp screw and carefully mark the joint shank position in relation to the threads on the rod. This will help to position the new joint as accurately as possible on replacement. Note also the position of the pin in relation to the one at the other end. Unscrew the joint from the rod, noting whether it is a left or right hand thread.

3 Before screwing a new joint on check the distance from the centre line of the pin to the end of the hollow threaded shank, in relation to the one you took off. These things can vary as the years go by and if you have marked the shank position on the rod, for replacement reference, and the shank on the new joint is a different length then compensation will have to be made as appropriate in the distance it is screwed on. Otherwise the overall length of the tie rod will be altered and the wheel alignment will change.

4 Clean the tapered hole in the arm and put the pin back in. If the pin turns when the nut is tightened pressure on the joint from a jack underneath will usually jam it sufficiently. Another dodge is to smear a little carborundum paste on the taper which will help the two surfaces to bite together.

5 When the taper pin nuts are tight check that the joint is central with the wheels in the straight ahead position and then tighten the clamp to lock it to the tie rod.

6 The track rod joints are not adjustable or detachable from the rod so the whole rod must be renewed if the joint at either end is worn. The joint pins are removed and refitted to the arms in the same way as for the tie rods (photo).

7 Provided there has been no attempt to compensate for wear by adjustment of the tie rods, renewal of the track rod does not require wheel alignment checking afterwards. With tie rods it is advisable to have the wheel alignment checked on a proper gauge whenever the joints are disturbed. The toe-in is the dimension

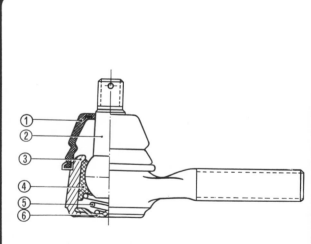

Fig.11.8. Part cross section through steering tie rod ball joint

1	Dust cover	4	Nylon bush
2	Taper pin	5	Spring
3	Socket	6	Cover plate

16.6. Fitting a track rod with ball joint to the idler arm

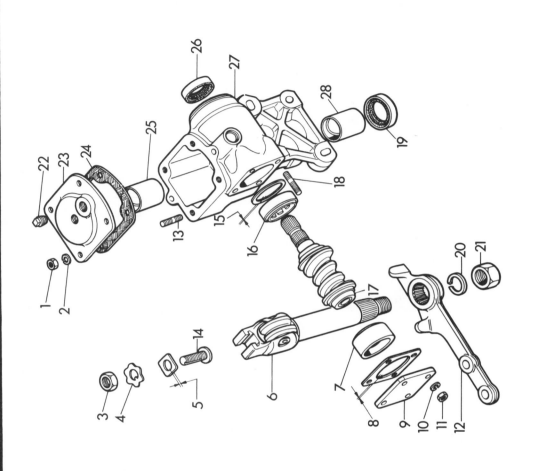

Fig.11.9. Steering box — Components

1	Cover nut	6	Roller shaft	10	Lockwasher	15	Shim ring (selective)	20	Lockwasher	25	Bush
2	Lockwasher	7	Bearing	11	Nut	16	Bearing	21	Nut	26	Oil seal
3	Locknut	8	Lock plate shim	12	Drop arm	17	Stud	22	Plug	27	Steering box casing
4	Lockwasher		(selective)	13	Stud	18	Worm shaft	23	Cover plate	28	Bush
5	Lock plate (selective)	9	Cover plate	14	Adjustment screw	19	Oil seal	24	Gasket		

affected. A fairly accurate check of toe-in can be carried out by the owner if he has two lengths of board - about 5 feet long and with one edge on each board planed perfectly straight. Wheels should be in the straight ahead position. Each board is raised on bricks or something equally suitable and lined up with a front wheel. The boards should be as near the centre as the hub will permit, and just touching the tyre walls. Both boards should project forwards (see sketch). If the distance between the two boards is then measured in two places 13 inches apart (13 inches is the wheel diameter) the difference should be 7 mm/.275 inches - the longer measurement being that nearest the wheels.

8 Adjustment may be made in the tie rod by slackening both joint clamps and turning the rod. One end of each rod has a left hand thread. This will effectively lengthen or shorten the rod and thus alter the alignment of the wheels. If both tie rods have been disturbed make any adjustment equally on each. It must be emphasised that this method is only rough and ready. Wheel alignment must be carried out at the central position and other checks made on various degrees of turn to be fully satisfactory. So adjustments the owner may carry out in emergency must be properly checked at the earliest opportunity.

17. Steering gear - adjustment, removal and replacement

1 It must be emphasised that adjustments to the steering gear are only minor adjustments and are not such that can compensate for progressive or excessive wear. In fact adjustments are normally carried out early in the life of the car as a result of the settling down or running in of the components. Such adjustments in the early life of the vehicle are important because if neglected, wear will occur at a greater rate than otherwise. This wear will then pass the point where adjustment is fully effective.

2 There are three places where slackness may occur, namely the bearings in which the worm shaft runs, the meshing of the worm and roller, and the bushes in which the roller shaft runs. The first two are adjustable. The third requires new bushes to be fitted and reamed.

3 The worm shaft bearings are pre-loaded by shims under the cover. Any end float may be decreased by decreasing the shims under the cover which consequently puts a greater load on the bearings when tightened down. Shims are available in thicknesses of 0.10 mm/.004 in and 0.15 mm/.006 inch.

4 The backlash between the worm and roller can be adjusted by means of the screw in the top cover plate. If the locknut is slackened the adjusting screw can be turned. This setting is best done with the tie rods disconnected from the drop arm. Set the drop arm in the central, (straight ahead) position and tighten the adjuster screw so that no play exists and that with a 30° movement either side of the WORM shaft (not the drop arm) the turning torque is ¾—1½ ft lbs/ 9—17 kgcm. Beyond the 30° point on each side the turning torque decreases to ½ ft lbs/7 kgcm.

5 If after adjustment of the worm to roller it is found that the turning torque in the central area does not range equally on each side, then the worm position has to be centralised by the transfer of shims from under the upper bearing to the lower bearing or vice versa. This involves dismantling.

6 If the steering gear is beyond adjustment it is necessary to remove it for overhaul or replacement. This is done by undoing the clamp bolt securing the worm shaft to the lower end of the steering column, disconnecting the tie rod and track rod from the drop arm and then releasing the three bolts securing it to the body frame. Note that there will probably be shims between the flange mounting of the steering gear and the body frame. This is because tolerances on a pressed steel body frame are not close enough to give the precise alignment necessary for the steering gear and column. Before refitting the same or new steering box make sure that the same shims are installed in the same position. It is advisable to slacken the mounting bolts at the upper end of the steering column also. Fit the steering box in position but do not tighten the mounting nuts. Then clamp the worm shaft to the column and fix the tie rods to the drop arm. With the front wheels off the ground, turn the steering from side to side a few times before finally tightening the steering box mounting bolts followed by the steering column upper bracket bolts.

7 Overhaul of the steering box is not a job within the competence of the average owner because bushes have to be fitted and reamed to suit the roller shaft. As an overhaul normally requires most parts to be renewed the economics need thorough investigation before stripping the box down with this in mind.

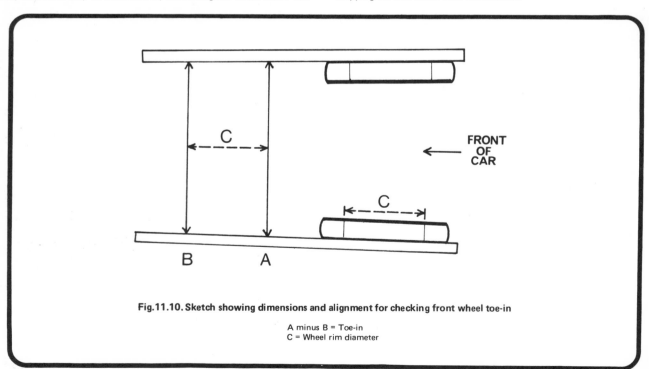

Fig.11.10. Sketch showing dimensions and alignment for checking front wheel toe-in

A minus B = Toe-in
C = Wheel rim diameter

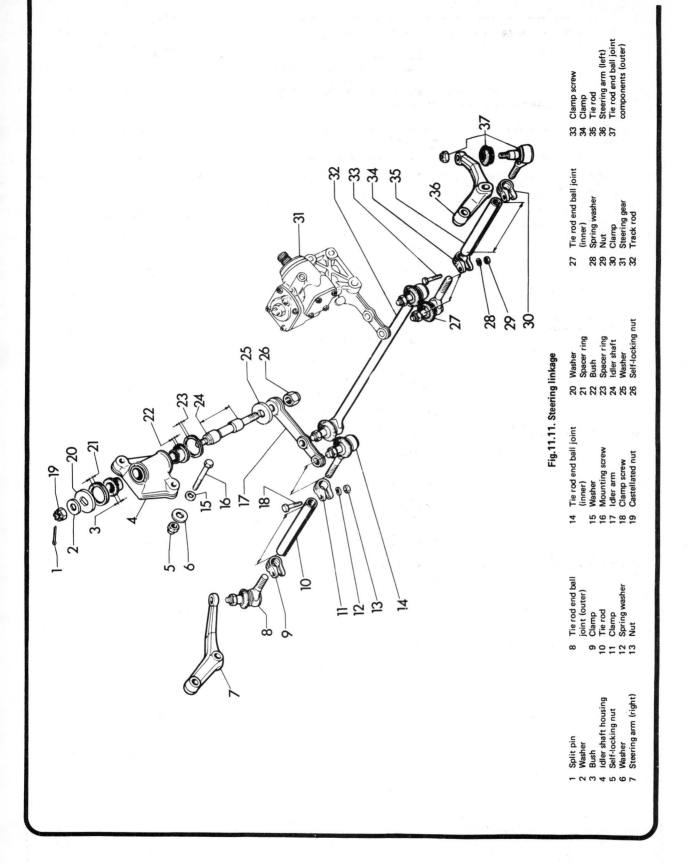

Fig.11.11. Steering linkage

1	Split pin
2	Washer
3	Bush
4	Idler shaft housing
5	Self-locking nut
6	Washer
7	Steering arm (right)
8	Tie rod end ball joint (outer)
9	Clamp
10	Tie rod
11	Clamp
12	Spring washer
13	Nut
14	Tie rod end ball joint (inner)
15	Washer
16	Mounting screw
17	Idler arm
18	Clamp screw
19	Castellated nut
20	Washer
21	Spacer ring
22	Bush
23	Spacer ring
24	Idler shaft
25	Washer
26	Self-locking nut
27	Tie rod end ball joint (inner)
28	Spring washer
29	Nut
30	Clamp
31	Steering gear
32	Track rod
33	Clamp screw
34	Clamp
35	Tie rod
36	Steering arm (left)
37	Tie rod end ball joint components (outer)

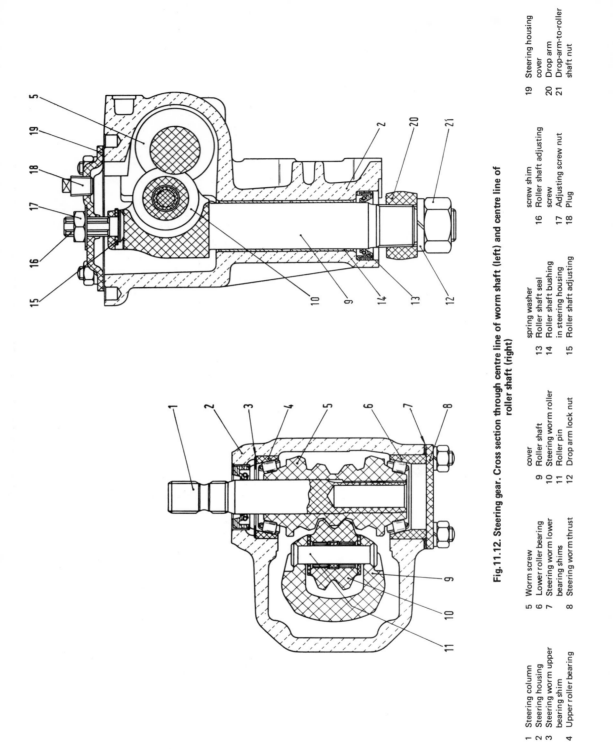

Fig.11.12. Steering gear. Cross section through centre line of worm shaft (left) and centre line of roller shaft (right)

1 Steering column
2 Steering housing
3 Steering worm upper bearing shim
4 Upper roller bearing
5 Worm screw
6 Lower roller bearing
7 Steering worm lower bearing shims
8 Steering worm thrust
9 cover
10 Steering worm roller
11 Roller pin
12 Drop arm lock nut
13 Roller shaft seal
14 Roller shaft bushing in steering housing
15 Roller shaft adjusting
16 Roller shaft adjusting screw
17 Adjusting screw nut
18 Plug
19 Steering housing cover
20 Drop arm
21 Drop-arm-to-roller shaft nut

screw shim
9 Roller shaft
spring washer

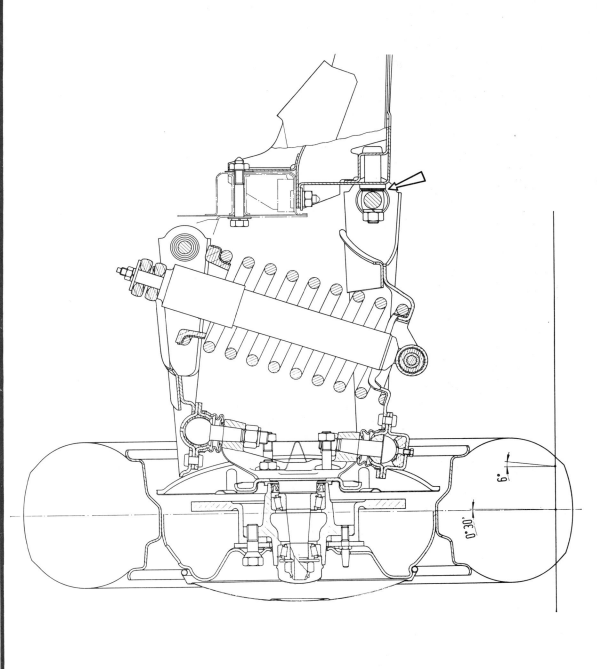

6°

0° 30′

Fig.11.13. Cross section through front suspension assembly. Arrow indicates shims for setting camber angle. Angles indicated are camber and steering pivot inclination

18. Steering idler arm - renovation

1   If examination shows that there is wear in the idler shaft bushes the unit should first be removed from the car by disconnecting the tie rods (see Section 16 for methods of removing the pins) and then unbolting it from the body side frame.

2   If the nuts are then removed from each end of the pivot shaft the bushes can be removed and new ones fitted.

19. Steering geometry - checking and adjustment

1   It is virtually impossible to regard each feature of the steering geometry independently. Apart from the wheel alignment (toe-in) which is considered when tie rod ball joints are renewed, (see Section 16) the castor angle, camber angle and steering pivot inclination are other factors which all depend on the state of the suspension wishbone bushes and ball joints and spring condition. The checking of these angles needs specialised equipment and can only then serve any useful purpose provided the suspension is in a good state of repair. If not then the suspension must first be over-hauled. Apart from the adjustable length steering tie rods for setting the toe-in, the only other form of steering adjustment is incorporated in the variable shims packed behind the lower wishbone pivot bar where it bolts to the front axle. The only time when these would need alteration is where damage required the replacement of any main part of the front suspension.

2   If therefore, you experience abnormal tyre wear or unsatisfactory handling do not assume that the wheel alignment is the sole cause. It may be wear in one or more of the various bushes and ball joints in the suspension and steering system. A proper check of the whole system is the only sure way of curing any problems.

20. Steering wheel - removal and replacement

1   Disconnect the battery.

2   Remove the screws securing the horn ring and motif from behind the wheel spokes.

3   Unscrew the large nut in the centre of the steering wheel and after marking the column in relation to the wheel with a centre punch, pull the wheel off the splined column.

4   Replace the wheel so that the punch marks already made line up. If no marks have been made set the front wheels in the straight ahead position and replace the steering wheel with the spoke horizontal and in the lower half of the wheel.

21. Steering column and shaft - removal and replacement

1   The steering column is bolted by a bracket to the dash panel at the upper end and clamped to the steering box worm shaft by a splined collar at the lower end.

2   Once the lower coupling and upper bracket bolts have been loosened, and the wires disconnected from the ignition switch and headlamp flasher switch, the whole column complete with steering wheel can be removed from inside the car.

3   Later models are fitted with a central articulated section in the column. This can be disconnected at the upper or lower end depending on the reason for removing the column in the first place.

4   Although it is possible to line up the splined sections of the shaft later it is always good practice to mark each connection before separating it so that no mistake is made.

5   When refitting the column assemble all the mounting bolts loosely to start with so that the steering can be turned from side to side with the front wheels off the ground. Then tighten the mounting bracket bolts.

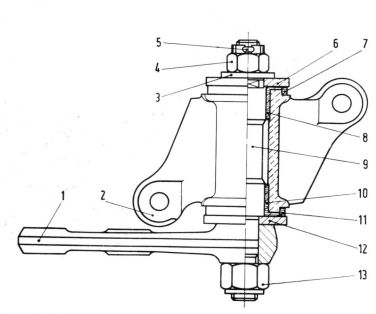

Fig.11.14. Part cross section through steering idler arm and bracket assembly

1 Idler arm	5 Split pin	8 Bush	11 Seal
2 Support bracket	6 Washer	9 Pivot shaft	12 Flat washer
3 Washer	7 Seal	10 Bush	13 Self locking nut
4 Nut			

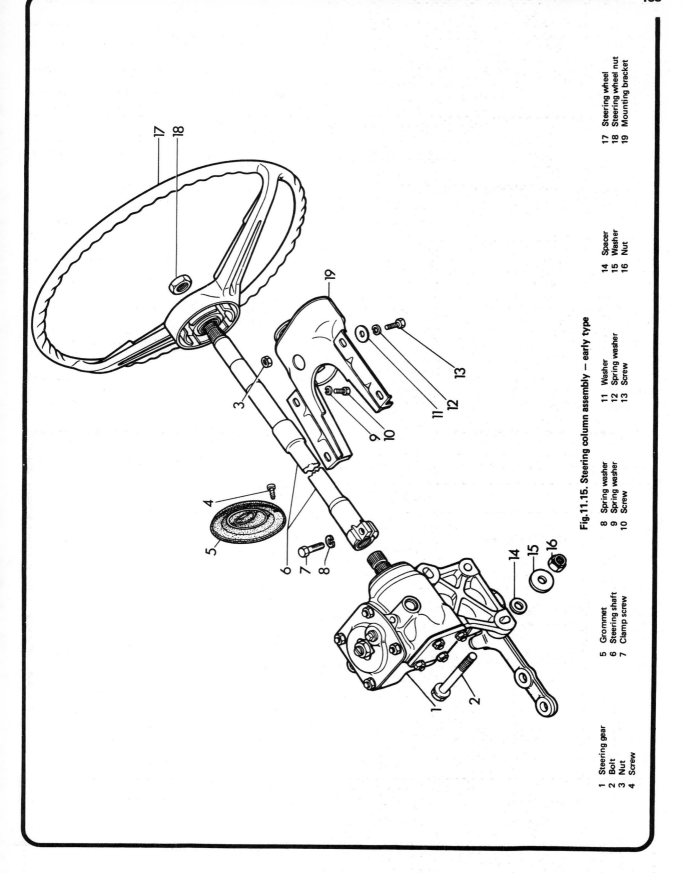

Fig.11.15. Steering column assembly — early type

1	Steering gear	8	Spring washer	11	Washer	17 Steering wheel
2	Bolt	9	Spring washer	12	Spring washer	18 Steering wheel nut
3	Nut	10	Screw	13	Screw	19 Mounting bracket
4	Screw	5 Grommet	14 Spacer			
		6 Steering shaft	15 Washer			
		7 Clamp screw	16 Nut			

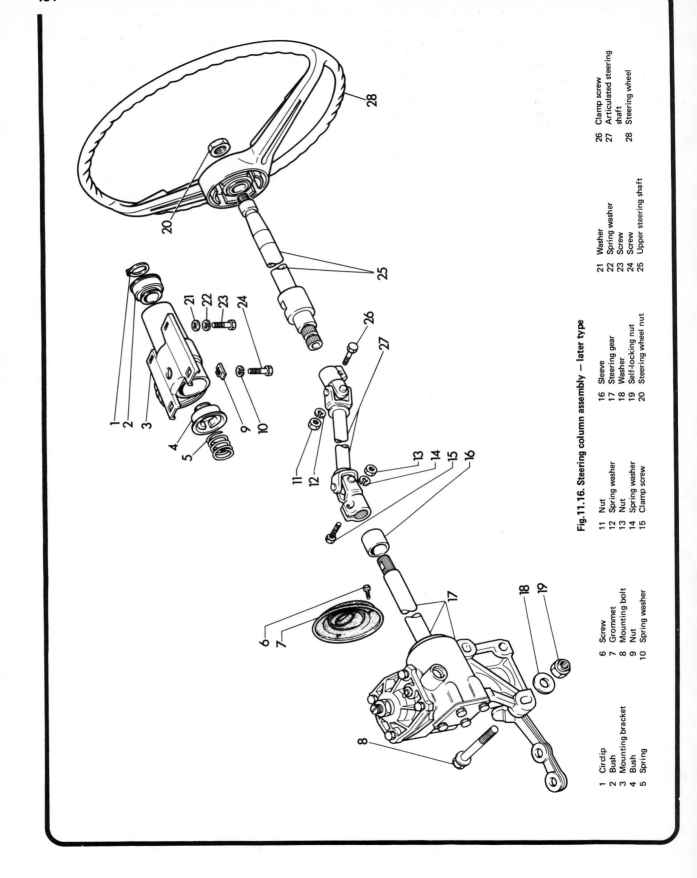

Fig.11.16. Steering column assembly — later type

1	Circlip	6	Screw	11	Nut
2	Bush	7	Grommet	12	Spring washer
3	Mounting bracket	8	Mounting bolt	13	Nut
4	Bush	9	Nut	14	Spring washer
5	Spring	10	Spring washer	15	Clamp screw

16	Sleeve
17	Steering gear
18	Washer
19	Self-locking nut
20	Steering wheel nut

21	Washer
22	Spring washer
23	Screw
24	Screw
25	Upper steering shaft

26	Clamp screw
27	Articulated steering shaft
28	Steering wheel

22. Wheels and tyres

1 To provide maximum tyre life the wheels should be repositioned on the car diagonally and the spare included at intervals of 6000 miles. However, most people prefer not to have to buy too many tyres at the same time and so let two wear out first. A new pair should always be fitted to the front wheels.

2 Radial tyres are standard fitting on saloons and should never be mixed with crossply. It is also bad practice to mix tread patterns from side to side so avoid this. If for any emergency reason a mixture of tyres is necessary the only possible combination is to have two radials on the rear and two crossplys on the front.

3 On estate cars radials may be used but mixtures are particularly to be avoided. A fully loaded estate can handle in a very peculiar manner if the tyres and pressures are incorrect.

4 Wheel checking and balancing should always be carried out when new tyres are fitted. Furthermore, wheels should be checked for balance whenever bad roads or inadvertent kerb thumping has occurred. Distorted wheels often go unnoticed by the driver and can contribute to excessive tyre wear and poor handling in certain situations.

23. Fault finding

Before assuming that the steering mechanism is at fault when mishandling is experienced make sure that the trouble is not caused by:—

1 Binding brakes
2 Incorrect mix of radial and crossply tyres
3 Incorrect tyre pressures
4 Misalignment of the body frame and rear axle

Therefore the following diagnosis guide will isolate the fault.

Symptom	Reason/s	Remedy
Steering wheel can be moved considerably before any sign of movement of the wheels is apparent	Wear in the steering linkage, gear and column coupling	Check movement in all joints and steering gear and overhaul and renew as required.
Vehicle difficult to steer in a consistent straight line - wandering	As above	As above
	Wheel alignment incorrect (indicated by excessive or uneven tyre wear)	Check wheel alignment.
	Front wheel hub bearings loose or worn	Adjust or renew as necessary.
	Worn ball joints, track rods or suspension arms	Renew as necessary.
Steering stiff and heavy	Incorrect wheel alignment (indicated by excessive or uneven tyre wear)	Check wheel alignment.
	Excessive wear or seizure in one or more of the joints in the steering linkage or suspension arm ball joints	Renew as necessary
	Excessive wear in the steering gear unit	Adjust if possible or renew.
Wheel wobble and vibration	Road wheels out of balance	Balance wheels.
	Road wheels buckled	Check for damage.
	Wheel alignment incorrect	Check wheel alignment.
	Wear in the steering linkage, suspension arm ball joints or suspension arm pivot bushes	Check and renew as necessary.
	Broken front spring	Check and renew as necessary.
Excessive pitching and rolling on corners and during braking	Defective dampers and/or broken spring	Check and renew as necessary.

Chapter 12 Bodywork and underframe

Contents

Weights and dimensions

Saloon

Kerb weight (with water, oil, fuel, spare wheel, tool kit and accessories) 855 kg/1885 lbs
Gross weight, fully laden.. ... ...   1255 kg/2767 lbs
Maximum trailer weight ... ...   740 kg/1628 lbs
Gross weight distribution   - front axle.. ... ...   555 kg/1224 lbs
                             - rear axle ... ...   700 kg/1543 lbs
Carrying capacity ... ...   5 adults plus 50 kg/110 lbs

Dimensions (all figures in millimetres) Height dimensions are for an unladen vehicle.

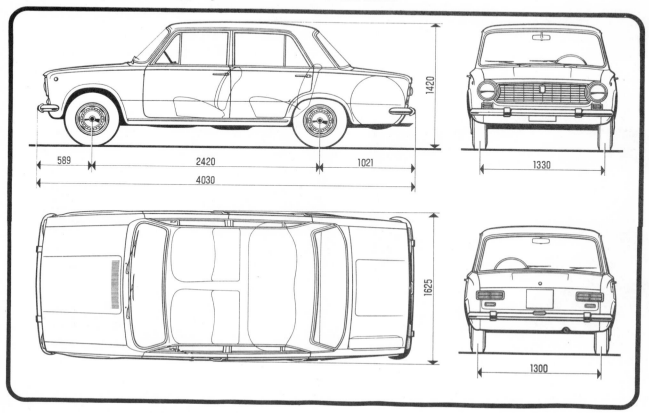

This sequence of photographs deals with the repair of the dent and scratch (above rear lamp) shown in this photo. The procedure will be similar for the repair of a hole. It should be noted that the procedures given here are simplified - more explicit instructions will be found in the text

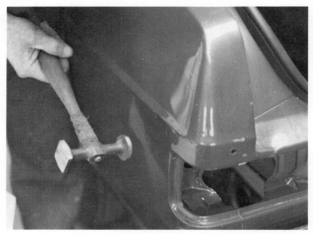

In the case of a dent the first job - after removing surrounding trim - is to hammer out the dent where access is possible. This will minimise filling. Here, the large dent having been hammered out, the damaged area is being made slightly concave

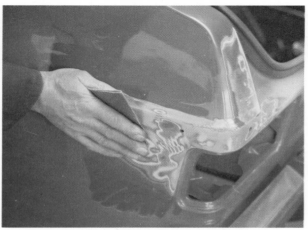

Now all paint must be removed from the damaged area, by rubbing with coarse abrasive paper. Alternatively, a wire brush or abrasive pad can be used in a power drill. Where the repair area meets good paintwork, the edge pf the paintwork should be 'feathered', using a finer grade of abrasive paper

In the case of a hole caused by rusting, all damaged sheet-metal should be cut away before proceeding to this stage. Here, the damaged area is being treated with rust remover and inhibitor before being filled

Mix the body filler according to its manufacturer's instructions. In the case of corrosion damage, it will be necessary to block off any large holes before filling - this can be done with zinc gauze or aluminium tape. Make sure the area is absolutely clean before ...

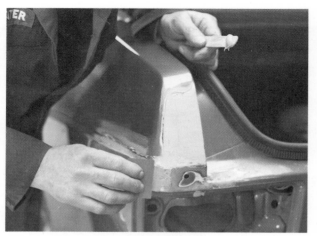

... applying the filler. Filler should be applied with a flexible applicator, as shown, for best results: the wooden spatula being used for confined areas. Apply thin layers of filler at 20-minute intervals, until the surface of the filler is slightly proud of the surrounding bodywork

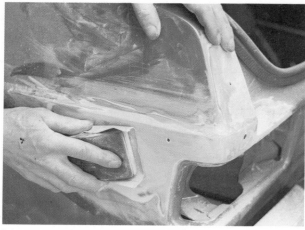

Initial shaping can be done with a Surform plane or Dreadnought file. Then, using progressively finer grades of wet-and-dry paper, wrapped around a sanding block, and copious amounts of clean water, rub-down the filler until really smooth and flat. Again, feather the edges of adjoining paintwork

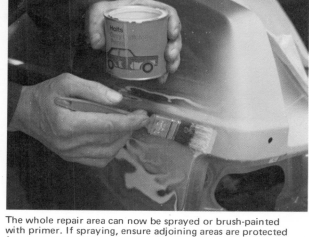

The whole repair area can now be sprayed or brush-painted with primer. If spraying, ensure adjoining areas are protected from over-spray. Note that at least one-inch of the surrounding sound paintwork should be coated with primer. Primer has a 'thick' consistency, so will fill small imperfections

Again, using plenty of water, rub down the primer with a fine grade of wet-and-dry paper (400 grade is probably best) until it is really smooth and well blended into the surrounding paint-work. Any remaining imperfections can now be filled by carefully applied knifing stopper paste

When the stopper has hardened, rub-down the repair area again before applying the final coat of primer. Before rubbing-down this last coat of primer, ensure the repair area is blemish-free - use more stopper if necessary. To ensure that the surface of the primer is really smooth use some finishing compound

The top coat can now be applied. When working out of doors, pick a dry, warm and wind-free day. Ensure surrounding areas are protected from over-spray. Agitate the aerosol thoroughly, then spray the centre of the repair area, working outwards with a circular motion. Apply the paint as several thin coats.

After a period of about two-weeks, which the paint needs to harden fully, the surface of the repaired area can be 'cut' with a mild cutting compound prior to wax polishing. When carrying out bodywork repairs, remember that the quality of the finished job is proportional to the time and effort expended

Estate

Kerb weight (with water, oil, fuel, spare wheel, tool kit and accessories)	910 kg/2005 lbs
Gross weight, fully laden..	1340 kg/3000 lbs
Carrying capacity	5 adults plus 80 kgs/176 lbs
or	1 adult plus 360 kgs/795 lbs *

*Load distributed over total floor area with rear seat flat

Dimensions (all figures in millimetres) Height dimensions are for an unladen vehicle.

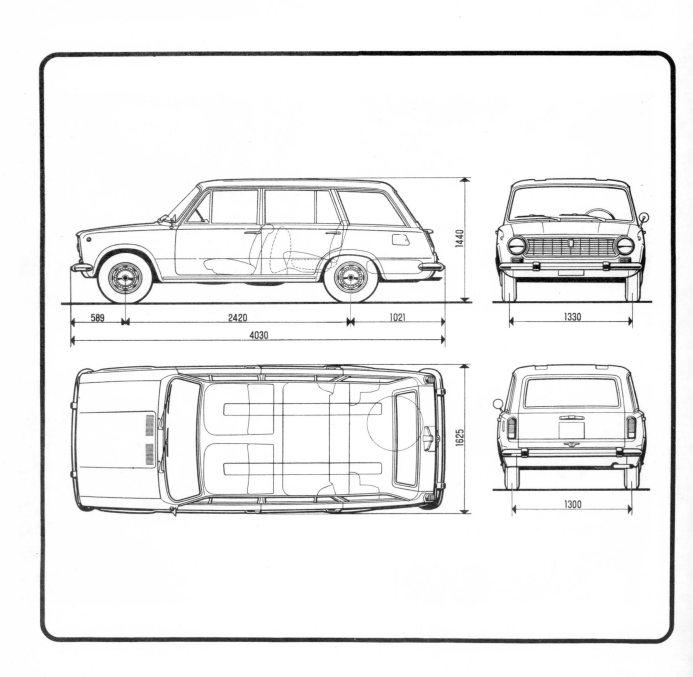

1. General description

The combined body shell and underframe is an all welded unitary structure of sheet steel. Openings in it provide for the engine compartment, luggage compartment, doors and front and rear windows. The rear axle is attached to the body by arms bolted directly to it on rubber bushes, and a detachable crossmember across the bottom of the engine compartment provides support for the engine and front suspension. A second detachable item is a central crossmember bridging the transmission tunnel which is the rear support of the engine/gearbox unit.

The estate model has four side doors and a full width single rear door hinged at the top.

2. Maintenance - bodywork and underframe

1 The general condition of a car's bodywork is the one thing that significantly affects its value. Maintenance is easy but needs to be regular and particular. Neglect, particularly after minor damage, can lead quickly to a further deterioration and costly repair bills. It is important also to keep watch on those parts of the car not immediately visible, for instance the underside, inside all the wheel arches and the lower part of the engine compartment. If your car is not fitted with mud flaps at the front, it is strongly recommended that they are installed. These protect the door undersills from grit slurry thrown up by the front wheels in wet weather.

2 The basic maintenance routine for the bodywork is washing — preferably with a lot of water, from a hose. This will remove all the loose solids which may have stuck to the car. It is important to flush these off in such a way as to prevent grit from scratching the finish. The wheel arches and underbody need washing in the same way to remove any accumulated mud which will retain moisture and tend to encourage rust. Paradoxically enough, the best time to clean the underbody and wheel arches is in wet weather when the mud is thoroughly wet and soft. In very wet weather the underbody is usually cleaned of large accumulations automatically and this is a good time for inspection.

3 Periodically, it is a good idea to have the whole of the underside of the car steam cleaned, engine compartment included, so that a thorough inspection can be carried out to see what minor repairs and renovations are necessary. Steam cleaning is available at many garages and is necessary for removal of accumulations of oily grime which sometimes cakes thick in certain areas near the engine, gearbox and back axle. If steam facilities are not available, there are one or two excellent grease solvents available which can be brush applied. The dirt can then be simply hosed off.

4 After washing paintwork, wipe it off with a chamois leather to give an unspotted clear finish. A coat of clear protective wax polish will give added protection against chemical pollutants in the air. If the paintwork sheen has dulled or oxidised, use a cleaner/ polisher combination to restore the brilliance of the shine. This requires a little more effort, but the condition is usually caused because regular washing has been neglected. Always check that door and ventilator opening drain holes and pipes are completely clear so that water can drain out. Bright work should be treated the same way as paintwork. Windscreens and windows can be kept clear of the smeary film which often appears if a little ammonia is added to the water. If they are scratched, a good rub with a proprietary metal polish will often clear them. Never use any form of wax or chromium polish on glass.

3. Maintenance - interior

1 Mats and carpets should be brushed or vacuum cleaned regularly to keep them free of dirt. If they are badly stained remove them from the car for scrubbing or sponging and make quite sure they are dry before replacement. Seats and interior trim panels can be kept clean by a wipe over with a damp cloth. If they do become stained (which can be more apparent on light coloured upholstery) use a little liquid detergent and a soft nailbrush to scour the grime out of the grain of the material. Do not forget to keep the head lining clean in the same way as the upholstery. When using liquid cleaners inside the car do not over wet the surfaces being cleaned. Excessive damp could get into the seams and padded interior causing stains, offensive odours or even rot. If the inside of the car gets wet accidentally, it is worthwhile taking some trouble to dry it out properly, particularly where carpets are involved. Do NOT leave oil or electric heaters inside the car for this purpose.

4. Minor repairs to bodywork

1 A car which does not suffer some minor damage to the bodywork from time to time is the exception rather than the rule. Even presuming the gatepost is never scraped or the door opened against a wall or high kerb, there is always the likelihood of gravel and grit being thrown up and chipping the surface, particularly at the lower edges of the doors and sills.

2 If the damage is merely a paint scrape which has not reached the metal base, delay is not critical, but where bare metal is exposed action must be taken immediately before rust sets in.

3 The average owner will normally keep the following 'first aid' materials available which can give a professional finish for minor jobs:

a) Matching paint in liquid form - often complete with brush attached to the lid inside (aerosols should only be bought for painting areas larger than 6 inches square - they are extravagant and expensive for anything less and give no better results. Spraying from aerosols is generally less perfect than the makers would have one expect).

b) Thinners for the paint (for brush application).

c) Cellulose stopper (a filling compound for small paint chips).

d) Cellulose primer (a thickish grey coloured base which can be applied and rubbed down in several coats to give a perfect paint base).

e) Proprietary resin filler paste (for larger volume of in-filling).

f) Rust inhibiting primer.

g) Wet dry paper of fine, medium and coarse grades.

4 Where the damage is superficial (i.e. not down to the bare metal and not dented), fill the scratch or chip with sufficient filler to smooth the area, rub down with paper and apply the matching paint.

5 Where the bodywork is scratched down to the metal, but not dented, clean the metal surface thoroughly and apply the primer (it does not need to be a rust inhibitor if the metal is rust free and clean) and then build up the scratched part to the level of the surrounding paintwork with the stopper. When the primer/stopper is hard it can be rubbed down with wet and dry paper. Keep applying primer and rubbing it down until no surface blemish can be felt. Then apply the colour, thinned if necessary. Apply as many coats as needed, rubbing down with the finest grade paper between each.

6 If the bodywork is dented, first beat out the dent as near as possible to conform with the original contour. Avoid using steel hammers - use hardwood mallets or similar and always support the back of the panel being beaten with a hardwood or metal 'dolly'. In areas where severe creasing and buckling has occurred it will be virtually impossible to reform the metal to the original shape. In such instances a decision should be made whether or not to cut out the damaged piece or attempt to re-contour over it with filler paste. In large areas where the metal panel is seriously damaged or rusted, the repair is to be considered major and it is often better to replace a panel or sill section with the appropriate part supplied as a spare. When using filler paste in largish quantities, make sure the directions are carefully followed. It is false economy to try and rush the job, as the correct hardening time must be allowed between stages or before finishing. With thick application the filler usually has to be applied in layers - allowing time for each layer to harden. Sometimes

the original paint colour will have faded and it will be difficult to obtain an exact colour match. In such instances it is a good scheme to select a complete panel - such as a door, or boot lid, and spray the whole panel. Differences will be less apparent where there are obvious divisions between the original and resprayed areas.

Finally a general word of advice. Do not expect to be able to prepare, fill, rub down and paint a section of damaged bodywork in one day and expect good results. It cannot be done. Give plenty of time for each successive application of filler and primers to harden before rubbing it down and applying the next coat.

5. Major repairs to bodywork

1 Where serious damage has occurred or large areas need renewal due to neglect, it means certainly that completely new sections or panels will need welding in and this is best left to professionals. If the damage is due to impact it will also be necessary to completely check the alignment of the body shell structure. Due to the principle of construction, the strength and shape of the whole can be affected by damage to a part. In such instances the services of a Fiat agent with specialist checking jigs are essential. If a body is left misaligned, it is first of all dangerous as the car will not handle properly - and secondly, uneven stresses will be imposed on the steering, engine and transmission, causing abnormal wear or complete failure. Tyre wear will also be excessive.

6. Front and rear bumpers - removal and replacement

1 The front bumper is held in the centre by two nuts which fit on the bumper studs through mounting brackets. At the outer ends of the bumper a bolt from inside the wing screws into the spacer attached to the bumper. Removal of the two bolts and the two nuts enables the bumper to be taken off.
2 The rear bumper is mounted in the same manner except that the fixing bolt for the outer ends are accessible inside the luggage compartment.
3 Over-riders are fitted to both bumpers and are secured by two nuts and bolts, the bolts being anchored in the over-riders.

7. Windscreen and fixed windows - removal and replacement

1 To remove the windscreen first remove the windscreen wiper arms. The glass is taken out by pressure from inside at the upper corners. On the back window apply the pressure at the lower corners. This releases the inner lip of the weatherstrip from the aperture flange and the whole screen can be removed with the strip still attached. Where a screen is broken simply remove the weatherstrip.
2 The weatherstrip may be re-used provided it is not split or otherwise damaged and the rubber still retains reasonable flexibility. It is essential to clean away all traces of sealing compound from both the weatherstrip and the aperture flange. The moulding must be removed from the weatherstrip before fitting the weatherstrip to the glass.
3 To replace the screen first fit the weatherstrip to the glass and then replace the moulding in the weatherstrip. A special tool with a loop and wheel to open the groove whilst the moulding is pressed in helps to carry out this operation speedily - however, with patience and care an old screwdriver, with the corners of the blade rounded off, will enable the moulding to be fitted in. Do not use any form of sealing compound when fitting the weatherstrip to the glass.
4 Next fit a piece of strong thin cord (fishing line is ideal) into the other groove of the weatherstrip, leave two ends crossed over at the centre top and bottom.
5 Place the glass in position centrally and whilst somebody holds it in place, draw on the cords from inside so that the lip of the weatherstrip is lifted over the aperture flange. There are two problems which usually arise. One is to avoid cutting the cord on the

edge of the flange, and the other is to avoid slicing off the lip of the weatherstrip with the cord. For this reason the angle at which the cord is withdrawn must be carefully maintained and no hurried jerks or excessive force must be used. If necessary use a blunt blade of some sort to assist in the tough spots. Above all do not try and rush it.
6 Provided the weatherstrip is in good condition and the aperture flange is not distorted in any way there should be a watertight seal. If experience shows that water is seeping in use a proprietary sealer of the thin clear type which can be injected with a thin flat nozzle. Inject this between the glass and weatherstrip on the outside all the way round. If this is inadequate inject more between the flange and the weatherstrip on the outside all the way round.

8. Instrument panel trim - removal

1 At each end of the trim remove the screw holding it to the windscreen pillar and then slide the trim ends up a little to disengage them from the pillars.
2 Remove the cowls round the direction indicator switch by undoing the four screws.
3 Take out the instrument cluster as described in Chapter 10.
4 Push out the cluster of three switches (lights, wiper, panel) as described in Chapter 10 and remove all the wire connections (make sure you note their positions).
5 Disconnect the wire to the glove compartment light and take away the windscreen washer pipes.
6 Remove the ashtray.
7 Remove the four screws holding the lower edge of the trim to dash panel.
8 Through the glove compartment and instrument cluster apertures undo the four nuts securing the upper edge of the trim to the dash panel. Take out also the two screws securing the glove compartment partition panel so that the heater ventilator cables can be disconnected from the levers which are attached to the trim panel.
9 Carefully lift the panel away.
10 When refitting the panel make sure the heater control cables are properly fitted to the levers.

9. Doors - checking and adjustments

1 Body rattles are often due to the doors and this can usually be traced to hinges, the door latch or the window mechanism inside the door.
2 Assuming that there has been no damage to the door or body it should be positioned centrally in its frame with an equal gap all round. If this is not the case the hinges may have moved on their attachments to the door pillar. The hinges should be marked around first with a pencil so that subsequent movement may be obvious. The two countersunk cross point securing screws are very tight and an impact screwdriver is essential both for loosening and tightening them. Move the door on the hinges until it is central in its aperture.
3 When the door is shut it should be flush with the body panel and not be movable. Also no excessive force should be needed to close the door - slamming should not be necessary - and hard pressure should not be needed on the catch release button to open it. The latch plate screwed to the door post can be moved in, out or up and down to improve these conditions. Mark the plate outline in pencil for a reference point and then slacken the three screws so that it can be moved. Move it in the direction required a little amount only and retighten the screws. Keep making small adjustments and testing until the desired position is reached.
4 Rattles which may be coming from inside the door will require some dismantling and this is dealt with in the next section.

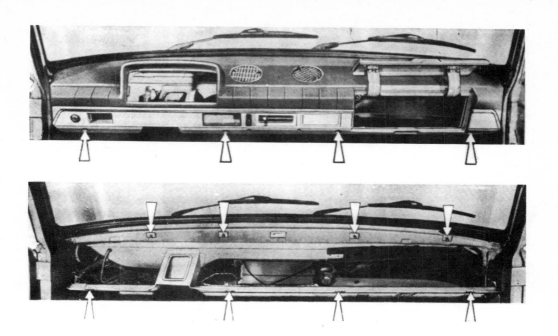

Fig. 12.3. Instrument panel trim in position and removed. Arrows indicate lower fixing screw and upper fixing nut positions

Fig. 12.4. Door hinge fixing

1   Countersunk hinge screws   2   Impact screwdriver
Arrow points to percussion point

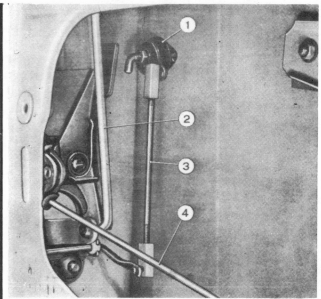

Fig. 12.5. Door latch linkage

1 Opening and locking device   3 Handle linkage
2 Plunger rod   4 Remote control rod

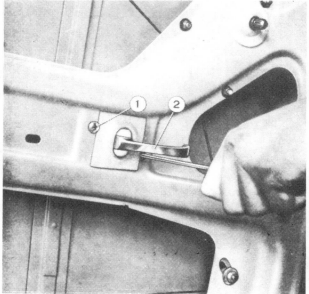

Fig. 12.6. Remote control handle

1 Fixing screw   2 Handle

Fig. 12.7. Door latch components

1 Plunger button
2 Plunger rod
3 Latch securing screws

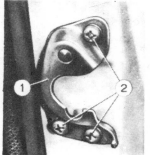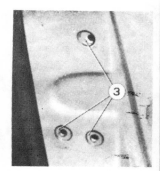

Fig. 12.8. Door latch striker plate mounting

1 Striker plate   3 Striker plate movable
2 Striker plate securing screws   mounting holes

10 Doors - removal and dismantling

1   If the doors are to be taken off the car, first mark the hinge positions. Disconnect the door check link and undo the four hinge screws with an impact screwdriver. Lift the door off.

2   Work on latches, windows and window winder mechanisms can all be carried out with the door in position on the car.

3   The window winder handles are held to the shafts with spring wire clips (see Fig. 12.9(. To remove these press back the escutcheon behind the handle and then use a wide blade to push them off. The handle can then be taken off.

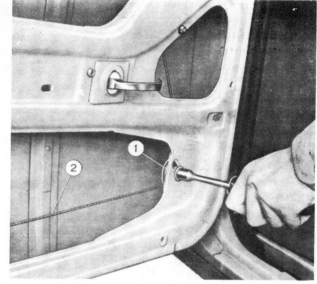

Fig. 12.10. Window regulator cable adjustment pulley

1   Pulley
2   Cable

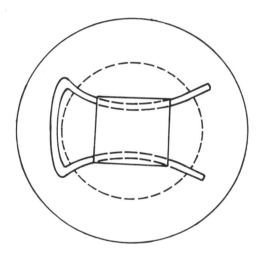

Fig. 12.9. Window winder handle. Diagram to show fixing clip arrangement

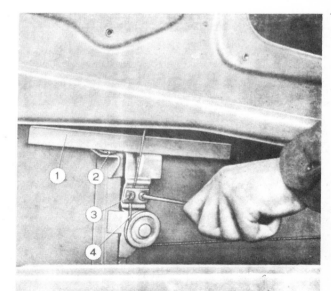

Fig. 12.11. Window regulator cable clamp

1   Glass support channel   3   Cable clamp screw
2   Lower stop   4   Cable

4   The inside remote door latches are fixed to the door inner panel. Remove the escutcheons by levering them off with a flat blade. Unscrew the armrest from the panel.

5   To remove the inner trim panel use a flat blade between the trim and door and lever out the press clips along the sides and bottom edge. The panel can then be drawn down and taken away.

6   The window mechanism is operated by a cable and there are two points of adjustment to ensure the window rises evenly and square. (See Fig. 12.10 and Fig. 12.11).

7   To remove the window the sill mouldings must be removed and the window lowered. The glass support channel is then detached from the cable clip and the lower guide channel taken out.

8   The quarter light can be removed after the main window lower guide channel is removed and the glass lowered. The screw in the quarter light door frame is taken out and the quarter light can then be taken out complete.

11 Bonnet and boot lids - adjustment and removal

1   The bonnet lid hinges at the front and each hinge is held to the body cross panel by two screws. The hinge holes are slotted so that the position of the lid can be altered as necessary. To remove it squeeze the legs of the wire prop together so as to release it from the bracket. Undo the hinge screws completely to lift the bonnet clear.

2   The boot lid is similar and the nuts securing the hinges to the lid may be slackened in order to reposition the lid in the aperture. The latch plate and catch positions are also adjustable if required in order to enable the lid to be closed without undue force.

12 Heating and ventilation system - description

1   The heater/ventilation unit is mounted centrally below the dash panel and incorporates a heater radiator supplied with hot water from the engine cooling system. A valve can shut off the supply of hot water and is controlled by a lever on the dash panel. Below the heater is a housing which contains an electrically powered blower fan. Air enters the car through two adjustable diffusers in the panel trim and through a shutter in the bottom of the fan housing. If the shutter is closed all air enters through the diffusers. Outside air enters through the grille in front of the windscreen into a plenum chamber and can then pass through a flap controlled aperture via the heater. In warm weather the heater valve being off, cool air will enter the car, if necessary with assistance from the blower. When the air inlet flap is closed no air passes through the heater housing.

13 Heating and ventilating system - repairs

1   Any repairs to the fan or heater radiator will require removal of the units from the car. First drain the engine cooling system making sure that the heater valve lever is in the 'hot' position so that all water will drain from the heater as well.

2   Loosen the hose clips on the pipes to the heater matrix.

3   Inside the engine compartment remove the rubber seals around the heater pipes by undoing the screws and washers securing them.

4   Slacken the clip holding the cable to the water valve and disconnect the cable.

5   Disconnect the yellow wire for the blower fan at the fan switch.

6   The lower half of the unit, the fan housing, is held to the upper part by four spring clips. Remove these and the fan housing can be taken off. The fan earth wire is connected to one of the heater mounting nuts.

7   The heater radiator is held to the body by four nuts. After removing these lower the radiator sufficiently to slacken the clamp screws which hold the operating cable to the air intake flap. The whole unit may then be removed.

8   The fan motor may be dismantled for examination and cleaning and renewal of carbon brushes. The water valve also may be taken off the heater radiator for checking and cleaning.

9   When refitting the heater unit it is important to make sure that all water seals are perfectly secure and that the fan motor runs freely. Test it on the bench in advance. Make sure that the fan electrical connections are made and that the gasket between the fan housing and body is correctly positioned.

10 When refilling the cooling system make sure that the water valve is open and after running the engine for a short time check the coolant level.

11 Poor heating performance in cold weather is usually due to a faulty thermostat in the engine cooling system. Check this first before anything else. Details are given in Chapter 2.

12 Failure of the blower fan may be due to a blown fuse. If this is the case the windscreen wipers and other items on fuse No. 1 will not work either (see Chapter 10). Check which item is blowing the fuse before assuming the fan motor is at fault.

Fig. 12.12. Quarter light removal. Undoing the frame screw

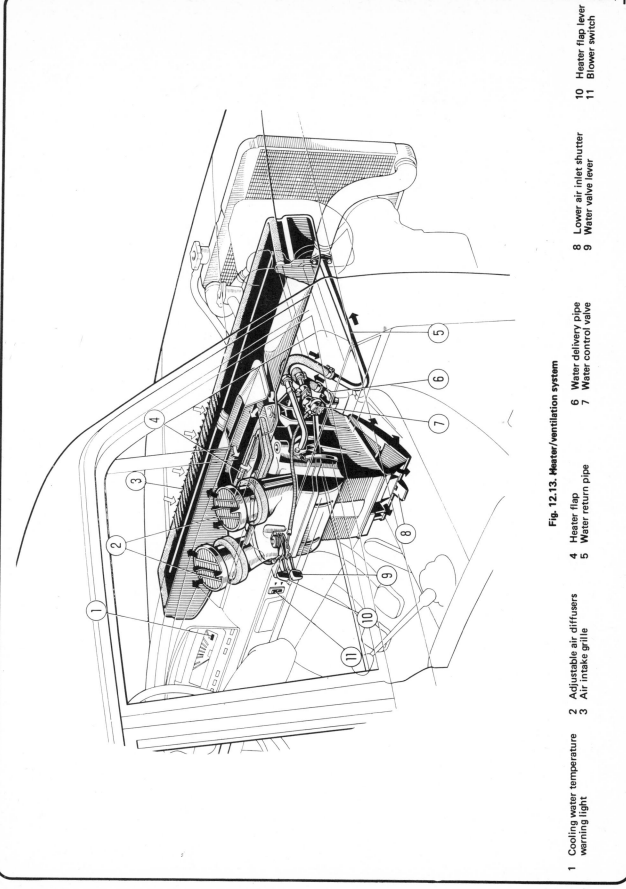

Fig. 12.13. Heater/ventilation system

1 Cooling water temperature warning light
2 Adjustable air diffusers
3 Air intake grille
4 Heater flap
5 Water return pipe
6 Water delivery pipe
7 Water control valve
8 Lower air inlet shutter
9 Water valve lever
10 Heater flap lever
11 Blower switch

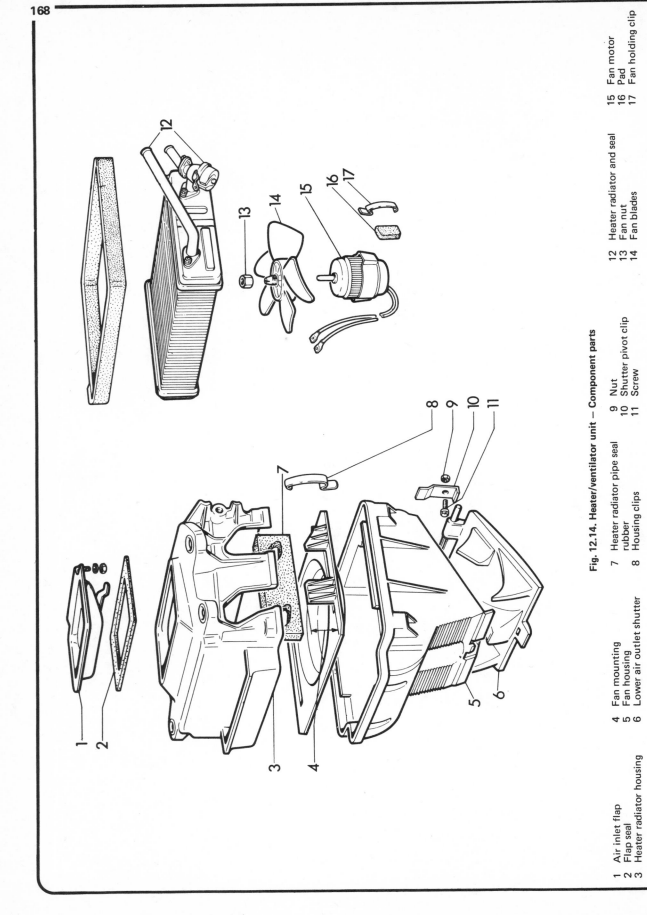

Fig. 12.14. Heater/ventilator unit – Component parts

1 Air inlet flap
2 Flap seal
3 Heater radiator housing

4 Fan mounting
5 Fan housing
6 Lower air outlet shutter

7 Heater radiator pipe seal rubber
8 Housing clips

9 Nut
10 Shutter pivot clip
11 Screw

12 Heater radiator and seal
13 Fan nut
14 Fan blades

15 Fan motor
16 Pad
17 Fan holding clip

Chapter 13 Supplement

Contents

Fig.13.1. North American version of the Fiat 124S wagon 1973 (without roof rack)

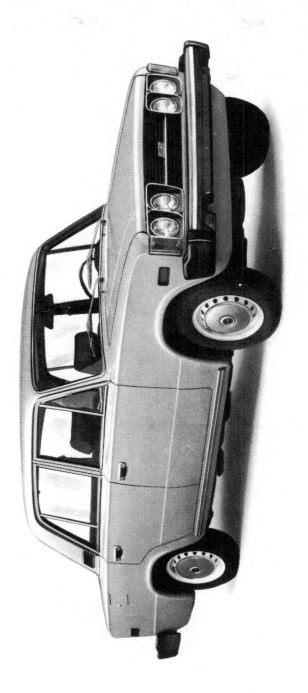

Fig.13.2. North American version of the Fiat 124S sedan 1973

Fig.13.3. European version of the Fiat Special T saloon 1974

Fig.13.4. North American version of the Fiat Special TC wagon 1974

1 Introduction

The purpose of this Supplement is to bring the information in the first twelve chapters of this manual up-to-date to include details of the Special T and Special TC Fiat 124 models.

Special thanks are due to Mr Jonathan Evans of the Ilminster Motor Company, Ilminster, Somerset, who was particularly helpful in the supply of information to the author.

2 Specifications

Engine (Special T and Special TC models — DOHC)

	124 AC 3.000	132 A.040.4
Manufacturers Type number:	**124 AC 3.000**	**132 A.040.4**
Swept volume	**1438 cc**	**1592 cc**
Bore	3.150 in (80 mm)	3.150 in (80 mm)
Stroke	2.815 in (7.15 mm)	3.12 in (79.2 mm)
Firing order	1-3-4-2	1-3-4-2
Compression ratio	8,9 : 1	8 : 1 (USA); 9.8 : 1 (UK)
Engine rotation	Clockwise when viewed from front	
Max. horsepower (DIN)	90 (1438cc)	78 (USA) — 1592cc; 104 (UK – 1592cc)

Crankshaft

Main journal diameter	1.9990 — 1.9998 in (50.775 — 50.795 mm)	2.0860 — 2.0868 in (52.985 — 53.005 mm)
Regrind diameters	minus 0.010 in (0.254 mm); minus 0.020 in (0.508 mm); minus 0.030 in (0.762 mm); minus 0.040 in (1.016 mm)	

Crankpin journal diameter:

Standard	1.7916 — 1.7924 in (45.508 — 45.528 mm)
Class A*	1.9997 — 2.0001 in (50.792 — 50.802 mm)
Class B*	1.9993 — 1.9997 in (50.782 — 50.792 mm)

Class 'A' identified by a red paint dot on crank. Class 'B' identified by a blue paint dot on crank.

Crankpin regrind diameters...	minus 0.010 in (0.254 mm); minus 0.020 in (0.508 mm); minus 0.030 in (0.762 mm); minus 0.040 in (1.016 mm)
Crankshaft endfloat	0.002 to 0.012 in (0.05 to 0.095 mm)
Maximum journal taper and ovality	0.0002 in (0.005 mm)

Main bearings:

Number	5
Diametrical clearance	0.002 — 0.0037 in (0.050 — 0.095 mm)
Undersizes	minus 0.010 in (0.254 mm); minus 0.020 in (0.508 mm); minus 0.030 in (0.762 mm); minus 0.040 in (1.016 mm)

Big end bearings:

Diametrical clearance	0.0010 — 0.0029 in (0.026 — 0.076 mm)

Pistons & gudgeon pins

Gudgeon pins:

	1438cc	1592 cc
Type	Clearance fit in piston	

Pin outer diameter:

	1438cc	1592 cc
Class 1**	0.8649 — 0.8651 in (21.970 — 21.974 mm)	0.8658 — 0.8659 in (21.991 — 21.994 mm)
Class 2**	0.8651 — 0.8653 in (21.974 — 21.978 mm)	0.8659 — 0.8660 in (21.994 — 21.997 mm)
Class 3**	0.8653 — 0.8654 in (21.978 — 21.982 mm)	

** Class indicated on pin end and on underside of piston boss

	1438cc	1592cc
Fit in piston	0.0004 — 0.0007 in (0.010 — 0.018 mm)	0.0001 — 0.0003 in (0.002 — 0.008 mm)
Pistons	Steel belted design	

Piston diameter (measured at same point as clearance with cylinder bore):

	1438 cc	1592cc
Class A***	3.1457 — 3.1461 in (79.9 — 79.91 mm)	3.1466 — 3.1470 in (79.925 — 79.935 mm)
Class C***	3.1465 — 3.1468 in (79.92 — 79.93 mm)	3.1474 — 3.1478 in (79.945 — 79.955 mm)
Class E***	3.1472 — 3.1476 in (79.94 — 79.95 mm)	3.1482 — 3.1486 in (79.965 — 79.975 mm)

*** Class indicated underneath piston skirt

	1438cc	1592cc
Oversize pistons	plus 0.0079 in (0.2 mm); plus 0.0157 in (0.4 mm); plus 0.0236 in (0.6 mm)	
Piston fit in bore measured at right angles to piston pin 2.057 in (52.25 mm) from piston crown	0.0035 — 0.0043 in (0.09 to 0.11 mm)	0.0025 — 0.0033 in (0.065 — 0.085 mm)

Piston rings (3 per piston):

Piston ring gap in bore		Piston ring/groove clearances	Width of grooves
Top No. 1	0.0118 — 0.0177 in (0.30 — 0.45 mm)	0.0018 — 0.0030 in (0.045 — 0.077 mm)	0.0604 — 0.0612 in (1.535 — 1.555 mm)
No. 2	0.078 — 0.0137 in (0.20 — 0.35 mm)	0.0011 — 0.0027 in (0.030 — 0.070 mm)	0.0798 — 0.0806 in (2.03 to 2.05 mm)
No. 3	0.078 — 0.0137 in (0.20 — 0.35 mm)	0.0011 — 0.0024 in (0.030 — 0.062 mm)	0.1561 — 0.1569 in (3.967 — 3.987 mm)

Piston ring thickness:

1st compression	... ...	0.0582 — 0.0587 in (1.478 — 1.490 mm)
2nd oil control	... ...	0.0780 — 0.0787 in (1.980 — 2.0 mm)
3rd oil control	... ...	0.1545 — 0.1550 in (3.925 — 3.937 mm)
Piston ring oversizes	... ...	as per pistons

Camshafts

		1438cc	1592cc
Journal diameters:			
Front	... ...	1.1789 — 1.1795 in (29.944 — 29.96 mm)	1.1788 — 1.1795 in (29.944 — 29.960 mm)
Centre	... ...	1.8006 — 1.8012 in (45.735 — 45.751 mm)	1.8013 — 1.802 in 45.755 — 45.771 mm)
Rear	... ...	1.8163 — 1.8169 in (46.135 — 46.151 mm)	1.8171 — 1.8178 in (46.155 — 46.171 mm)
Bearing inside diameter:			
Front	... ...	1.1815 — 1.1824 in (30.009 — 30.034 mm)	1.1814 — 1.1824 in (30.009 — 30.034 mm)
Centre	... ...	1.8031 — 1.8041 in (45.8 — 45.825 mm)	1.8031 — 1.8042 in (45.8 — 45.825 mm)
Rear	... ...	1.8189 — 1.8199 in (46.2 — 46.225 mm)	1.8189 — 1.8198 in (46.2 — 46.225 mm)
Endthrust	... ...	Taken on plate locating rear end of shaft	
Drive	... ...	Toothed belt and wheel	

Tappets

Type	... ...	Bucket with recessed top to accept tappet discs which can be changed to vary the tappet/camshaft gap
Tappet/camshaft clearance:		
inlet (cold)	... ...	0.018 in (0.45 mm)
exhaust (cold)	... ...	0.020 in (0.50 mm)
Tappet shims are supplied in the following thicknesses:	...	0.1299, 0.1339, 0.1378, 0.1417, 0.1457, 0.1496, 0.1535, 0.1575, 0.1614, 0.1654, 0.1693, 0.1732, 0.1772, 0.1811, 0.1850 in (3.30, 3.40, 3.50, 3.60, 3.70, 3.80, 3.90, 4.00, 4.10, 4.20, 4.30, 4.40, 4.50, 4.60, 4.70 mm)
Tappet bore in housing	... ...	1.4567 — 1.4576 in (37 — 37.025 mm)
Tappet bucket outside diameter	... ...	1.4557 — 1.4565 in (36.975 — 36.995 mm)

Valves

Seat angle (Inlet and Exhaust)	... ...	$45^{\circ} \pm 5'$	
Head diameter (approx.):			
Inlet	... ...	1.6299 in (41.4 mm)	
Exhaust	... ...	1.4173 in (36 mm)	
Valve stem diameter:			
Inlet	... ...	0.3140 — 0.3146 in (7.975 — 7.990 mm)	
Exhaust	... ...	0.3142 — 0.3148 in (7.980 — 7.995 mm)	
Stem to guide clearance:			
Inlet	... ...	0.0013 — 0.0026 in (0.032 — 0.065 mm)	
Exhaust	... ...	0.0011 — 0.0024 in (0.027 — 0.060 mm)	
		1438cc	**1592cc**
Valve lift	... ...	0.3268 in (8.3 mm)	0.3765 in (9.564 mm)

Valve guides

Valve guide seat bore in cylinder head	... ...	0.5886 — 0.5896 in (14.95 — 14.977 mm)
Outer diameter of valve guide	... ...	0.5905 — 0.5912 in (14.998 — 15.016 mm)
Oversize guide outside diameter	... ...	+ 0.0079 in (+ 0.2 mm)
Valve guide bore	... ...	0.3158 — 0.3165 in (8.022 — 8.040 mm)

Snap-ring on guide outer surface sets the height of the guide above the cylinder head

Valve springs

Number per valve	... ...	2
Free height:		
Inner	... ...	1.6457 in (41.8 mm)
Outer	... ...	2.1220 in (53.9 mm)
Spring stiffness under load:		
Inner	... ...	length 1.2205 in (31 mm) — load 32 lbs (14.9 kg)

| Outer | ... | ... | ... | ... | ... | ... | ... | length 1.4173 in (36 mm) — load 85.8 lbs (38.9 kg) |

Valve timing

								1438cc (and UK 1592cc)	1592cc (USA only)
Timing marks	...	...	...	...	...	...	...	Holes on camshaft wheels	
Timing angles:									
Inlet valve:									
Opens ...	...	...	...	...	...	...	...	26° before TDC	22° before TDC
Closes ...	...	...	...	...	...	...	...	66° after BDC	70° after BDC
Exhaust valve:									
Opens ...	...	...	...	...	...	...	...	66° before BDC	70° before BDC
Closes ...	...	...	...	...	...	...	...	26° after TDC	22° after TDC

Auxiliary driveshaft

Bush bores in crankcase:								
Front	...	...	...	...	...	...	...	2.0126 — 2.0138 in (51.12 — 51.15 mm)
Rear	...	...	...	...	...	...	...	1.6547 — 1.6559 in (42.03 — 42.06 mm)
Inside bore of bushes:								
Front	...	...	...	...	...	...	...	1.893 — 1.8938 in (48.084 — 48.104 mm)
Rear	...	...	...	...	...	...	...	1.5354 — 1.5362 in (39 — 39.02 mm)
Shaft journal diameter:								
Front	...	...	...	...	...	...	...	1.8903 — 1.8913 in (48.013 — 48.038 mm)
Rear	...	...	...	...	...	...	...	1.5326 — 1.5336 in (38.929 — 38.954 mm)
Journal/bore clearance	...	...	...	...	...	...	0.0018 — 0.0036 in (0.046 — 0.091 mm)

Lubrication system

Pressure-running	...	...	...	...	...	...	...	57 — 85 psi
Sump oil capacity (incl. filter)	...	...	...	...	...	6.5 Imp. pints; 4 US qts; 3.75 litres
By-pass valve spring:								
Length	...	...	...	...	...	...	...	0.886 in (22.5 mm)
Load (min.)	...	...	...	...	...	...	...	9.5 lb (4.3 kg)

Oil pump:

Clearance gears/pump cover	...	...	...	...	...	0.0012 — 0.0045 in (0.031 — 0.116 mm)
Clearance gears/pump housing wall	...	...	...	...	0.0043 — 0.0071 in (0.110– 0.180 mm)

Fuel system and carburettor (N. America ohv models only)
General data

Exhaust emission control carburettor type	...	...	...	Weber 32 DHSA
Idling speed:				
Manual gearbox ...	...	...	...	...	...	...	850 rev/min
Automatic transmission	...	...	...	...	...	750 rev/min (in 'D')
Fast idle speed	...	...	...	...	...	...	...	1600 rev/min
Exhaust emission CO level (at idling speed)	...	...	...	3% ± 0.5%
Fuel tank capacity:				
Saloon	...	...	...	...	...	...	...	10.3 gallons (46 litres)
Estate	...	...	...	...	...	...	...	12.5 gallons (57 litres)

Fuel system and carburettors (ohc models only)
General data

Carburettor type	...	...	...	...	...	...	...	Weber 32 DHS13; Holley 32 DHS13; Solex 32 EIES 32; Weber 32 DMSA
Idling speed (manual gearbox)	...	...	...	...	...	800 – 900 rpm
Idling speed (automatic gearbox)	...	...	...	...	700 – 750 rpm (in 'D')
Fast idle speed (manual gearbox)	...	...	...	...	1550 — 1650 rpm
Fast idle speed (automatic gearbox)	...	...	...	1250 — 1350 rpm (in 'N')
Exhaust emission CO level (at idling speed)	...	...	...	0.5% ± 0.3%
Fuel tank capacity:				
UK models	...	...	...	...	...	...	...	8.5 Imp. gallons (39 litres)
USA (saloon)	...	...	...	...	...	...	...	9.6 US gallons (36.5 litres)
USA (estate)	...	...	...	...	...	...	...	11.4 US gallons (43 litres)

Ignition system
Spark plugs

Spark plug types:				
All ohv and USA ohc models	...	...	...	...	Champion N9Y, AC42XLS, Marelli CW7LP
UK ohc models	...	...	...	...	...	...	Champion N7Y, Bosch W215T30, Marelli CW78LP
Electrode gap	...	...	...	...	...	...	...	0.020 — 0.024 in (0.5 — 0.6 mm)

Distributor

Distributor points gap:				
ohv models	...	...	...	...	...	...	0.017 — 0.019 in (0.44 — 0.48 mm)
UK ohc models ...	...	...	...	...	...	...	0.017 — 0.019 in (0.44 — 0.48 mm)
USA ohc models (with single contact set)	...	...	...	0.016 — 0.018 in (0.42 — 0.48 mm)

USA ohc models (with dual contact set):

Main contacts	Set by dwell as stated below
Additional contacts	0.012 — 0.014 in (0.31 — 0.49 mm)

Dwell angle:

All types (except USA dual contact set)	$60^{\circ} \pm 3^{\circ}$
USA ohc models (with dual contact set)	$55^{\circ} \pm 3^{\circ}$

Static (timing) advance:

USA (ohc and ohv models)	0° (TDC)
UK (ohv and ohc models)	10° BTDC

Electronic ignition system (available as option on certain models):

Type	Marelli AEC103A, capacitor discharge system

Cooling system (Special T and Special TC)
Fan
Electro-magnetic cooling fan (operating temperatures):

Cut-in	$92^{\circ} \pm 2^{\circ}$C ($198^{\circ} \pm 3.5^{\circ}$F)
Cut-out	$82^{\circ} \pm 2^{\circ}$C ($180^{\circ} \pm 3.5^{\circ}$F)

Automatic transmission
General data

Type	3 speeds and reverse, fluid drive with torque converter
Multiplication range	Between 2.4 : 1 and 1 : 1

Speed ratios:

1st	2.40 : 1
2nd	1.48 : 1
3rd	1 : 1
Reverse	1.92 : 1

Kick-down shift speed limits:

To 2	Below 57 mph (92 kph)
2 to 1	Below 31 mph (50 kph)

Automatic downshift speeds:

D to 2	Below 65 mph (105 kph)
2 to 1	Below 31 mph (50 kph)

Upshift speeds (Accelerator fully depressed):

1 to 2	42 mph (68 kph)
2 to D	65 mph (105 kph)
Fluid capacity	5 pints (2.84 litres) on refill*. 9 pints (5.11 litres) from dry state

Torque converter retains fluid on normal draining of automatic transmission

Electrical system
Voltage regulator (alternator)

Current for thermal stabilisation	7 amps
Second stage test current	2 to 12 amps
Second stage voltage setting	14.2 ± 0.3 V
First stage test current	25 to 35 amps
First stage voltage setting (differential from 2nd stage voltage setting)	Lower by 0.2 to 0.7 V
Resistance between terminal '15' (see Fig.) and earth at ambient temperature of 25°C $\pm 10^{C}$ (77°F $\pm 18^{\circ}$)..	28 ± 2 ohms
Resistance between terminals '15' and '67' with contacts open	5.65 ± 0.3 ohms
Armature air gap	0.059 in ± 0.002 in (1.5 ± 0.05 mm)
Second stage contact gap	0.018 in ± 0.004 in (0.45 ± 0.1 mm)

Cut-out (charge indicator relay)

Field winding resistance	29 ± 2 ohms
Desensitising resistor	220 ± 22 ohms
Contact opening voltage	5.3 ± 0.4V
Contact closing voltage	0.2 to 0.9V

Fuses
Later USA ohv models:

Fuse No.	Circuits Protected
1 (16 amps)	Driving mirror light, horns, cigar lighter
2 (8 amps)	Windscreen wiper and heater blower
3 (8 amps)	L.H. main headlight beam and warning light
4 (8 amps)	R.H. main headlight beam
5 (8 amps)	L.H. main headlight beam
6 (8 amps)	R.H. dipped headlight beam
7 (8 amps)	Front L.H. side light; rear R.H. side light; side light warning lamp; number plate (left hand bulb); cigar lighter lamp; instrument panel lamp; luggage boot lamp
8 (8 amps)	Front R.H. side light; rear L.H. side light; number plate (right hand bulb); reversing lights
9 (8 amps)	Oil pressure warning light; water temperature gauge; fuel gauge and

| | | | reserve indicator bulb; direction indicator and warning light; glovebox light; brake stop lights; brake circuit failure lamp; heated rear window switch and relay |
| 10 (8 amps) | ... ... | | Voltage regulator |

Separate 16 amp fuse for heated rear window and its indicator light

USA Special TC models

1 (16 amps)	... ...	Engine cooling fan; horns and horn relay
2 (8 amps)	... ...	Windscreen washer pump; windscreen wipers; heater fan motor
3 (8 amps)	... ...	Left-hand headlights — main beams; main beam indicator lamp
4 (8 amps)	... ...	Right-hand headlights — main beams
5 (8 amps)	... ...	Left-hand outer headlight — dipped beam
6 (8 amps)	... ...	Right-hand outer headlight — dipped beam
7 (8 amps)	... ...	Front left/rear right side marker lamps; front left parking lamp; parking and tail lights indicator; rear right tail light; number plate light bulb (left); luggage compartment illumination light; cigar lighter housing illumination; ideogram illumination optical fibres light source; hazard warning switch illumination
8 (8 amps)	... ...	Front right parking lamp; front right/rear left side marker lamps; rear left tail light; number plate light bulb (right); instrument cluster illumination
9 (8 amps)	... ...	Reversing lights; low oil pressure indicator; fasten seat belts indicator; starter/belt interlock control; ignition mode selection relay; remove ignition key and fasten seatbelts buzzer relay; coolant temperature gauge; fuel gauge and reserve indicator; glove compartment illumination light; turn signal and indicator; stoplights; heated rear window relay and switch (where applicable); brake system effectiveness and handbrake 'ON' indicator; electrovalve for EEC system
10 (8 amps)	... ...	Voltage regulator; alternator field winding

Separate in-line fuses:

16 amps	... ...	Cigar lighter; pillar-lamps; hazard warning system (except switch)
16 amps	... ...	Heated rear window and indicator (where applicable)
3 amps	... ...	Remove key and fasten seatbelts buzzer; starter interlock control unit

UK Special T models

1 (16 amps)	... ...	Courtesy light; horn; cigar lighter
2 (8 amps)	... ...	Windscreen wiper and heater blower
3 (8 amps)	... ...	Left-hand main beam and headlamp warning light
4 (8 amps)	... ...	Right-hand main beam
5 (8 amps)	... ...	Left-hand dipped beam
6 (8 amps)	... ...	Right-hand dipped beam
7 (8 amps)	... ...	Left-hand side light; side light warning lamp; right-hand rear light; left-hand number plate light; boot light; panel light; cigar lighter illumination
8 (8 amps)	... ...	Right-hand side light; left-hand rear light; right-hand number plate light; reversing light
9 (8 amps)	... ...	Oil pressure warning light; water temperature gauge; fuel gauge and warning light; glovebox illumination; direction indicator and warning light; stoplight
10 (8 amps)	... ...	Voltage regulator, alternator field winding
Separate in-line fuse (16 amps)	... ...	Heated rear screen and warning light (where applicable)

Suspension and steering
General data

Turning circle	... ...	35 ft 1 in. (10.7 m)
Tyres:		
Saloon	... ...	150 SR or 155 SR x 13 in radial
Estate	... ...	165 SR x 13 in radial

Bodywork and underframe
General data

	UK models	USA models
Saloon (typical):		
Overall length	13.3 ft (4.059 metres)	13.9 ft (4.236 metres)
Overall width	5.29 ft (1.611 metres)	5.39 ft (1.644 metres)
Overall height	4.66 ft (1.42 metres)	4.66 ft (1.420 metres)
Wheelbase (all models)	7.94 ft (2.42 metres)	
Kerb weight*	2040 lbs (925 kg)	2060 lbs (934 kg)
* Manual transmission models	*Add 70 lbs (31.78 kgs) for automatic transmission*	
Estate (typical):		
Overall length	13.27 ft (4.045 metres)	13.81 ft (4.21 metres)

Overall width	...	...	...	...	...	...	...	5.29 ft (1.611 metres)	5.39 ft (1.644 metres)
Overall height	...	...	...	...	...	...	...	4.72 ft (1.44 metres)	4.72 ft (1.44 metres)
Wheelbase	...	...	...	...	...	...	...	7.94 ft (2.42 metres)	7.94 ft (2.42 metres)
Kerb weight**	...	...	...	...	...	...	...	2050 lbs (930 kg)	3070 lbs (1393.7 kgs)

** *Manual transmission models*   *Add 70 lbs (31.78 kgs) for automatic transmission*

Torque wrench settings

								lb.f.ft	kg.f.m
Engine (DOHC models):									
Cylinder head bolts	...	...	...	...	...	...		61.5	8.5
Manifold nuts	...	...	...	...	...	...		18	2.5
Camshaft housing nuts	...	...	...	...	...	...		14.5	2
Camshaft timing wheel bolts	...	...	...	...	...			86.8	12
Idler/tensioner wheel retaining nut	...	...	...	...				32.5	4.5
Auxiliary shaft wheel	...	...	...	...	...	...		87	12
Crankshaft timing/pulley wheelnut	...	...	...	...				87	12
Connecting rod cap nuts	...	...	...	...	...			36	5
Main bearing cap bolt (small)	...	...	...	...	...			57.8	8
Main bearing cap bolt (large)	...	...	...	...	...			83	11.5
Flywheel to crankshaft bolts	...	...	...	...	...			61.5	8.5
Automatic transmission:									
Flexplate to torque converter	...	...	...	...	...			42	5.8
Flexplate to crankshaft	...	...	...	...	...			25	3.5
Converter housing to transmission case	...	...	...					25	3.5
Extension housing to transmission case	...	...	...					20	2.8
Oil pan (sump) bolts	...	...	...	...	...	...		7	1.0

3 Routine maintenance

In addition to the tasks listed on pages 6, 7 and 8 of the manual, the following should be added, where applicable:

3000 miles (5000 km)
1 Check the automatic transmission fluid level and top-up as necessary.

6000 miles (10 000 km)
2 Check condition and tension of air pump drivebelt, renew as and when found necessary (USA models only).
3 Renew in-line fuel filter (where applicable).

12 000 miles (20 000 km)
4 Dismantle and clean crankcase emission control system, renew faulty components.
5 Check fuel evaporative emission control system, renew any faulty components.
6 Check all lines, manifolds and valves of the exhaust emission control system, renew faulty components.
7 Check operation of air pump.

24 000 miles (40 000 km)
8 Renew activated carbon trap
9 Renew timing belt*
10 Drain automatic transmission fluid and renew

36 000 miles (60 000 km)
11 Renew timing belt (DOHC models)*

*FIAT recommend that the timing belt be renewed at 24 000 miles (40 000 km) intervals. 36 000 miles (60 000 kms) is the maximum permissible mileage limit.

4 Engine (DOHC type)

General description
The U.K. versions of the FIAT 124 Special T utilise the 1438cc double overhead-camshaft (DOHC) engines, whilst the USA FIAT 124 Special TC versions are only fitted with the 1592cc engine. The engines fitted to the models mentioned above were also fitted to the FIAT 124 Sport models.

The DOHC engines are similar to the OHV engines fitted to the smaller FIAT 124 models: the chief differences lying in the cylinder head and the drive to the camshafts. Where reference to a particular component cannot be found in this Chapter, it is reasonable to assume that it is covered by the previous Chapters (1—12).

Major operations — engine in place
The following major operations can be carried out with the engine in-situ:
 1 *Removal and refitting of cylinder head assembly.*
 2 *Removal and refitting of the sump.*
 3 *Removal and refitting of the timing belt.*
 4 *Removal and refitting of the big-end bearing shells.*
 5 *Removal and refitting of the camshafts.*
 6 *Removal and refitting of the water pump.*
 7 *Removal and refitting of the oil pump.*
 8 *Removal and refitting of the pistons and connecting rods.*

Major operations — engine removed
The following operations can only be carried out with the engine removed from the car:
 1 *Removal and refitting of the main bearings.*
 2 *Removal and refitting of the crankshaft.*
 3 *Removal and refitting of the auxiliary driveshaft.*
 4 *Removal and refitting of the flywheel.*

Methods of engine removal
The engine can be removed attached to the gearbox or disconnected from it. Both procedures are described in Chapter 1. The method described in Chapter 1 does not, however, include specific details covering models with emission control equipment or automatic transmission. Where any significant variations are found refer to this Chapter for the relevant disconnection or removal details. In respect of extra wiring connections the safest method, to ensure correct refitting at a later date, is to attach labels to each connector.

Engine dismantling — general
Refer to the procedures given in Chapter 1, Section 7, for details of preparing the engine for dismantling.

Engine dismantling — ancillary components
1 Details of the components to be removed are given in Chapter 1, Section 8.
2 In addition to the ancillaries detailed all components relating to the emission control equipment will have to be removed. De-

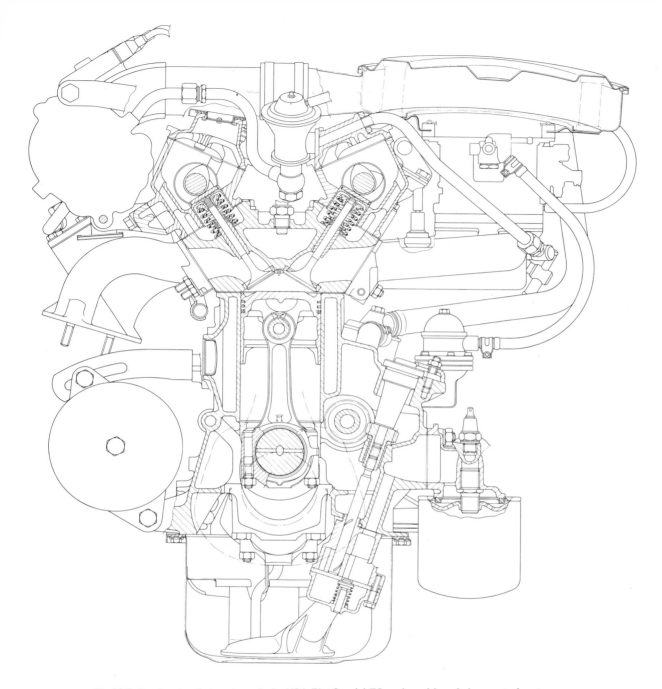

Fig.13.5. Sectional end view through the USA Fiat Special TC engine with emission control systems

tails of these components are given in this Chapter.

3 The timing belt and its associated gearwheels will have to be removed, the sequence is given in this Chapter.

4 Now remove the oil/vapour separator from the cylinder block below the inlet manifold. The separator is retained by a single bolt through its centre and rubber elbow hoses at its side.

5 The tensioner idler wheel and spring can be removed by undoing the nut and bolt securing it to the face of the cylinder block.

6 Remove the engine oil level dipstick and its tube. The dip-

stick tube is located by a bracket at the top and by a sleeve nut, screwed into the cylinder block, at its base.

Timing belt — removal, refitting and adjustment

   The timing belt will need to be renewed at 3 yearly or 36 000 mile (60 000 km) intervals, at the most, and will therefore be one of the more frequent major tasks undertaken. FIAT state that the timing belt cannot be reused and if at any time the tension on the belt is relieved it must be renewed.

8 Begin by draining the cooling system and removing the radia-

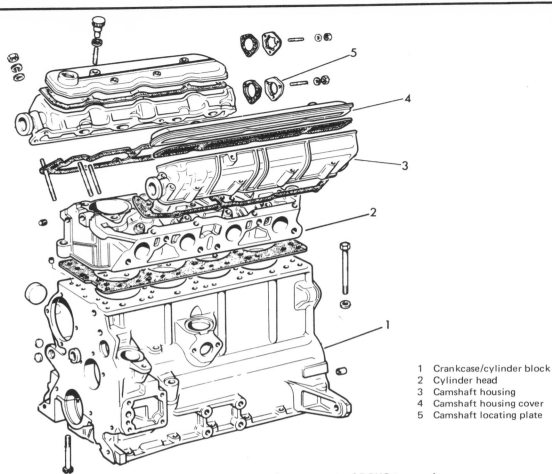

1 Crankcase/cylinder block
2 Cylinder head
3 Camshaft housing
4 Camshaft housing cover
5 Camshaft locating plate

Fig.13.6. Main static components of DOHC type engine

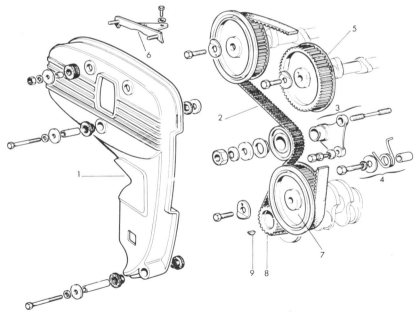

Fig.13.7. Timing belt components (DOHC engine)

1 Timing belt cover
2 Timing belt
3 Idler wheel bearing bracket

4 Idler wheel spring
  tensioner assembly
5 Camshaft timing wheel

6 Upper support bracket for
  timing cover-with pointers
7 Auxiliary shaft wheel

8 Crankshaft timing wheel
9 Woodruff locating key

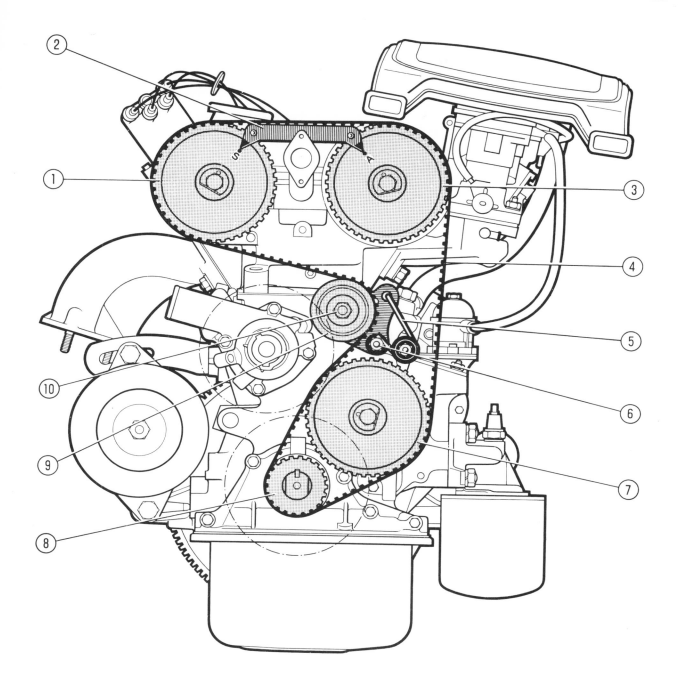

Fig.13.8. Typical layout of timing gear and auxiliary drive (DOHC engine)

1	Exhaust camshaft wheel	4	Toothed belt	7	Auxiliary drive wheel	9	Tensioner pulley
2	Timing pointers	5	Tensioning pulley assembly	8	Crankshaft wheel/sprocket	10	Tensioner nut
3	Inlet camshaft wheel	6	Idling clamping nut				

tor.

9   Now disconnect one end of the hose between the thermostat and water pump. Also remove the two bolts securing the water pipe elbow (photo) to the front of the cylinder head. The union elbow can now be removed complete with attached hoses and thermostat.

10   Remove the timing belt cover (photo). It is retained by three

bolts and a nut.

11   Remove the spark plugs and set the engine at TDC with No. 4 cylinder on the compression stroke. A check will show that the timing marks on the camshaft gearwheels are aligned with the pointers on the fixed timing bracket attached to the front of the cylinder head.

12   On USA models, with an air pump, proceed to slacken the

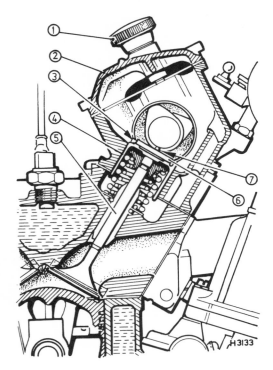

Fig.13.9. Cross-section of the inlet side of the cylinder head (DOHC engine)

1   Camshaft cover retaining bolt
2   Camshaft housing cover
3   Notch in tappet barrel for extracting tappet shim
4   Tappet barrel
5   Inlet valve
6   Tappet shim
7   Cam/tappet clearance gap

air pump mounting bolts and remove the air pump drivebelt.

13   Loosen the nut at the centre of the tensioner idler wheel and the bolt attached to the tensioner spring (photo).

14   Press the idler wheel back to release the belt tension and with the idler so held retighten the nut to hold it away.

15   Remove the timing belt and check that the timing marks are still aligned. The hole drilled into the auxiliary shaft wheel should be in approximate alignment with the bolt for the tensioner spring.

16   Fit the new timing belt taking care to ensure that the slack part of the belt is between the exhaust camshaft gearwheel and the idler wheel tensioner.

17   Loosen the nut on the tensioner to take up the slackness in the belt.

18   Rotate the engine crankshaft through two complete turns to bring the timing marks back into alignment. Should one of the camshaft gearwheels not be in alignment with the fixed pointer then it will be necessary to reset the timing after releasing the tension from the timing belt.

19   Assuming that the timing is set correctly tighten the nut on the idler wheel and the bolt on the tensioner spring.

20   Finally recheck that the timing marks on the camshaft gearwheels, auxiliary shaft pulley and crankshaft pulley are still properly aligned.

21   Reassembly is now a reversal of the dismantling procedure.

Cylinder head removal — engine in car

22   Drain the cooling system and remove the radiator having first disconnected the battery negative (earth) lead.

23   Slacken the generator mounting and adjuster bolts and remove the drivebelt.

24   Now remove the timing belt cover, as described in this Chapter, followed by removal of the timing belt.

25   Remove all HT ignition leads to the spark plugs and label them as necessary. Remove the electrical connections to the various sender units fitted into the cylinder head, and label them too.

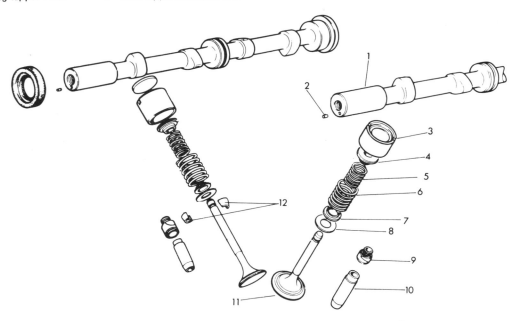

Fig.13.10. Valve operating mechanism components (DOHC engine)

1   Camshaft
2   Camshaft/wheel locating dowel
3   Tappet
4   Spring cover/cap
5   Inner spring
6   Outer spring
7   Inner spring seat
8   Outer spring seat
9   Oil seal
10   Valve guide
11   Valve
12   Collets

4.9 The water pipe elbow fitted to the front of the cylinder head

4.10 Removing the timing belt cover

4.13 The idler wheel tensioner assembly. The arrows indicate the bolt and nut which have to be loosened when releasing the belt tension

26 Remove the air cleaner assembly and disconnect the accelerator rod linkage.

27 On models with full emission control equipment, it may be found far simpler to remove the carburettor from the manifold and place it to one side complete with its attached hoses. However, make a careful note of the location of each of the hoses. On other models, it will be found satisfactory to simply disconnect the hoses and to leave the carburettor in-situ.

28 Release the exhaust manifold flange connection and separate the downpipe from the manifold.

29 Where applicable remove the vacuum servo hose from the inlet manifold connection.

30 On models with full emission control equipment disconnect the metal pipe, flexible hose and bracket from the EGR valve assembly.

31 Ancillaries such as the distributor (when driven from the exhaust camshaft), air pump (where applicable), exhaust and inlet manifolds can be removed before removing the cylinder head.

32 Remove the pipes, unions and brackets attached to the cam housing cover plates.

33 Now remove the ten bolts and washers holding the cylinder head in position. Slacken the bolts off evenly and in the reverse order to that used for tightening (See Fig. 13.12).

34 Before removing the cylinder head ensure that all attaching brackets, pipes and electrical wires are removed.

35 Finally, lift the cylinder head assembly off. If the head appears to be stuck to the cylinder block, under **no** circumstances attempt to free it by levering it off with a screwdriver or chisel. Tap the head firmly with a plastic or wooden-headed hammer.

36 The mild shocks from such a tool should break the bond between the cylinder head, gasket and cylinder block, allowing the head to be lifted clear.

37 Under **no** circumstances attempt to free the cylinder head by turning the engine over on the starter and using the cylinder compressions. Remember that the timing belt has been removed and piston/valve contact will most certainly occur if you should attempt this method!

Cylinder head removal — engine out of car

38 Follow the instructions given in paragraphs 22—37 of this Section, ignoring the parts which do not apply.

Cylinder head — dismantling

39 The cylinder head assembly is made of aluminium alloy and comprises three sub-assemblies, the head and the two overhead camshaft assemblies. The head comprises the combustion chambers, inlet and exhaust ports and the valve assemblies. The two camshaft assemblies comprise the camshafts, camshaft housings, tappets and housing covers.

40 Once the cylinder head has been removed from the engine, place it on a clean bench and commence removal of the inlet and exhaust manifolds, unless they have already been removed.

4.43 Detaching the water extension elbow and upper timing cover support bracket

41 The inlet manifold is retained by four bolts and two nuts and the exhaust manifold is retained by four nuts.

42 Once the manifolds have been removed, the camshaft housing covers are next removed with the aid of a large Allen key.

43 Now remove the bolts that retain the water extension elbow to the front of the cylinder head. Detach the elbow and the upper timing cover support bracket (photo).

44 The camshaft housings are each located on the cylinder head by ten studs and retained by nuts. The tappet barrels should remain in their bores when the camshaft housings are removed.

Valves — removal

45 Valve removal on the DOHC engine is identical to the valve removal sequence described in Chapter 1, Section 11.

Valve guides — inspection and renewal

46 Refer to Chapter 1, Section 12.

Camshafts, camshaft gearwheels and tappets — removal

47 Since the camshafts are withdrawn from the rear end of the housings, it will be necessary to remove the camshaft gearwheel at the forward end first. FIAT recommend that their special service tool be used to hold the camshaft gearwheel steady when removing the lock bolt. An alternative method is given in the following text.

48 The gearwheels are locked to their respective camshafts by a single bolt. Grasp the gearwheel gently in a vice which is fitted with soft covers on the jaws and undo the bolt.

49 Remove the bolt and washer which keeps the wheel/shaft alignment dowel peg in position. Ease the wheel off the shaft and take care not to lose the alignment dowel.

50 Next, at the rear of the housing, the camshaft retaining plate

is held by three nuts. Once removed the camshaft can be carefully withdrawn from the rear of the housing.

51 Be careful not to damage the camshaft bearing bores in the housing when removing the shaft. The housing is of aluminium alloy whereas the shaft is of hardened steel.

52 The tappets can be pushed out of their bores, and, as with the valves, it is wise to store them and their shims separately so that they may be refitted into their original locations.

Sump — removal

53 Refer to Chapter 1, Section 13, for details of removing the sump.

54 After removing the sump, assuming that the engine is being dismantled, remove the two bolts and washers retaining the oil tube. Now draw the tube out.

Oil pump — removal

55 Refer to Chapter 1, Section 19, for details of the oil pump removal.

Auxiliary shaft — removal

56 Remove the engine from the car (referring to Chapters 1 and 13).

57 Remove the timing belt (Chapter 13).

58 Remove the sump (Chapter 1).

59 Remove the distributor (only on models where the distributor is driven from the auxiliary shaft).

60 Remove the oil pump (Chapter 1).

61 Remove the auxiliary shaft gearwheel. The gearwheel can be prevented from rotating by wrapping the old timing belt around it while the securing bolt is undone.

62 Now remove the gearwheel taking care not to lose the locating dowel which should still be in place on the end of the auxiliary shaft.

63 Undo the four bolts securing the auxiliary shaft cover housing and remove it.

64 Now remove the clamp plate and remove the blanking cap (models with distributor driven from exhaust camshaft) followed by the oil pump drive gear. To facilitate easy removal of the gear, rotate the auxiliary shaft and draw the gear out through the casing using a pair of long-nosed pliers.

65 Now undo the two bolts holding the auxiliary shaft retainer plate in position.

66 With the 'U' shaped retainer plate now removed, the auxiliary shaft can be withdrawn from the cylinder block. Take great care when drawing the shaft out to prevent damage to the auxiliary shaft bearings fitted into the cylinder block.

Pistons, connecting rods and big-end bearings — removal

67 Refer to Chapter 1, Section 15, for details of the removal sequence.

Pistons — removal from connecting rods

68 Refer to Chapter 1, Section 16, for details.

Piston rings — removal

69 Refer to Chapter 1, Section 17, for details.

Flywheel — removal

70 Refer to Chapter 1, Section 18, for details.

Crankshaft and main bearings — removal

71 Refer to Chapter 1, Section 22, for details.

Crankshaft — examination and renovation

72 Refer to Chapter 1, Section 23, for details.

Big-end (connecting rod) bearings and main bearings — examination and renovation

73 Refer to Chapter 1, Section 24, for details.

Cylinder bores — examination and renovation

74 Refer to Chapter 1, Section 25, for details.

Pistons and rings — examination and renovation

75 Refer to Chapter 1, Section 26, for details.

Camshafts and camshaft bearings — examination and renovation

76 Carefully examine the camshaft bearings for wear. If the bearings are obviously worn or pitted or the metal underlay is just showing through, they must be renewed. This is an operation for your local FIAT agent or automobile engineering works, as it demands the use of specialised equipment. The bearings are removed using a special drift after which the new bearings are pressed in, care being taken that the oil holes in the bearings line up with those in the block. With another special tool the bearings are then reamed.

77 The camshafts themselves, should show no signs of wear, but if very slight scoring marks on the cams are noticed, the score marks can be removed by gentle rubbing with very fine emery cloth or an oil stone. The greatest care should be taken to keep the cam profiles smooth.

Timing wheels and belt — examination

78 The belt has a rubber surface and is reinforced for strength. As a consequence it is most unlikely that the wheels will need anything more than a clean in an oil/grease solvent and wiping dry.

79 The idler wheel which maintains the tension in the timing belt, runs on a pre-packed ball bearing race. Whenever the timing belt is being changed or attended to, it is advisable to check for excessive play of the wheel and bearing. The wheel bearing assembly should be renewed if discernible play is felt.

80 The belt however, does not wear but fatigues, and because failure of this belt would be catastrophic for the engine, it must be renewed at regular intervals even though superficially it may appear serviceable.

81 The timing belt must be renewed at intervals **NOT** exceeding 36 000 miles (60 000 kms) — FIAT, justifiably, recommend that it should be renewed every 25 000 miles (40 000 kms).

82 It is important to remember that when handling a new belt bending it too sharp an angle should be avoided or the fibres which reinforce the belt will be seriously weakened.

Tappets — examination and renovation

83 Examine the bearing surface of the tappets which lie on the camshaft. Any indentations in this surface or cracks indicate serious wear, and the tappets should be renewed. Thoroughly clean them out removing all traces of sludge. It is most unlikely that the sides of the tappets will be worn, but, if they are a very loose fit in their bores and can be readily rocked, they should be discarded. It is very unusual to find worn tappets and any wear present is likely to occur only after very high mileages or through engine abuse.

Connecting rods — examination and renovation

84 Refer to Chapter 1, Section 31, for details.

Flywheel starter ring gear — examination and renovation

85 Refer to Chapter 1, Section 32, for details.

Oil pump — dismantling, examination and renovation

86 Refer to Chapter 1, Section 33, for details.

Decarbonisation

87 Refer to Chapter 1, Section 34, for details.

Valves, valve seats and valve springs — examination and renovation

88 Refer to Chapter 1, Section 35, for details.

Cylinder head — examination

89 Refer to Chapter 1, Section 36, for details.

Engine reassembly — general

90 Refer to Chapter 1, Section 37, for details

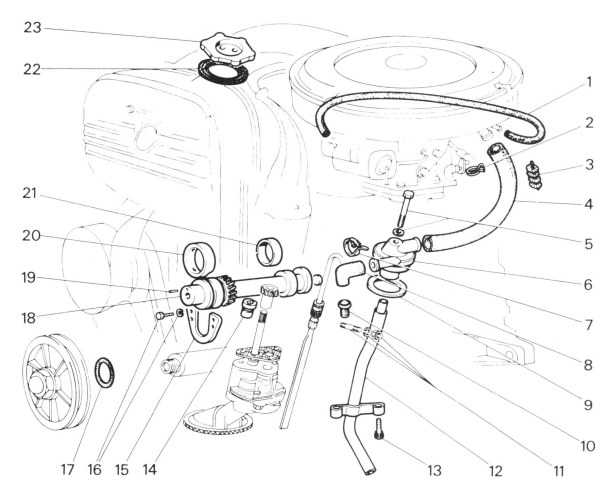

Fig.13.11. The auxiliary shaft, oil pump and oil vapour separator assemblies (DOHC engine)

1 Blow-by gas and oil vapour hose	7 Hose clip	12 Breather tube	18 Auxiliary shaft
2 Hose clip	8 Elbow hose	13 Bolt	19 Dowel peg
3 Flame trap	9 Gasket	14 Drive gear bush	20 Front bush
4 Breather pipe	10 Cylinder block connection pipe	15 Retainer plate	21 Rear bush
5 Retainer bolt and washer		16 Bolt and spring washer	22 Seal
6 Oil vapour separator body	11 Stud, spring washer and nut	17 Washer	23 Oil filler cap

Crankshaft — refitting
91 Refer to Chapter 1, Section 38, for details.

Pistons and connecting rods — reassembly
92 Refer to Chapter 1, Section 39, for details.

Piston rings — refitting
93 Refer to Chapter 1, Section 40, for details.

Pistons — refitting to cylinder
94 Refer to Chapter 1, Section 41, for details.

Connecting rod to crankshaft — reassembly
95 Refer to Chapter 1, Section 42, for details.

Crankshaft front and rear plates
96 When overhauling the engine it is always advisable to renew

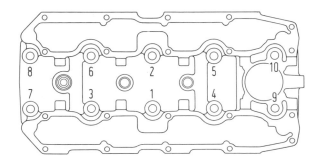

Fig.13.12. Cylinder head retaining bolts tightening sequence (DOHC engine)

4.107 Fitting the distributor drive housing blanking piece (DOHC models where the distributor takes its drive from the exhaust camshaft)

4.113 The oil vapour separator unit

4.126 Tightening down the camshaft housing nuts to the specified torque setting using a torque wrench

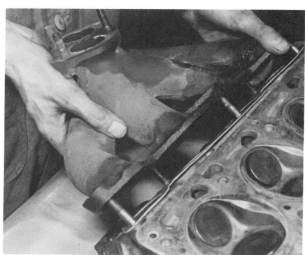

4.132 Installing the exhaust manifold

4.139 The tappet shim plate can be removed with the tappet barrel being held down with a bent screwdriver, and the cam pointing directly away from the tappet

4.147 Timing holes in camshaft wheels in correctly 'timed' position ready for the cylinder head to be refitted

the oil seals. The crankshaft has a front and rear oil seal fitted into a housing bolted to each cylinder block end.

97 The two seals are pressed into their respective housings and rest against centralising lugs at the rear.

98 With the housings removed from the cylinder block drive the seals out from their housings.

99 Correct fitting of the new oil seals is essential. The seals are marked with an arrow to denote the direction of rotation of the crankshaft. The seals should be fitted so that the arrow is visible from the outside of the seal and should be checked for correct crankshaft rotation in relation to the arrow.

100 When refitting the housing always use new paper gaskets taking care that the retaining bolts are tightened evenly. **Note:** It is also recommended that the crankshaft surface on which the lip of the seal will run is lubricated with engine oil prior to fitting the housings.

101 With the covers now in position, refit the crankshaft gearwheel followed by the crankshaft pulley fitted with a new rubber 'O' ring.

102 Tighten the crankshaft pulley retaining nut to the recommended torque setting.

Auxiliary shaft — refitting

103 Lubricate the auxiliary shaft cylinder block bushes and refit the auxiliary shaft.

104 Refit the 'U' shaped retainer plate securing it with two bolts and washers.

105 Fit a new oil seal to the auxiliary shaft cover plate and refit the cover plate along with a new gasket ensuring that the mating faces are clean.

106 Refit the auxiliary shaft gearwheel ensuring that the dowel peg locates with the hole drilled in the gearwheel. Refit the securing bolt and washer and tighten the bolt to the recommended torque setting. The gearwheel can be prevented from rotating while the bolt is being tightened by holding the gearwheel with the old timing belt.

Oil pump — refitting

107 Refer to Chapter 1, Section 46, for details. Note that the DOHC engine has the auxiliary shaft fitted where the OHV engine has its camshaft fitted. Remember, too, that not all the DOHC engine models have a distributor which is driven from the auxiliary shaft. Where this is not so, the distributor will be driven from the exhaust camshaft and the hole in the cylinder block will be covered by a blanking piece (photo).

Sump — refitting

108 Before refitting the sump as detailed in Chapter 1, Section 47, ensure that the oil tube, and front and rear crankshaft cover plates are in position.

Flywheel and clutch assembly — refitting

109 Refer to Chapter 1, Section 49, for details of the flywheel refitting procedure.

110 Refer to Chapter 5 for details of refitting the clutch assembly.

Water pump and oil separator — refitting

111 Refer to Chapter 2, for details of refitting the water pump.

112 Now fit the rubber elbow hose and breather pipe to the separator and clean the mating faces of the housing and cylinder block.

113 Fit a new gasket to the separator and position the assembled separator onto the cylinder block (photo).

114 Now refit the single bolt retaining the separator to the cylinder block.

115 Finally tighten the elbow hose and breather pipe clips.

Valves and valve springs — reassembly to cylinder head.

116 Refer to Chapter 1, Section 50, for details.

Camshafts, tappets and camshaft gearwheels — refitting

117 Wipe the camshaft bearing journals and liberally lubricate with engine oil.

118 Likewise wipe and lubricate the inside bearing bores of each camshaft housing.

119 Carefully slide the camshafts into their housings, taking care not to scratch the surfaces of the bearings with the cam lobes as they pass through.

120 Fit the camshaft endplates and tighten the securing bolts to the specified torque setting.

121 Refit the respective camshaft gearwheel onto the shaft projecting through the front of the housing. The wheel is located by a dowel pin and secured by a single bolt. A tab washer is fitted beneath the bolt and this serves not only to lock the bolt when it is tightened later, but also to retain the dowel pin in its bore.

122 Generously lubricate the tappets internally and externally and insert them into the bores from which they were removed.

Cylinder head — reassembly

123 The cylinder head comprises:

A Basic head casting with valves and springs fitted.
B The two camshaft assemblies.
C The camshaft housing covers.
D Water outlet.
E Spark plugs.
F Water temperature sender unit.
G Exhaust manifold.
H Inlet manifold, carburettor and various sender switches fitted into the inlet manifold (where applicable).

Before commencing reassembly, ensure that the correct gaskets have been obtained. Compare their shape with the old gaskets and joint faces to which they are to be fitted. When purchasing new gasket sets always quote the engine type and serial number.

124 Clean the mating faces of the cylinder head and camshaft housing.

125 Place the camshaft assembly onto the cylinder head, over the studs which locate it in position, having first fitted a new gasket.

126 Now fit the spring washers and nuts, progressively tightening them to the specified torque setting (photo).

127 Do not fit the camshaft housing covers until the tappet/cam clearance has been adjusted. This operation is described later in this Chapter.

128 The water elbow and cylinder head mating faces should be cleaned and the elbow refitted along with a new gasket.

129 Secure the elbow with nuts and spring washers and tighten to the specified torque setting.

130 Next, the spark plugs should be screwed into the cylinder head and tightened to the recommended torque setting.

131 The water temperature sender unit can also be refitted at this stage assuming that it was removed during the dismantling sequence.

132 The exhaust manifold can now be refitted using a new gasket (photo), having first checked that both the mating faces of the cylinder head and manifold are clean and free from the remains of the old gasket. The exhaust manifold gasket should be fitted without any jointing compound, and the retaining nuts tightened to the recommended torque setting.

133 The inlet manifold may, or may not, be fitted with the carburettor assembly, but in any event use new gaskets and ensure that all mating surfaces are free from fragments of the old gasket and are scrupulously clean. Air leaks in the inlet manifold will cause running problems and, at its worst, a seized engine! Again tighten the securing nuts to the recommended torque setting.

Tappet/camshaft clearance setting — engine in, or out of, car

134 Remove the camshaft housing covers.

135 Rotate the camshaft (by rotating the crankshaft — if this task is performed with the engine in the car) until the cam lobe which moves the tappet to be checked is perpendicular to the tappet face and the valve is closed.

136 Using a set of feeler gauges measure the existing tappet clearance and record the measurement so that the required thickness of the tappet shim can be calculated.

137 If the clearance gap is not between 0.017–0.019 in (0.43–

Fig.13.13. Checking the tappet/camshaft clearance

1 Cam lobe	3 Tappet barrel
2 Tappet shim plate	4 Feeler gauge set

0.48 mm) inlet valve and 0.019—0.021 in (0.48—0.53 mm) exhaust valve when the engine is cold proceed as follows.

138 Rotate the camshaft until the valve is fully open then insert FIAT tool A60318 or a bent screwdriver to hold the tappet barrel down.

139 Rotate the camshaft again so that the tappet shim may be extracted from the top of the tappet barrel with a thin small screwdriver inserted into the grooves in the side of the tappet barrel (photo).

140 Etched onto one face of the tappet shim is its thickness, alternatively measure the thickness with a micrometer. Add, or subtract, as appropriate, the difference between the measured gap (paragraph 135) and the desired gap (paragraph 136) from the thickness of the tappet shim to obtain the thickness which is required to produce the desired clearance.

141 The specification section lists the range of thicknesses of tappet shims available from FIAT dealers. There are 15 different thicknesses from 0.1299—0.1850 in (3.3—4.7 mm) in increments of 0.004 in (0.1 mm).

142 Insert the new tappet shim into the recess in the top of the tappet barrel with the side of the tappet shim marked with the thickness dimension facing the tappet barrel.

143 Turn the camshaft again so that the spacing tool or bent screwdriver (paragraph 138) can be extracted. Turn the camshaft once more to the position indicated in paragraph 135, and check that the desired tappet/cam clearance has been achieved.

144 Repeat this procedure for the remaining seven valves.

145 Finally refit the camshaft housing covers.

Cylinder head — refitting to cylinder block

146 It is essential to position the camshafts in the cylinder head and the crankshaft in the cylinder block in their correct relative (timed-up) positions (photo) before the cylinder head is lowered onto the cylinder block. Once the cylinder head has been fitted it is equally important that the camshafts are not rotated until they have been 'timed' and coupled to the crankshaft by the timing belt. There could be severe, possibly damaging, mechanical collision of valves and pistons if these precautions are not taken.

147 Turn the camshafts until the datum marks on their front faces

are in alignment with the fixed pointers bolted to the cylinder head (photo). The cylinder head is now ready for refitting to the cylinder block.

148 Turn the crankshaft until No.1 and No.4 pistons are at top-dead-centre (TDC). The pistons and crankshaft are now in the correct position to accept the cylinder head.

149 Place a new cylinder head gasket onto the cylinder block, having smeared it, sparingly, with a little grease first. The gasket is marked as to which way up it should be.

150 Lower the head carefully onto the cylinder block. Take care not to knock the open valves against the engine block face, they may possibly bend or chip.

151 Two temporary studs, one screwed into either end of the cylinder block will assist in locating the gasket and aid the task of lowering the cylinder head safely onto the cylinder block.

152 Once the head is in position the securing bolts may be screwed in finger-tight and then tightened evenly, as described in Chapter 1, in the sequence shown in Fig 13.12. When tightening the cylinder head down it is advisable to set the torque wrench to a much lower setting than that indicated in the Specifications Section of Chapter 13 and gradually increase the torque wrench setting until the specified torque is reached after several stages. Following this procedure will reduce the possibility of distorting the cylinder head.

153 The timing belt and tensioner should now be refitted, as described in paragraphs 154 and 155.

Timing belt, and tensioner — reassembly

154 Having checked the condition of the tensioner idler wheel bearing, and overhauled the tensioner as necessary, refit it loosely to the block face.

155 Now fit the new rubber timing belt, as described in paragraphs 7 to 21, of this Chapter.

Final assembly

156 Refit the water pump pulley.

157 Refit the air pump and drivebelt (where applicable).

158 Refit the generator and its drivebelt.

159 Refit the distributor.

160 Refit the oil filter adaptor housing along with a new oil filter. Finally, refit any other ancillary which may be fitted more easily with the engine removed. It is recommended that the carburettor is fitted after the engine has been fitted in the car, to prevent damage.

Engine — refitting and initial starting after overhaul or major repair

161 Whether, or not, the engine has been removed together with the gearbox it is easier to refit them as individual units.

162 Place a sling around the engine so that it stays horizontal when lifted and lower it carefully into the engine compartment.

163 It is important when connecting the engine to the gearbox that no strain is imposed on the gearbox primary (input) shaft when it is being engaged in the clutch assembly (for automatic transmission refer to a later Section of this Chapter for details).

164 It may be necessary to turn the engine a little to engage the primary shaft in the clutch assembly but if the clutch assembly has been aligned correctly (see Chapter 5) there should be little difficulty.

165 Refit the bellhousing to gearbox bolts and refit and tighten the engine mountings.

166 Now refit all the ancillaries, wiring connections, controls and hoses etc.

167 Before attempting to start the engine ensure that the battery is fully charged, and that all coolants, lubricants and fuel are replenished.

168 If the fuel system has been dismantled it will require several revolutions of the engine on the starter motor to pump the petrol up to the carburettor. The easiest method is to remove the spark plugs and spin the engine. This will ensure that oil will be pumped around the system before the initial start.

169 As soon as the engine fires, allow it to run at a fast idle only, and bring it up to the normal operating temperature.

170 As the engine warms-up there will be odd smells and some smoke from parts getting hot and burning off oil deposits. The signs to look for are water and oil leakage which will be obvious if serious. Check also the exhaust pipe and manifold connections, as they do not always 'find' their exact gastight positions until the warmth and vibration of the engine have acted upon them, and it is almost certain that they will need further tightening This should be done, of course with the engine stopped.

171 When the normal running temperature has been reached, adjust the engine idling speed as described in Chapter 3.

172 Stop the engine and wait a few minutes to see if any lubricant or coolant is dripping out when the engine is stationary.

173 Road test the car to check that the timing is correct and that the engine is giving the necessary smoothness and power. **Do not race the engine** — if new bearings and/or pistons have been fitted it should be treated as a new engine and run-in at a reduced speed for the first 500 miles (850 km).

Fault diagnosis — engine
174 Refer to Chapter 1, Section 58, for details.

---

5 Cooling System

Electro-magnetic clutch driven fan

1 This device is mounted on the water pump pulley hub and provides for the fan to be driven only when current is supplied via the thermal switch in the bottom of the radiator. It is not an electric motor, but an electrically generated magnetic field which links the pump pulley to the fan so that the fan is rotated by the pulley. When there is not any current flowing through the clutch windings in the pulley hub, no magnetic field is formed to couple the fan to the pulley. The fan will then merely feather around in the draught from the radiator.

2 The checks necessary on a suspect electro-magnetic clutch do not necessitate its removal from the engine.

    A *Examine the condition of the brush, which is on the pump, and contact ring on the water pump side of the pulley. Renew the brush if worn to a stub, and clean the contact ring with fine emery and a dry cloth.*

    B *There should be a gap of 0.010 in (0.25 mm) between the pulley hub and electric winding body and the response face of the fan hub. See paragraph 3, for adjustment procedure.*

    C *Finally, the electric windings of the clutch may be checked for a short or open circuit. Should zero or infinite resistance be measured across the contact ring and pump body the clutch unit should be renewed.*

3 The air gap between the clutch electrical winding body and the response plate on the fan hub is adjusted as follows:

    A *There are three square-headed adjusting bolts which are found on the front face of the fan hub. The bolts have locking nuts fitted.*

    B *Unscrew the locknuts and turn the adjusting bolts to move the response plate on the pump side of the fan hub so that the air gap is between 0.010 and 0.013 in (0.25—0.33 mm). Insert the feeler gauges opposite the bolts that have been adjusted.*

    C *Once the adjustment has been made the adjusting bolts are locked by tightening the locknuts.*

4 In the event that the clutch is found faulty it may be removed from the pump as follows:

5 Remove the radiator as described in Section 5 of this chapter and then proceed to undo the central nut on the pump shaft that retains the fan clutch assembly on that shaft. Lift aside the brush in contact with the clutch.

6 The fan hub and clutch assembly may then be pulled off the shaft. Do not lose the key which locates the fan on the shaft.

7 The refitting of the fan and clutch assembly is the reversal of the removal procedure.

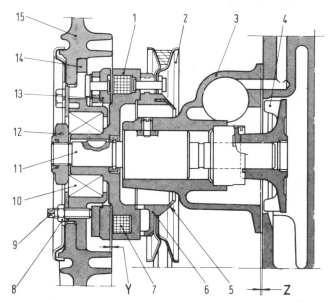

Fig.13.14. The section of the electro-magnetic fan drive system and water pump

1 Pump pulley hub and electro-magnetic coil	9 Fan drive ring position adjuster screws
2 Water pump drive pulley	10 Fan bearing
3 Pump body	11 Water pump shaft
4 Water pump impellor	12 Fan drive securing nut
5 Contact ring	13 Electro-magnetic armature
6 Contact ring hub	14 Fan hub
7 Electro-magnetic coil	15 Fan
8 Locknut	

Y = 0.010—0.014 in (0.25—0.35 mm); Z = 0.039 in (1 mm)

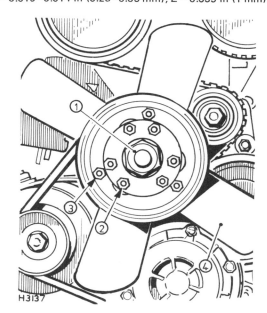

Fig.13.15. Front view of electro-magnetic fan drive

1 Fan hub assembly securing nut
2 Electro-magnetic drive gap adjusting screws
3 Screws fixing fan to hub
4 Fan

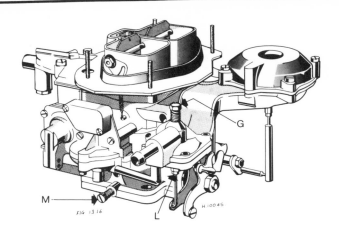

Fig.13.16. Weber 32 DHSA Carburettor

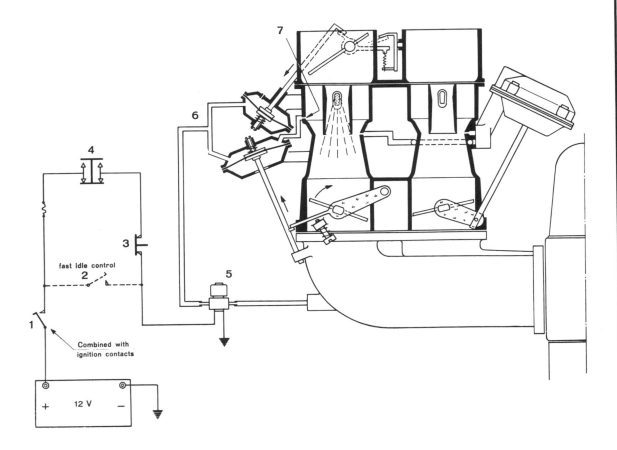

Fig.13.17. Diagram of the exhaust emission control system as fitted to later Fiat 124 OHV North American models

1 Switch in circuit with ignition contacts
2 Fast idle control switch
3 'Clutch engaged' switch
4 3rd and 4th gear engaged switch
5 Weber electrically-operated valve
6 Diaphragm capsules to maintain slight opening of main throttle and choke valves on deceleration (dependant on setting of switches '3' and '4')
7 Bypass orifice to neutralise vacuum action capsule diaphragms when valve '5' closes

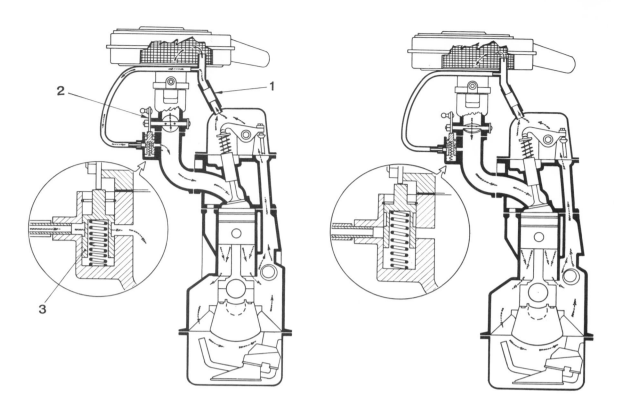

Fig.13.18. Crankcase emission control system (OHV model)

Left - throttle set wide open or beyond idling, gases routed through line '1' to air cleaner and partially through valve '3' (opened by cam lever '2') to inlet manifold.
Right - engine at idling speed, valve '3' closed and all gases directed through carburettor venturi

---

6 Carburation; fuel, exhaust and emission control systems

Weber 32 DHSA carburettor (North America OHV models) — slow-running adjustment

1   Refer to Fig.13.16. and note the location of the three adjustment screws.
2   Check that the ignition system is correctly adjusted; also the valve clearances.
3   Run the engine until it reaches normal operating temperature.
4   Adjust the idle metering screw (M) until the smoothest idle is obtained then adjust the slow-running screw (L) until the engine speed is between 850 and 950 rpm.
5   Actuate the fast idle by-pass switch (2) (Fig.13.17) and adjust the fast idle screw (G) (Fig.13.16) until the engine speed is 1600 rpm.
6   With the fast idle switch tripped and the choke inoperative and the engine having resumed its normal idling speed of 850 to 950 rpm, check the exhaust emission with an exhaust gas analyser strictly following the manufacturer's instructions. Re-adjust the carburettor screws fractionally if necessary to bring the exhaust emission level within that specified. (3% CO).

Emission control systems — general description

7   The emission control systems enable cars, manufactured for the North American market, to conform with all Federal Regulations governing the emission of hydro-carbons, carbon monoxide, nitric oxide and fuel vapours from the crankcase, exhaust and fuel systems.

Crankcase breather system

8   A brief description of this system is given in Chapter 3 for early models, but a slightly different system is fitted to the DOHC models.
9   Crankcase breathing and removal of 'blow-by' vapours is achieved by making use of the inherent partial vacuum in the carburettor. In this way, emissions are burnt in the combustion process. An oil/vapour separator unit is fitted into the crankcase and a connecting pipe joins the separator to the air filter and carburettor. A control valve fitted to the carburettor diverts some of the vapours directly into the carburettor at wide throttle openings the remainder being routed to the 'clean' side of the air cleaner. When the throttle is closed the vapours are drawn directly into the inlet manifold via the control valve. A flame-trap is fitted into the pipeline joining the carburettor to the separator unit.

Air injection and EGR system

10   This sytem is used to reduce the emissions of hydrocarbons, nitric oxide and carbon monoxide in the exhaust gases, and comprises an air pump, diverter valve, check valve and air manifold.
11   A rotary vane type pump is belt-driven from the engine and delivers air to each of the four exhaust ports, thus creating conditions favourable for re-combustion of the exhaust gases.
12   The diverter/relief valve ejects air from the pump to atmosphere during deceleration, being controlled in this operation by the inlet manifold vacuum. Excessive pressure is discharged to atmosphere by operation of the relief valve.
13   The check valve is a diaphragm — spring operated non-return valve. Its purpose is to protect the pump from exhaust gas press-

6.23 The activated carbon trap (typical example)

6.27 The air pump attached to the exhaust camshaft housing. Note the outlet pipe

6.35 The air distribution manifold showing the four manifold union nuts

6.41 The check valve (arrowed)

6.49 The EGR valve

ures both under normal conditions and in the event of a drive-belt failure.

14 The air manifold is used to direct the compressed air into the engine exhaust ports.

Fuel evaporative emission control system

15 This system prevents the release of fuel vapours from the fuel tank and carburettor into the atmosphere. The fuel tank and carburettor are vented through an activated carbon trap. This unit absorbs the vapours which are then drawn into the intake manifold and burnt in the combustion process. The system comprises the following units:

    A Sealed fuel tank filler cap.
    B Limited filling tank.
    C Tank outlet vapour/liquid separator unit.
    D Carburettor vent pipe line.
    E Activated carbon trap.
    F Three-way control valve.

16 The activated carbon trap is simply a canister filled with carbon and positioned in the engine compartment. There are three pipe connections, one from the fuel tank vent system, one from the inlet manifold, and one from the air filter. The fuel vapours 'soak' into the carbon, which is then purged of the vapour when the engine is running. The vacuum in the inlet manifold draws warm air from the air filter unit through the carbon taking the

vapour into the engine through the inlet manifold pipe. Between the petrol tank and the carbon canister is a three-way valve. The valve allows air into the vent system to compensate for consumption of fuel. The valve also allows vapours to pass along the vent line to the carbon canister and engine. The third mode of operation of the valve is to allow vapour to vent directly to atmosphere in the event of a blockage in the vent pipe to the canister.

Exhaust gas recirculation (EGR) system

17 To minimise nitric-oxide exhaust emissions, the peak combustion temperatures are lowered by circulating a metered quantity of exhaust gas through the inlet manifold.
18 A control signal is taken from the throttle edge tapping of the carburettor. At idle or full-load no recirculation is provided, but under part-load conditions a controlled amount of recirculation is provided according to the vacuum signal profile of the metering valve. The EGR valve is attached to the inlet camshaft cover.
19 An EGR thermovalve control unit is attached to the inlet manifold and cuts the vacuum signal when the choke is in operation.

Throttle positioner system (fast idling system)

20 The object of this system is to maintain a flow of air through the carburettor. This will allow the carburettor to meter the fuel efficiently and not give a slightly rich mixture as normally occurs in engine over-run and slow idling conditions.

Oil/vapour separator unit — removal, cleaning and refitting

21 The removal and refitting of this unit is detailed in Section 4, of this Chapter.
22 After removing the unit and cleaning it inspect the joining hoses for damage, and remember to clean the flame-trap fitted into the hose joining the separator to the air filter.

Activated carbon trap — removal and refitting

23 Disconnect the three pipes noting their exact positions (photo).
24 Undo and remove the two mounting bolts and lift the unit free.
25 Refitting the unit is the reverse of the removal operation.

Air pump — removal

26 Remove the timing belt cover.
27 Disconnect the hose from the rear of the air pump (photo).
28 Remove the air pump drivebelt.
29 Undo the nut holding the pump to the upper support bracket.
30 Undo the nut and bolt and remove the shield holding the pump to the cylinder head.
31 Lift the pump away.
32 It will be noted that the air pump drivebelt is not adjustable so if it is worn, or stretched, it must be replaced by a new belt.
33 Refitting the air pump is straightforward and follows the reverse of the removal sequence. Remember to fit the shield to the rear of the mounting lug.

Air distribution manifold — removal and refitting

34 Remove the air filter assembly.
35 Disconnect the hose to the check valve (photo).
36 Undo the nut and bolt securing the air manifold to the support bracket fitted to the cam housing cover.
37 Using a specially cranked spanner or FIAT tool A50146, undo the four manifold union nuts.
38 The manifold, complete with check valve, can now be removed.
39 If necessary, hold the manifold in a vice, and unscrew the check valve.
40 Refitting is the reverse of the removal procedure.

Check valve — removal, testing and refitting

41 Disconnect the air hose at the check valve (photo).

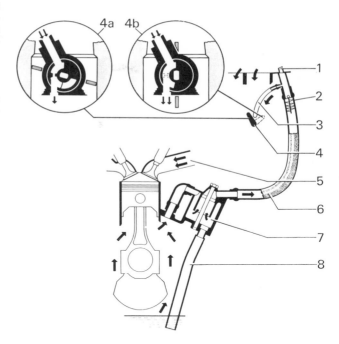

Fig.13.19. Crankcase emission control system (fitted to all DOHC models)

1	Emission feed to air cleaner		above idling
2	Flame trap	5	Inlet manifold
3	Air cleaner to control valve line	6	Oil separator to air cleaner line
4a	Control valve - engine idling	7	Liquid/vapour separator unit
4b	Control valve - engine speed	8	Oil drain pipe back to sump

42 Using an open spanner, unscrew the check valve but take care not to put undue strain on the manifold.
43 If necessary, the valve can be checked by blowing air (by mouth only) through the valve. Air should pass through from the hose connection end, but not from the manifold end. Renew the valve if defective.
44 Refitting is the reverse of the removal procedure.

Diverter and relief valve — removal and refitting

45 The diverter valve and its activating electro-valve are fixed to a bracket attached to the right-hand upper strut mounting.
46 Release the hose connections and remove the nuts and bolts retaining it to the bracket.
47 The diverter valve electro-valve is fixed to the bracket by two bolts, and is removed once the two electrical connections and hoses have been released.
48 Refitting is a reversal of the removal procedure.

Exhaust gas recirculation (EGR) valve — removal and refitting

49 Loosen the clip and remove the hose from the EGR valve (photo).
50 Undo the metal pipe union to the EGR valve.
51 Remove the nut, bolt and washer holding the EGR valve pipe bracket to the exhaust camshaft housing.
52 Remove the two bolts and spring washers retaining the EGR valve to the camshaft cover.
53 Remove the EGR valve and gasket.
54 Refitting is the reverse of the removal procedure.

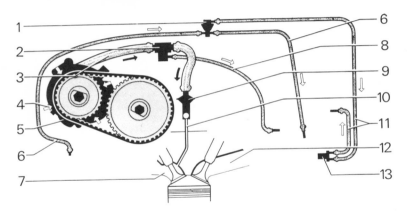

1	Exhaust gas recirculation (EGR) control valve
2	Diverter valve
3	Air hose connecting air pump to diverter valve
4	Air intake
5	Air pump
6	Exhaust gas recirculation line
7	Exhaust port in cylinder head leading to exhaust manifold
8	Vacuum line tapping in inlet manifold for diverter valve
9	Non-return valve
10	Air injector
11	Vacuum tapping line in carburettor for EGR valve
12	Inlet manifold
13	EGR control valve thermo-valve

Fig.13.20. Air injection and EGR system (North American DOHC model shown)

Fault diagnosis — emission control systems

Symptom	Reason/s
Low CO content of exhaust gases (weak or lean mixture)	Fuel level incorrect in carburettor Incorrectly adjusted carburettor
High CO content of exhaust gases (rich mixture)	Incorrectly adjusted carburettor Choke control mechanism sticking Activated carbon trap blocked Fuel level incorrect in carburettor Air injection system fault
Noisy air injection pump	Belt worn or stretched Faulty relief valve Faulty diverter valve Faulty check valve

7 Ignition System

Electronic ignition

1 As stated in the Specifications this system was offered as an optional extra on certain models and functions as described below.

2 The electronic ignition system comprises a transistorized switching circuit and a special ignition coil. The purpose of the switching circuit is to use a small current flowing through the contact breaker mechanism to trigger a larger current flowing through the primary windings of the coil. The interruption of the larger current in the primary winding will induce a greater voltage in the secondary, and hence the sparks will be more powerful. A transistor switching system is necessary because if the contact breaker mechanism were required to interrupt larger currents the wear and erosion would increase to impractical levels. The larger primary winding current is not only desired because of the more powerful sparks produced, but also because the larger current will offset the effect of the coils impedance which tends to reduce the energy of sparks at high engine speeds.

Dual contact distributor

3 The dual contact distributor is fitted to certain USA models and consists of main and additional contact sets.

4 The additional contact set produces an ignition setting 10° advanced for cold starting purposes, but as the engine reaches a predetermined temperature, after the warm-up period, the main contacts are brought into operation which provide an ignition setting of 0° or TDC.

5 This system is controlled by a vacuum temperature control valve which, when the engine is cold, closes and thus cuts off the vacuum to the distributor vacuum capsule. During this condition the timing is advanced 10°.

6 As the engine warms-up so the vacuum temperature control valve opens, thus allowing vacuum to act upon the delay valve. The delay valve slows down the flow of vacuum acting on the distributor vacuum capsule.

7 When eventually the full effect of the vacuum is allowed to react on the distributor vacuum capsule the timing will be retarded 10°.

8 FIAT do not give a contact breaker gap setting for the main contact set and therefore it is recommended that a dwell angle meter is used. The specification given is a dwell angle reading.

9 Procedure for inspection, removal and installation of both contact sets is identical to the information for the conventional set as covered in Chapter 4. Note that in some instances the distributor cap may be retained by screws and not spring clips, as indicated in Chapter 4.

8 Gearbox (manual type) — later USA ohv models, Special T & TC

Gearbox ratios

1 Later USA ohv models and all FIAT 124 Special T and Special TC models have gearboxes with the following ratios:

First	*3.79 : 1*
Second	*2.17 : 1*
Third	*1.41 : 1*
Fourth	*1 : 1*
Reverse	*3.65 : 1*

Final drive ratios

Saloon	*4.1 : 1*
Estate	*4.3 : 1*

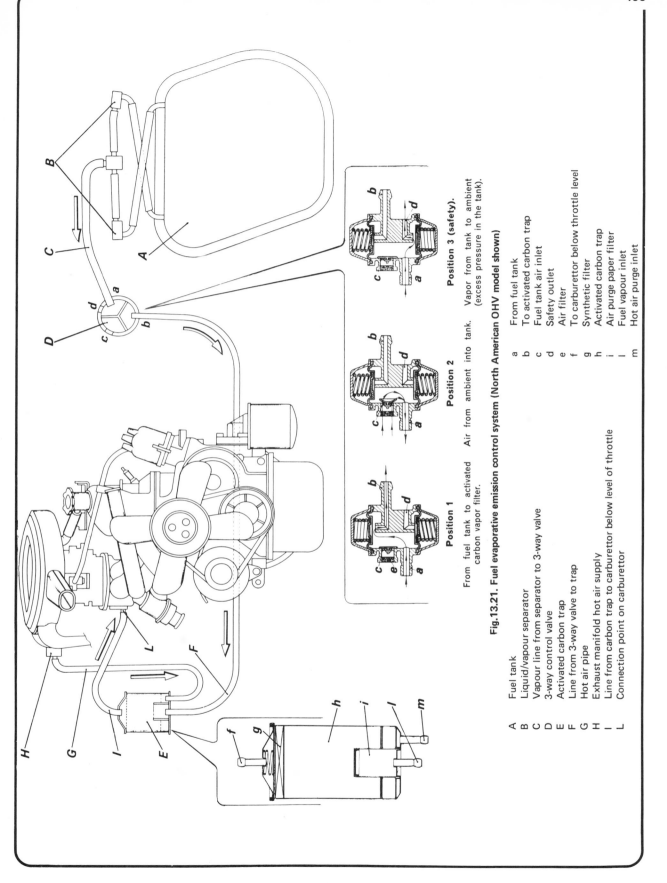

Position 1

From fuel tank to activated carbon vapor filter.

Position 2

Air from ambient into tank.

Position 3 (safety).

Vapor from tank to ambient (excess pressure in the tank).

Fig.13.21. Fuel evaporative emission control system (North American OHV model shown)

A Fuel tank
B Liquid/vapour separator
C Vapour line from separator to 3-way valve
D 3-way control valve
E Activated carbon trap
F Line from 3-way valve to trap
G Hot air pipe
H Exhaust manifold hot air supply
I Line from carbon trap to carburettor below level of throttle
L Connection point on carburettor

a From fuel tank
b To activated carbon trap
c Fuel tank air inlet
d Safety outlet
e Air filter
f To carburettor below throttle level
g Synthetic filter
h Activated carbon trap
i Air purge paper filter
l Fuel vapour inlet
m Hot air purge inlet

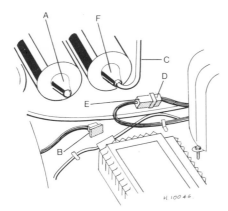

Fig.13.22. Electronic ignition

A   Coil socket (Auxiliary ignition circuit only)
B   Connector (Auxiliary ignition circuit only)
C   HT lead (Common) fitted to electronic ignition circuit
       coil
D   Connector (Common)
E   Connector (Electronic ignition circuit only)
F   Coil socket (Electronic ignition circuit only)

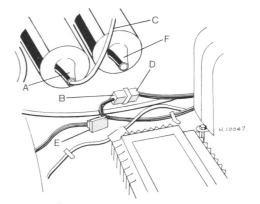

Fig.13.23. Auxiliary ignition circuit

A   Coil socket (Auxiliary ignition circuit only)
B   Connector (Auxiliary ignition circuit only)
C   HT lead (Common) fitted to auxiliary ignition circuit
       coil
D   Connector (Common)
E   Connector (Electronic ignition circuit only)
F   Coil socket (Electronic ignition circuit only)

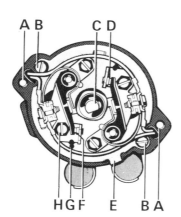

**Fig.13.24. The internal layout of the two contact distributor
fitted to later North American DOHC models**

A   Tapped holes for cap retaining screws
B   Baseplate retaining screws
C   Rotor shaft
D   Main contact breaker points
E   Cap locating slot
F   Starting contact breaker points
G   Slotted hole for inserting screwdriver when adjusting
       points gap
H   Fixed contact plate adjuster securing screw

**Fig.13.25. Typical engine timing marks (OHV model shown -
DOHC model identical)**

1   Crankshaft pulley moving datum mark
2   10° BTDC
3   5° BTDC
4   0° (TDC)

9   Automatic Transmission

General description

1   Three speed automatic transmission of General Motors design,
is now available as an option on both saloon and estate wagon
versions. The transmission unit provides an infinitely variable ratio between 2.4:1 and 1:1. It provides three forward speeds and
reverse.

2   Due to the complexity of the automatic transmission unit, if
performance is not up to standard, or overhaul is necessary, it is
recommended that this is left to a main FIAT agent having the
special equipment to carry out the work.

Transmission fluid — topping-up and renewal

3   Every 3000 miles (5000 km) check the level of the transmission fluid on the dipstick. This must be carried out after a run of
at least 6 miles (8 to 10 km) in order that the fluid will be at

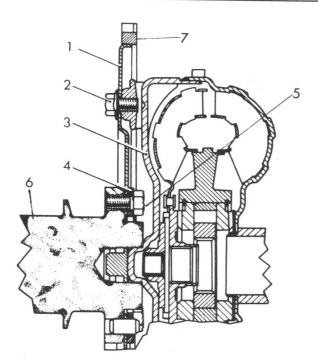

Fig.13.26. Cross-sectional view of the torque converter and flex-plate

1 Flexplate
2 Flexplate to torque converter bolt
3 Torque converter
4 Distance plate
5 Flexplate to crankshaft bolt
6 Crankshaft
7 Starter ring gear on flexplate

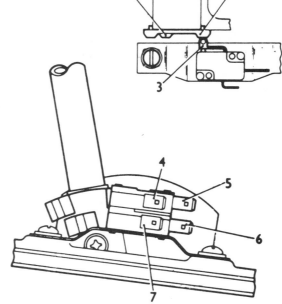

Fig.13.27. Automatic transmission speed selector lever, starter inhibitor and reversing lamp switch detail (typical)

1 Neutral cam
2 Park cam
3 Upper switch roller
4 Starter inhibitor connector (red wire)
5 Starter inhibitor connector
6 Reversing lamp connector (blue/white wire)
7 Reversing lamp connector (white wire)

    (grey/red wire)

Adjust switch so that the cams ('1' and '2') actuate switch lever when moved to neutral and park positions. Refer to appropriate wiring diagram

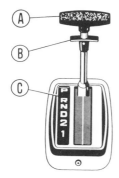

Fig.13.28. The floor-mounted automatic transmission selector lever

A Selector lever B Trigger C Illuminated index

Fig.13.29. Location of the automatic transmission dipstick and filler tube (DOHC model shown but OHV model is identical)

operating temperature.

4 With the engine idling, move the speed selector lever to 'N' or 'P' and then withdraw the dipstick. Wipe it clean, insert it into the filler tube, withdraw it again and check that the level is between the 'Min' and 'Max' marks otherwise top-up using only the recommended fluid.

5 Every 24 000 miles (40 000 km) drain the fluid while it is hot and refill with the correct quantity of specified fluid. If the old fluid is badly discoloured renew the filter and its seal which are located in the transmission valve assembly.

Automatic transmission — operating principles

The automatic transmission replaces the conventional clutch and gearbox, and occupies the same space in the same way being bolted onto the rear of the engine. It comprises two basic parts - the torque converter and the three speed epicyclic gearbox.

The torque converter is a form of oil operated turbine which transmits the engine power from a multi-bladed rotor (the pump) directly connected to the crankshaft to another multi-bladed rotor (the turbine) directly connected to the input shaft of the transmission. At low engine revolutions, the oil driven by the pump has little force imparted to it, so the turbine does not move. When the pump speed increases, so the force of the oil is transferred to the turbine.

An intermediate multi-bladed rotor (the stator) regulates the flow of oil back to the pump after it has done its work through the turbine.

The gearbox consists of a Ravignaux planetary gear set in constant mesh and the selection of the gears is by braking one or more of the components of this gear set.

This braking is effected by one of the three servo operated multi-plate clutches and a band, literally a brake band, which can be applied to the outer ring gear of the set. The automatic operation of three clutches and the low speed band is the complicated part, involving a servo hydraulic pump system controlled by road speed, inlet manifold vacuum and the position of the accelerator.

The capabilities of the automatic transmission are different from the manual system and in order that those unfamiliar with them may understand the difference, a full description of the function at starting, parking and stopping, in all of the five or six selector positions is given below.

'P' Park. In this position with the engine either stopped or running, no gears are 'engaged' and the gearbox output shaft is mechanically locked which in effect means that the propeller shaft and rear axle are also locked. The car cannot be moved, therefore. The engine may be started in this position, the selector lever trigger must be fully depressed. Do not select 'P' if the car is moving. Damage will result.

'N' Neutral. The conditions for neutral are the same as for 'P' except that the gearbox output shaft is not mechanically locked. The car will, therefore, roll with the engine either running or stopped.

'R' Reverse. The trigger on the selector lever must be depressed to engage 'R'. In this position reverse gear is 'engaged'. If the engine is not running, it cannot be started unless the selector lever is moved to 'P' or 'N'. With the brakes applied the car will not move. With the brakes off, increase in engine speed will move the car backwards. When the engine speed is decreased, the engine will act as a brake through the transmission. If the car is standing with the brake off, it may roll at low engine speed in either direction. Reverse should not normally be selected whilst the car is moving.

'D' Drive. The selector position for normal driving requirements. In this position first gear is initially 'engaged' but, at low engine speed with the brakes off, the car may roll in either direction. The engine cannot be started in this position. With the engine speed increased, the car will move forward in low gear.

When the speed and load conditions are right, the transmission will automatically move to second gear 'engagement' and then subsequently to top gear. When speed decreases, the gears will automatically shift back down as far as first, again according to speed and load situation.

'2' Second. To select this position the lever trigger need not be depressed. When selected, the automatic transmission will operate as in 'D' except that it will not move up out of 2nd. It should not be used in excess of 60 mph.

It is possible to change to '2' when the vehicle is moving. It will immediately put the vehicle in 2nd gear until speed or throttle position may cause it to change down to first. The in-

termediate range is normally used in traffic or on uphill sections where one would tend to get a lot of changing going on between 2nd and top if in the 'D' position. Move from '2' to 'D' without depressing the lever trigger.

'1' First. To select this position, the selector lever trigger is fully depressed. This position should not be selected above 35 mph. It would normally be used to provide engine braking on steep downhill sections of road, or to avoid unnecessary changing between 1st and 2nd in dense traffic or on continuous slow uphill climbs.

Some points to bear in mind in the operation of automatic transmission are:

A. It is possible to obtain a quick change down to provide acceleration by depressing the accelerator fully. This change will not take place, however, if the vehicle is already in excess of the maximum speed of the gear below.

B. Where continuous engine braking on overrun is wanted '1' or '2' ranges must be selected. It follows, therefore, that when shifting into these ranges when on the move, engine braking will take place if the car speed is high. On slippery surfaces the possibility of skids occurring must, therefore, be considered due to the sudden braking effect on the rear wheels.

C. It is not possible to push start the car.

D. If the car is to be towed for any reason, the speed must be kept below 30 mph (48 km/h) and the selector be put in 'N'. Not more than 30 miles (48 km) should be covered. If there is a suspected fault in the transmission, the car should not be towed at all unless the propeller shaft is disconnected or the driving wheels raised to prevent the transmission being ruined.

E. Engine tuning and smooth running is much more significant where automatic transmission is fitted.

F. Transmission fluid normally heats up in use. Severe or abusive use, or failure to keep cooling areas clean, can cause overheating and damage.

Automatic transmission — adjustments and tests

6 Internal adjustments of the unit are not recommended. External adjustments comprise the following: (i) the speed selector mechanism, (ii) the downshift cable, (iii) the starter inhibitor/reversing lamp switch.

7 Adjustment of the speed selector mechanism should be maintained so that with the floor mounted selector lever tested in all positions, the selector arm on the transmission unit will be in the corresponding detent without tension in either direction. The simplest way to carry out the test is to disconnect the linkage at the transmission unit selector arm. Place the selector lever in 'P' and the selector arm in the corresponding position. Now offer up the linkage when the connecting cotter pin should be a sliding fit. If this is not so, adjust the length of the link rod. Repeat the procedure in all other speed selector positions.

8 The downshift cable is actuated when the accelerator pedal is fully depressed. Adjustment is maintained simply by ensuring that with the pedal in the fully released position, the downshift cable is not under tension and neither has it any slackness. Adjust the cable stop as necessary. Remember that idling speed adjustment affects the adjustment of the downshift cable and this should be correctly set as specified (750 rpm in 'D').

9 A cross section of the selector lever mechanism and starter inhibitor switch is given so that adjustment can be made to ensure that the operation of the selector lever button and the safety start cut out are correct. It should not be possible to start the engine when the selector lever is in the 'D', '2', '1', or 'R' positions. Similarly it should only be possible to select '1' or 'P' when the selector trigger is fully depressed, and '2' and 'R' when it is partially depressed.

Details are given in the next Section on how to remove the transmission unit but, it must be emphasised that full testing can only be carried out when it is installed. Thus removal and replacement should only be carried out when it is known that the unit is beyond repair in its installed position and when all faults have been identified.

10 The test which the owner may carry out, if he suspects that there is either slip or otherwise, is the stall test. However, it will be necessary for a tachometer to be fitted to the engine. With the transmission fully warmed-up, apply the brakes fully (chock the wheels too for safety), engage a drive range and press the accelerator to the floor. The engine speed should settle at 2100-2150 rpm. Do not maintain the test for more than 10 seconds or overheating will result. If the engine rpm are too high then the torque converter oil supply should be suspect, and then the low band servo in the transmission itself. If the rpm are too low then the engine is not delivering full power or the torque converter unit is faulty.

11 The lower part of the torque converter housing is fitted with a perforated metal cover to permit cooling air into the housing. It is important to keep this clean as any restriction could result in overheating and loss of efficiency and damage.

Automatic transmission — removal and installation

12 Before making any attempt to remove the transmission, make sure your reasons are valid. In other words, get expert diagnosis first if transmission malfunctioning is the reason.

13 If you are removing the engine from a car with automatic transmission, the two should be separated at the flexplate which connects the crankshaft to the torque converter. Do not try and separate the torque converter from the gearbox.

14 All the normal precautions for gearbox removal, as described in Chapter 6, Section 2, should be taken. It must be remembered that they are heavier than conventional gearboxes — approximately 110 lbs (50 kg) and therefore, adequate support must be provided.

15 Drain the transmission fluid and retain it for future use if required.

16 Disconnect the speedometer drive cable.

17 Disconnect the speed selector linkage at the transmission unit end.

18 Remove the dipstick and oil filler tube.

19 Disconnect the exhaust pipe from the gearbox bracket.

20 Remove the starter motor heat shield and then unscrew the three starter motor securing bolts. Pull the starter motor as far forward as possible to clear the starter drive from the transmission flexplate ring gear.

21 Disconnect the propeller shaft and swing it to one side, as described in Chapter 7, Section 2.

22 Remove the semi-circular plate which covers the lower half of the torque converter housing.

23 Unscrew and remove the three bolts (now exposed) which secure the flexplate to the torque converter. It will be necessary to rotate the engine to enable each of these bolts to be reached. These three bolts must be removed before the main housing bolts securing the transmission to the engine are undone, otherwise, a strain could be put on the flexplate which would distort.

24 Once the flexplate bolts are removed, the casing bolts can come out with the whole unit properly supported, the transmission is then drawn a little to the rear and lowered in the normal way.

25 If the flexplate is to be renewed, it may be unbolted from the crankshaft flange. Seal the bolts on replacement as for the flywheel.

26 When replacing the transmission, proceed in the reverse order of removal. Line up the painted balance marks on torque converter and flexplate.

27 Refill the transmission unit with the correct type and quantity of fluid.

---

10 Braking system — dual hydraulic circuit

General description

1 The saloon and estate wagon versions are now fitted with a dual hydraulic circuit including vacuum servo assistance. The remote type fluid reservoir is partly divided and the fluid level should be maintained at a level above the separator. Overhaul of

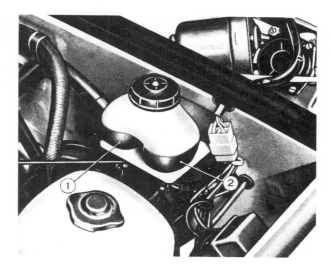

Fig.13.30. The brake fluid reservoir for tandem type master cylinder

1 Fluid for rear brake circuit
2 Fluid for front brake circuit

the main braking system components is already described in Chapter 9.

Brake warning light switch

2 Vehicles exported to North America incorporate a warning light switch located within the engine compartment. This is essentially a piston type valve interposed between the front and rear hydraulic circuits. The piston is normally held in balance by the equal pressures of the two circuits but in the event of a leak in either one of the two circuits the piston is displaced and makes contact to close an electrical circuit and illuminate the facia mounted warning lamp.

3 The brake warning lamp will almost certainly illuminate during bleeding of the hydraulic system but this should be ignored. When bleeding is complete however, if the lamp still remains on then it is an indication of a pressure differential between the two circuits and is probably due to air still trapped on one circuit.

Vacuum servo unit

4 The tandem type master cylinder is bolted directly to the front face of the servo unit.

5 The changed specification for piston rod protusion should be noted in comparison with Fig.13.31.

---

11 Electrical system

Battery

1 A 60 amp-hour battery is now fitted to all USA and automatic transmission models.

Alternator

2 The FIAT 12 M/124/12/42M alternator is now fitted to all models as standard equipment. A voltage regulator and cut-out unit are mounted separately from the alternator within the engine compartment.

Alternator — fault tracing and rectification

3 With the engine set to the specified idling speed, the charge indicator lamp (ignition warning lamp) should just be illuminated. Rev the engine and check that the lamp goes out. If it stays on, or comes on intermittently, check the following items.

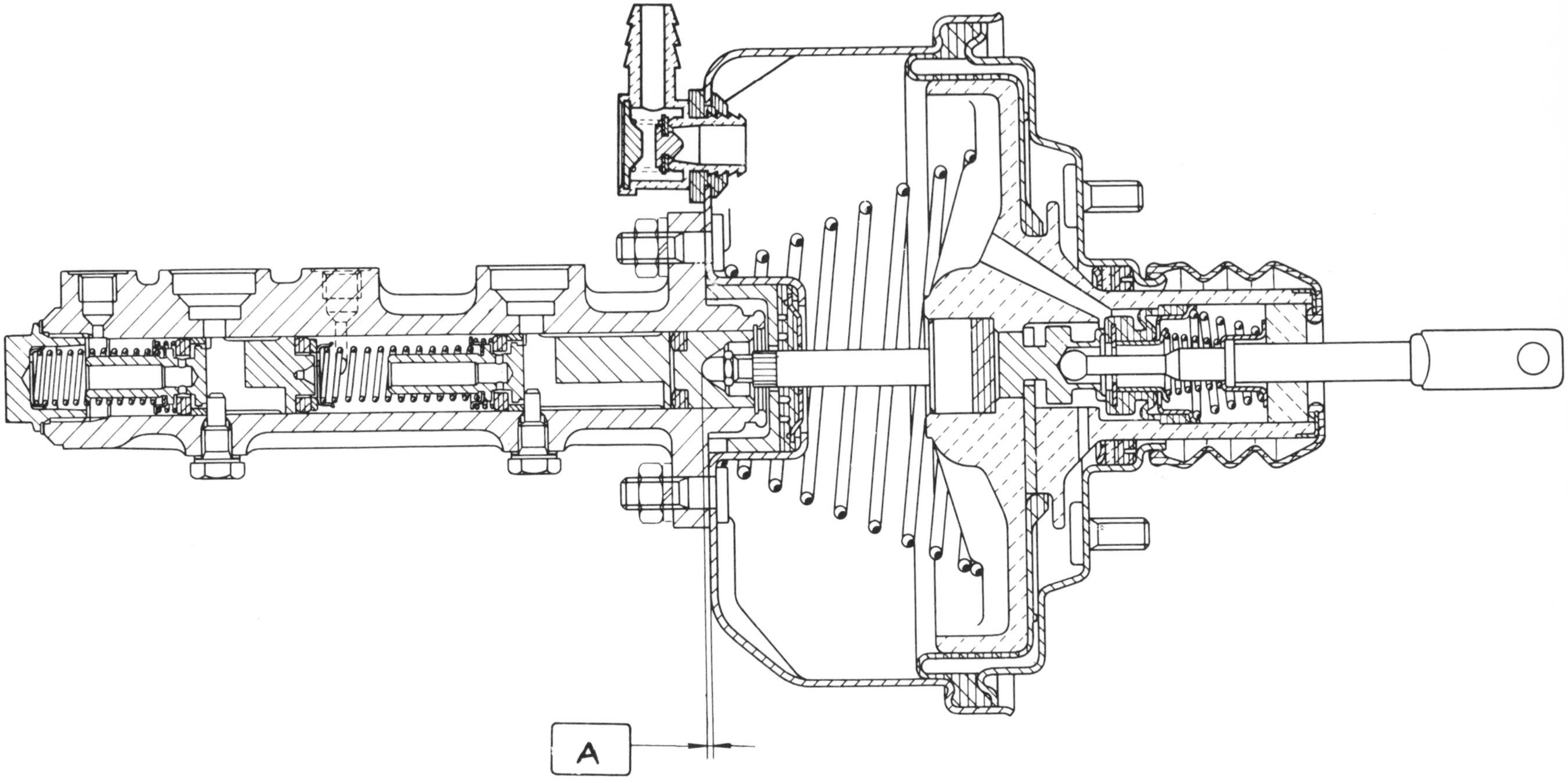

Fig. 13.31. Sectional view of brake vacuum servo booster unit

A = 0.050 to 0.073 in (1.26 to 1.85 mm) for later OHV models
A = 0.041 to 0.051 in (1.05 to 1.25 mm) for DOHC models

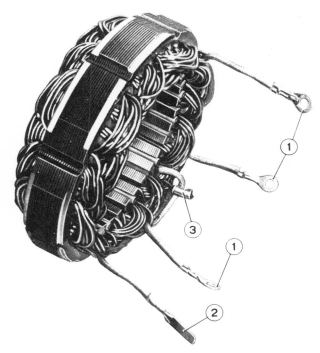

Fig.13.32. Alternator stator

1 Stator coil phase end terminals
2 Cut-out spade connector
3 Stator coil 'Y' centre connection

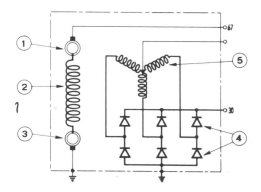

Fig.13.33. Alternator wiring diagram (internal)

1 Slip ring   2 Rotor coil
3 Slip ring   4 Rectifier diodes
5 Stator coil

4   Check the drivebelt adjustment. This should be installed to give a total deflection of between 3/8 in. and 5/8 in. (9.5 to 15.9 mm) at the centre of its upper right-hand run (alternator pulley to water pump pulley).

5   Check the security of the electrical leads to the alternator and voltage regulator terminals.

6   Check for wear in the alternator brushes as described in the next section.

7   Check that the voltage regulator 8 amp fuse is not blown.

8   Suspect that the cut-out is faulty, or out of adjustment, and rectify as described later.

9   If on switching on the ignition the warning lamp does not illuminate, check that the indicator bulb has not burned out.

10   Check the security of all electrical lead connections to the alternator, voltage regulator and indicator lamp.

11   Suspect a faulty cut-out and check and adjust as described later.

Alternator — brush renewal

12   Detach the leads from the rear cover alternator terminals.

13   Unscrew and remove the securing screw from the brush holder/mounting assembly on the stator housing.

14   New brushes complete with holder are supplied as an assembly and it is recommended that this method of renewal is carried out rather than attempt to renew the brushes only.

15   Before fitting the new brush assembly, blow out any carbon dust from the alternator interior and wipe away any dirt or grease from the slip rings.

Alternator — dismantling and reassembly

16   Unscrew the drive pulley securing nut. In order to prevent the pulley turning during this operation, temporarily refit the drivebelt and grip the belt close to the pulley. If necessary grip the belt in a vice but use two pieces of wood as protectors.

17   Remove the pulley and fan.

18   Remove the single retaining screw and withdraw the brush holder complete with brushes.

19   Prise out the Woodruff key from the shaft.

20   Unscrew and remove the nuts from the tie-bolts which hold the stator housing and drive end cover together.

21   Pull off the drive end cover and withdraw the stator.

22   From the interior of the stator housing, unscrew the three securing nuts from the stator coil phase and terminals.

23   Disconnect the cut-out lead spade connecting plug.

24   Withdraw the stator from its housing.

25   Further dismantling of the alternator is not recommended but simple tests for serviceability of the major components may be carried out in the following manner and new components installed where necessary.

26   Test the rotor coil for an open circuit by connecting a circuit tester between the two slip rings located at the rear of the rotor. The indicated resistance should be from 4.1 to 4.3 ohms but if there is no conductance then the coil is open and the rotor must be renewed as an assembly.

27   Connect the tester between each slip ring in turn and the rotor shaft. If the tester needle moves then the rotor is earthed and must be renewed.

28   Inspect the rotor bearing for wear and if necessary remove it from the shaft using a two-legged puller.

29   Clean the surfaces of the slip rings and rotor segments with a solvent (methylated spirit) moistened cloth.

30   Test the insulation of the stator coil by connecting the tester between the stator coil and the stator core. If the tester needle moves then the coil is earthed due to a breakdown in insulation and it must be renewed.

31   Check the stator coil leads for conductance. If the tester needle does not flicker then the coil has an open circuit and it must be renewed.

32   The testing of rectifiers should be restricted to measuring the resistance between their leads and holders in a manner similar to that described in the preceding paragraph. This test will indicate short or open circuited diodes but not rectifying or reverse flow characteristics which can only be checked with specialised equipment.

33   If more than one of the preceding tests proves negative then it will normally prove desirable to exchange the alternator for a reconditioned unit rather than to renew more than one component.

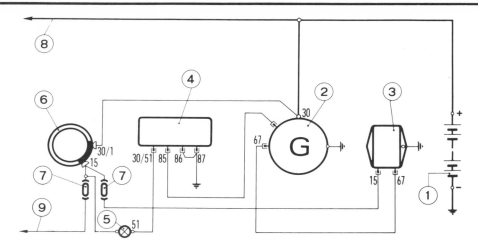

Fig.13.34. Alternator charging circuit

1 Battery
2 Alternator
3 Voltage regulator
4 Cut-out relay

5 Ignition warning
(charge indicator)
lamp

6 Slip ring
7 Fuses
8 Lights and instruments

9 Direction indicators

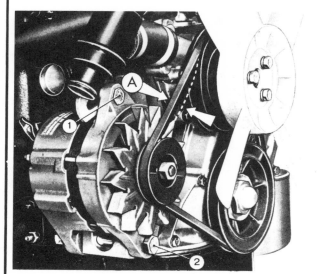

Fig.13.35. Alternator drive belt tension diagram

A Total belt deflection 3/8 to 5/8 in (9.5 to 15.9 mm)
1 Adjustment strap bolt   2 Pivot mounting bolt

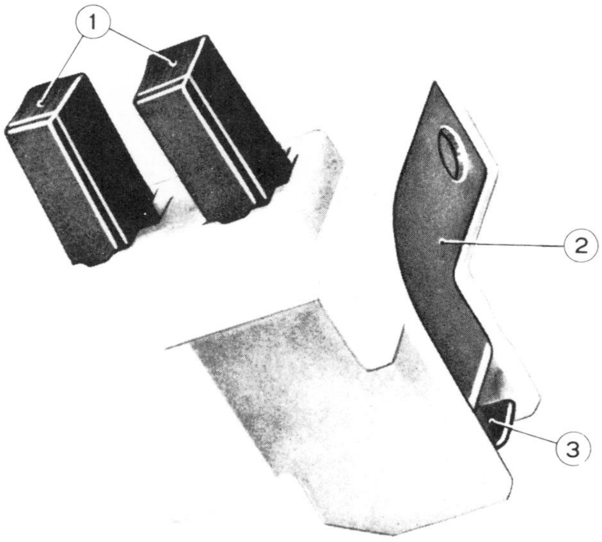

Fig.13.36. Alternator brush and holder assembly

1 Carbon brushes
2 Negative terminal
3 Positive terminal

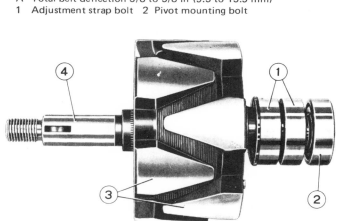

Fig.13.37. Alternator rotor assembly

1 Slip rings
2 Bearing
3 Pole shoes
4 Shaft

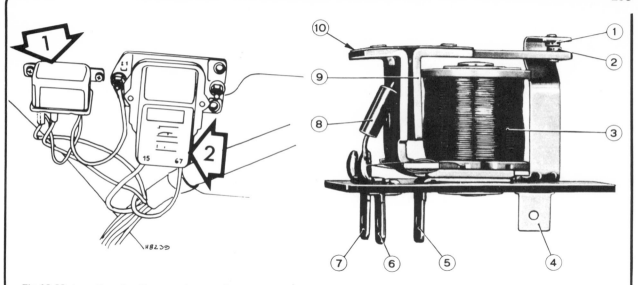

Fig.13.38. Location of voltage regulator and cut-out

1 Cut-out relay unit   2 Voltage regulator

Fig.13.39. Cut-out unit with cover removed

1 Stationary contact
2 Movable contact
3 Field coil
4 Spade connector ('87')
5 Spade connector ('30'/'51')
6 Spade connector ('85')
7 Spade connector ('86')
8 Desensitising resistor
9 Contact arm
10 Contact arm spring

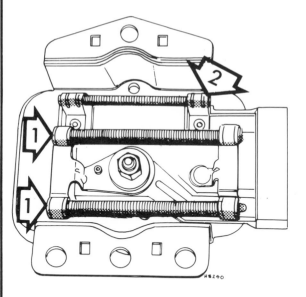

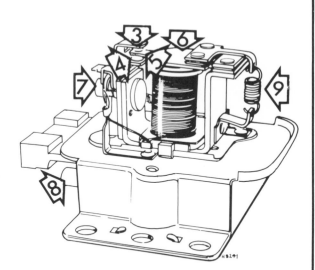

Fig.13.40. Voltage regulator viewed from above and below

1 Resistors
2 Field coil resistor
3 First stage stationary
  contact
4 Second stage stationary
  contact
5 First stage movable
  contact
6 Contact arm
7 Contact holder
  adjustment nut
8 Resistor
9 Setting spring

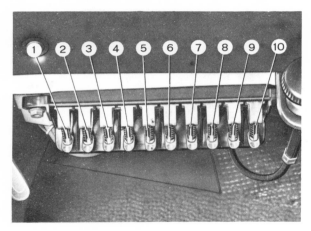

Fig.13.41. Layout of fuses (for circuit identification see Specifications)

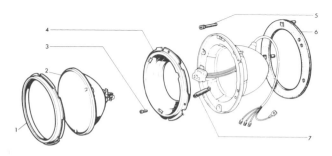

Fig.13.42. Components of sealed beam type headlamp unit (US models)

1	Rim	5	Adjusting screw
2	Sealed beam unit	6	Gasket
3	Securing screw	7	Tension spring
4	Rim		

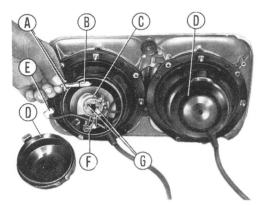

Fig.13.43. Removing a halogen type headlamp bulb (UK Special T)

A	Bulb holder	E	Wiring connector
B	Halogen bulb	F	Spring
C	Retainer	G	Holder
D	Dust cover		

34 Reassembly is a reversal of dismantling but pack the rotor bearing with high melting point grease before assembling it to the stator housing. Check that the brushes contact the face of the slip ring squarely.

Voltage regulator and cut-out — servicing

35 In the event of a fault developing in the remotely located voltage regulator or cut-out, it is not recommended that full electrical testing or adjustment is carried out due to the need for special instruments. However, the following simple servicing and testing can be implemented. If this action does not remedy the faults, the unit should be removed and a new one installed and adjusted by your FIAT dealer.

36 Remove the cover from the voltage regulator by unscrewing its retaining screws. Renew the cover sealing gasket if it has deteriorated.

37 Unhook the small setting coil spring and then loosen the locknut on the slotted contact holders and push the contacts as far from each other as possible.

38 Using a fine file smooth the face of each contact to free it from pits, burns or pips. Finally clean each contact face with methylated spirit.

39 Tighten the locknut only finger-tight and reconnect the setting spring.

40 Adjust the two sets of contacts so that they are in perfect face contact alignment. Using feeler gauges their air gaps are as follows:

$$\text{Armature air-gap } 0.059 \pm 0.002 \text{ in } (1.5 \pm 0.05 \text{ mm})$$
$$\text{2nd stage contacts } 0.018 \text{ in} \pm 0.004 \text{ in } (0.45 \pm 0.1 \text{ mm})$$

41 Tighten the contact locknut fully.

42 In the event of a fault developing in the cut-out unit (warning light not coming on or going out at the correct time) check the section — 'Alternator — fault tracing and rectification' earlier in this Chapter.

43 The cut-out is a factory set unit and in the event of a fault, the only servicing which can be carried out is to clean the contact faces with fine glass paper (not emery) and wipe them with methylated spirit and to check the security of the leads to the spade terminals.

Fuses

44 On all later models the fusebox is now located at the base of the instrument panel. The fuses, ratings and circuits protected are listed in the Specifications section at the beginning of this Chapter.

Headlamps (USA models)

45 On models operating in the USA, the headlamps will be of the sealed beam type. Some versions will be found with a dual system (4 lamps) while others will have single units (2 lamps).

46 The procedure for removal and alignment of this type of unit is similar to that already detailed in Chapter 10, for bulb type headlamps.

Headlamps (UK Special T model) with halogen bulbs

47 This type of headlamp bulb is of greater efficiency when compared with the regular tungsten bulb and sealed beam type units.

48 Removal of the halogen type bulb is facilitated by removing the dust cover and pulling off the wiring connector.

49 Depress and slightly turn the bulb retainer spring.

50 Pull out the bulb holder and bulb.

51 If the bulb is still serviceable, avoid touching the glass part of the bulb with your fingers. In the event of touching either a serviceable or new bulb wipe it immediately with a soft-cloth which has been dampened with methylated spirits.

52 Installation of the bulb/holder is the reverse of removal.

Front direction indicator lamps, rear lamps, reversing lamp (saloon)

53 The bulbs are accessible for renewal in all these components after removal of the lens securing screws as illustrated.

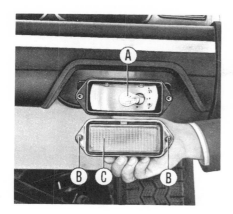

Fig.13.44. Removing lens from front direction indicator (USA Special TC model shown)

    A Bulb
    B Lens retaining screws
    C Lens

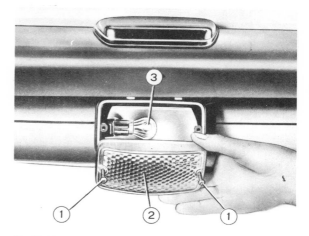

Fig.13.45. Removing the lens from a reversing lamp (typical)

    1 Lens retaining screws
    2 Lens
    3 Bulb

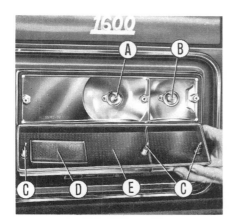

Fig.13.46. Removing the lenses from a rear lamp cluster

    A Tail and brake stoplamp bulb
    B Direction indicator bulb
    C Lens securing screws
    D Lens (reflector part)
    E Lens

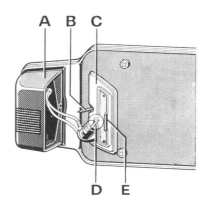

Fig.13.47A. Component parts of license plate lamp as fitted to USA Special TC models

    A Lamp body
    B Lens retaining screw
    C Bulb holder integral with lens
    D Bulb
    E Fixing lug for lens fastening

Rear number plate, side marker and repeater lamps
54 Access to this bulb for renewal is obtained by slipping off the cover retaining clips.
55 Access to repeater or side marker lamps is obtained from under the front wings.

Windscreen wiper switch
56 The switch is now of the 3-position type and is operational when the ignition key is in position '1' or '3'.

Instrumentation (USA models)
57 Estate wagon versions exported to the USA are fitted with rectangular instrument clusters, while the saloon has the round or binnacle type instruments.
58 The layout of the instruments and controls is similar to that shown in Fig. 13.50, but certain extra items such as the brake circuit warning lamp, battery charge indicator and heated

rear window indicator lamps may be found on some models.

Instrumentation (UK Special T)
59 The layout of the instrument panel is similar to that shown in Fig.13.51, but the right-hand instrument panel also houses a tachometer (rev-counter) as shown in Fig. 13.52.

Seatbelt interlock system (USA models)
60 This system comprises basically an electronic control unit, seatbelt retractor switches, seat switches, indicator and buzzer warning system and a relay.
61 If the front seats are occupied but either seatbelt has not been fastened, the car cannot be started and a warning buzzer and indicator are actuated if any attempt is made so to do.
62 The engine can be started for maintenance or tuning operations by reaching in through the window so that no weight is placed on either of the front seats.

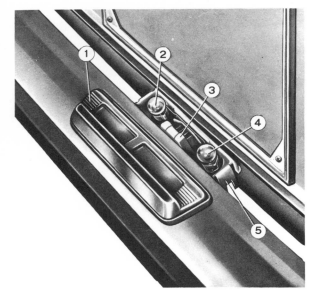

Fig.13.47B. Component parts of number plate lamp (alternative type)

1 Cover   (partly removed)
2 Bulb   4 Bulb
3 Bulb socket holder   5 Spring clips

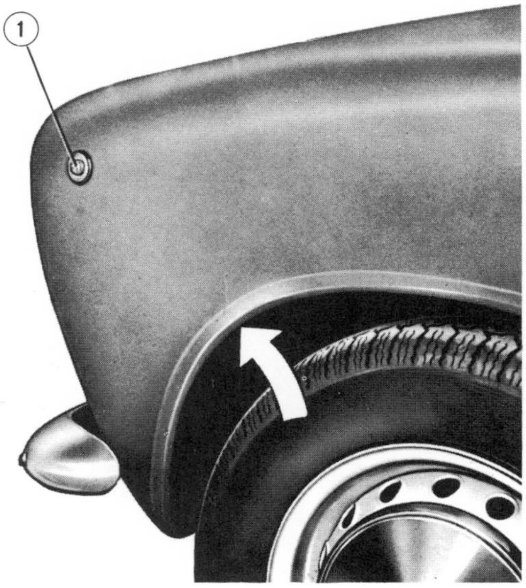

Fig.13.48. Location and accessibility of side repeater lamps. These may in certain applications be square in section

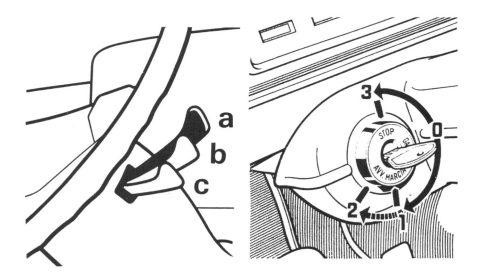

Fig.13.49. Windscreen wiper and ignition switch positions

a	OFF	O	OFF (key removable)		energise	3	Steering locked, key
b	Intermittent operation	1	Ignition On auxiliaries	2	Starter energised		removable, parking
c	Continuous operation						lights ON

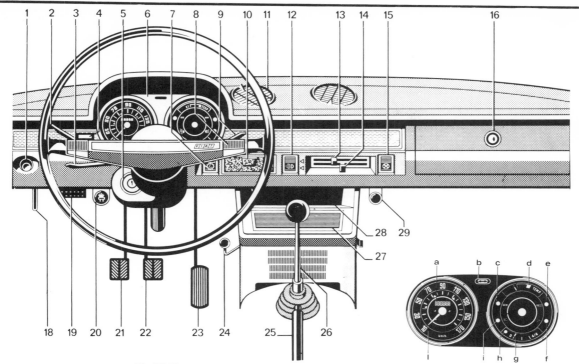

Fig.13.50. LHD instrument and control layout (OHV models)

1 Windscreen washer
2 Headlamp control
3 Direction indicators
4 Heated rear window switch and warning lamp
5 Ignition/starter switch
6 Instrument panel (see inset)
7 Panel switch
8 Horn
9 Windscreen wiper
10 Ashtray
11 Air vents
12 Lights
13 Ventilation control
14 Heater control
15 Heater blower
16 Glove compartment
18 Bonnet release
19 Fuse block
20 Choke knob
21 Clutch
22 Brake
23 Accelerator
24 Heater flap
25 Handbrake
26 Gearshift lever
27 Radio
28 Parcels shelf
29 Cigar lighter
a Mileage recorder
b Direction indicator warning lamp
c Ignition warning lamp (charge indicator)
d Water temperature
e Oil pressure
f Indicator lamp
g Fuel
h Fuel (low level) warning lamp
i Headlamp (main beam) warning lamp
l Speedometer

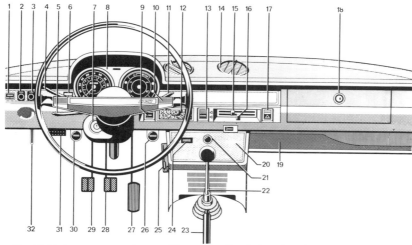

Fig.13.51. Instrument and control layout for North American Special TC models

1 Fasten seatbelts indicator
2 Brake system effectiveness indicator
3 Hazard warning indicator
4 Headlamp control
5 Direction indicators
6 Heated rear window switch and warning lamp
7 Ignition switch/steering lock
8 Instrument panel
9 Heater fan/speed switch
10 Horn
11 Windscreen wash/wipe switch
12 Ashtray
13 Main lighting switch
14 Air vents
15 Ventilation control
16 Air temperature control
17 Hazard warning switch
18 Glove compartment
19 Shelf
20 Radio housing blanking panel
21 Cigar lighter
22 Gearchange lever
23 Handbrake
24 Panel light rheostat switch
25 Heater flap
26 Throttle control knob
27 Accelerator pedal
28 Footbrake pedal
29 Clutch pedal
30 Choke knob
31 Fusebox
32 Bonnet release catch

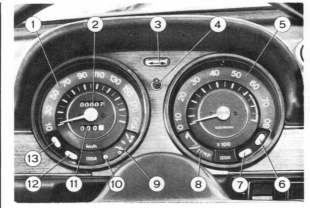

Fig.13.52. Instrument cluster (UK 124 Special T model)

1 Speedometer
2 Total odometer
3 Direction signal repeater (green)
4 Trip odometer setting knob
5 Tachometer
6 No charge indicator (red)
7 Low oil pressure

indicator (red)
8 Temperature gauge
9 Fuel gauge
10 Low fuel indicator (red)
11 Trip odometer
12 Headlight high beam indicator (blue)
13 Parking light indicator (green)

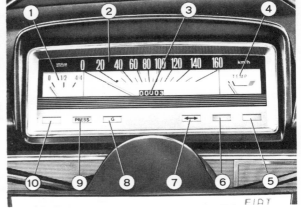

Fig.13.53. Instrument cluster (rectangular type)

1 Fuel gauge
2 Speedometer
3 Mileage recorder
4 Water temperature
5 Headlamp (main beam) warning lamp (blue)
6 Parking lamp indicator lamp (green)

7 Direction indicators warning lamp (green)
8 Ignition warning lamp (red)
9 Oil pressure warning lamp (red)
10 Fuel (low level) warning lamp (red)

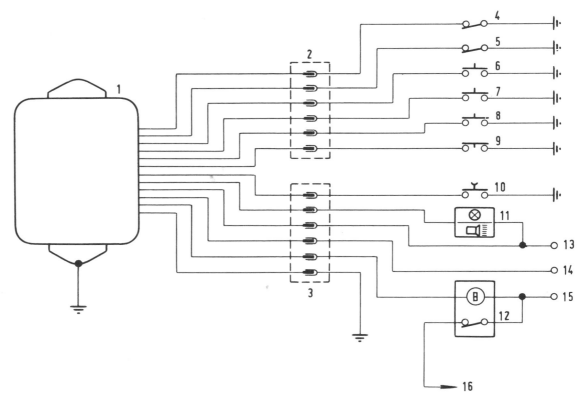

Fig.13.54. Seatbelt interlock system wiring diagram (USA models only)

1 Electronic control unit
2 Red junction box
3 White junction box
4 Driver belt retractor switch
5 Passenger belt retractor

switch
6 Driver seat switch
7 Passenger seat switch
8 Transmission switch
9 Oil pressure sender unit

10 Interlock bypass switch
11 Indicator and buzzer warning system
12 Relay
13 Ignition
14 To battery positive

terminal
15 Starting
16 To starter motor solenoid

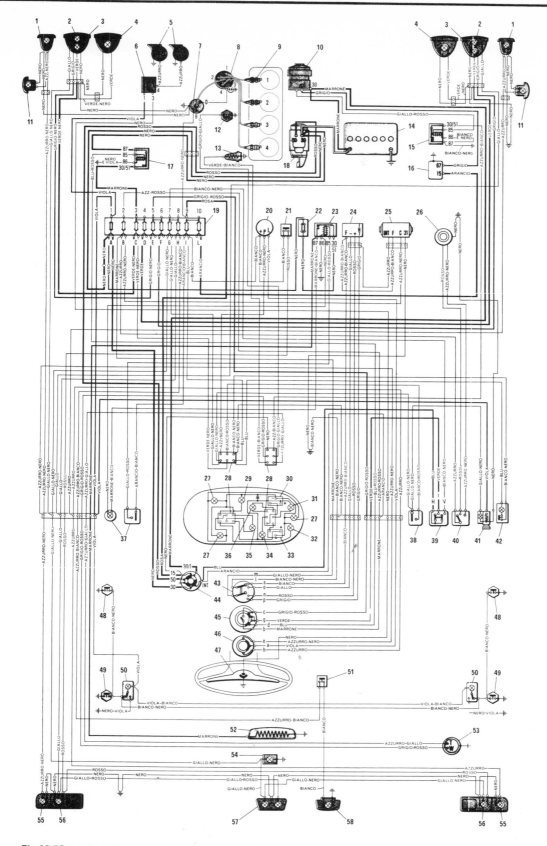

Fig.13.58A. Wiring diagram — North American OHV models. Also for vehicles with automatic transmission

Key to Fig.13.58A.

1	Front direction indicators	30	Water temperature gauge
2	Side lights	31	Oil pressure W/L (red)
3	Main and dipped beams	32	Side light W/L (green)
4	Main beams	33	Fuel gauge
5	Horns	34	Fuel W/L (red)
6	Horn relay	35	Headlamp W/L (blue)
7	Coil	36	Ignition W/L (red)
8	Distributor	37	Heated backlight switch and W/L (if fitted)
9	Spark plugs	38	Panel light switch
10	Alternator	39	Lighting switch
11	Repeater lights	40	Blower switch
12	Oil pressure transmitter	41	Cigar lighter/lamp
13	Water temperature transmitter	42	Glove box light/switch
14	Battery	43	Wiper switch
15	Ignition W/L relay	44	Ignition switch
16	Voltage regulator	45	Headlamp control/flasher switch
17	Headlamp relay	46	Direction indicator switch
18	Starter	47	Horn switch
19	Fuse unit	48	Front door switch
20	Direction indicator flasher	49	Rear door switch
21	Stop light switch	50	Courtesy light/switch
22	Heated backlight fuse (if fitted)	51	Reversing light switch
23	Heated backlight relay (if fitted)	52	Heated backlight (if fitted)
24	Wiper interrupter relay	53	Fuel transmitter
25	Wiper motor	54	Boot light
26	Blower	55	Rear direction indicators
27	Panel lights	56	Rear/stop lights
28	Connectors	57	Number plate lights
29	Direction indicator W/L (green)	58	Reversing light

Cable Colour Code

Arancio	=	Amber	Marrone	=	Brown
Azzurro	=	Light blue	Nero	=	Black
Bianco	=	White	Rosa	=	Pink
Blu	=	Dark blue	Rosso	=	Red
Giallo	=	Yellow	Verde	=	Green
Grigio	=	Grey	Viola	=	Mauve

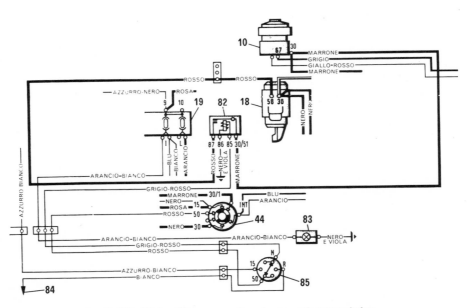

Fig.13.58B. Wiring diagram — optional automatic transmission

10 Alternator	44 Ignition switch	83 Gear indicator	switch (in place of
18 Starter	82 Starter inhibitor switch	84 To reversing light	reversing light switch
19 Fuse unit	relay	85 Starter/reverse inhibitor	'51')

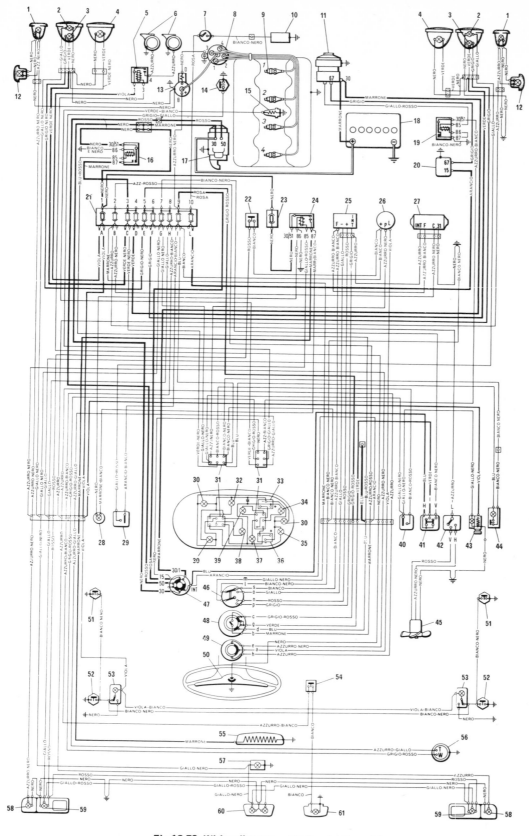

Fig.13.59. Wiring diagram – UK Special T models

Key for Fig. 13.59

1	Front direction indicators	32	Direction indicator w/l (green)
2	Sidelights	33	Water temperature gauge
3	Main and dipped beams	34	Oil pressure w/l (red)
4	Main beams	35	Sidelight w/l (green)
5	Horn relay	36	Fuel gauge
6	Horns	37	Fuel w/l (red)
7	Fan clutch control switch	38	Headlamp w/l (blue)
8	Distributor	39	Ignition w/l (red)
9	Spark plugs	40	Panel light switch
10	Fan clutch contact brush	41	Lighting switch
11	Alternator	42	Blower switch
12	Repeater lights	43	Cigar lighter/lamp
13	Coil	44	Glovebox light/switch
14	Oil pressure transmitter	45	Blower
15	Water temperature transmitter	46	Wiper switch
16	Headlamp relay	47	Ignition switch
17	Starter	48	Headlamp control/flasher switch
18	Battery	49	Direction indicator switch
19	Ignition w/l relay	50	Horn switch
20	Voltage regulator	51	Front door switch
21	Fuse unit	52	Rear door switch
22	Stoplight switch	53	Courtesy light/switch
23	Heated backlight fuse (if fitted)	54	Reversing light switch
24	Heated backlight relay (if fitted)	55	Heated backlight (if fitted)
25	Wiper interrupter relay	56	Fuel transmitter
26	Direction indicator flasher	57	Boot light
27	Wiper motor	58	Rear direction indicators
28	Heated backlight w/l (if fitted)	59	Rear/stop lights
29	Heated backlight switch (if fitted)	60	Number plate lights
30	Panel lights	61	Reversing light
31	Connectors		

Cable Colour Code

Arancio	=	Amber		Marrone	=	Brown
Azzurro	=	Light blue		Nero	=	Black
Bianco	=	White		Rosa	=	Pink
Blu	=	Dark blue		Rosso	=	Red
Giallo	=	Yellow		Verde	=	Green
Grigio	=	Grey		Viola	=	Mauve

Key for Fig. 13.60

1	High/low beam headlights	63	Low oil pressure indicator (red)
2	Front turn signal lamps	64	Turn signal indicator (flashes green)
3	Parking lamps	65	Fasten belts indicator (red)
3/1	Front side marker lamps	65/1	Vehicular hazard warning indicator (flashes red)
5	Alternator	65/2	Brake system effectiveness indicator (red)
6	Voltage regulator	66	Battery charge indicator (red)
9	Ignition distributor	67	Parking and tail lights indicator (green)
10	Ignition coil	69	High beams indicator (blue)
10/1	Ignition mode selection relay	72	Glove compartment light with switch
12	Starter motor	74	Cigar lighter with housing indicator
14	Horns	76	Handbrake ON switch
15	Horn relay	79	Horn button
17	Engine water temperature gauge sending unit	84	Washer pump motor
18	Low oil pressure indicator sending unit	87	Courtesy light jamb switches
18/1	Brake system effectiveness indicator switch	87/1	Remove key indicator jamb switch (driver's door)
23	Battery	89	Courtesy lights
25	Back-up lamp switch	93	Fuel gauge sending unit
26	Stoplight switch	95	Trunk light
28	8-amp fuses	98	Tail, turn signal, and stoplights unit
28/1	16-amp fuse	98/1	Rear side markers lamps
28/2	3-amp in-line fuse	99	License plate lamps
28/3	16-amp in-line fuse	100	Back-up lamp
30	Turn signal flasher	104	Thermostatic switch (on radiator) for motor '37/1'
32	Vehicular hazard warning signal flasher	121	Ignition mode selection relay control switch
35	Two-speed windshield wiper motor	126/1	Fasten belts and remove key buzzer
37	Two-speed heater fan motor	128	Battery charge relay
37/1	Engine fan motor	128/1	High beams relay
39	Relay for motor 37/1	128/2	Relay for buzzer '126/1'
40	Ideogram lighting potentiometer	128/3	Starter relay
42	Turn signal indicator switch	161	Light source, optical fibre illumination
42/1	High/low beams change-over switch	189	Interlock system electronic control unit
42/2	Wiper/washer three-position switch	190	Exhaust gas recirculation control valve
44	Steering lock ignition switch	191	Button switch on clutch for EGR valve control
46	Lighting switch (controls also headlights and instrument cluster lights)	192	Button switch on transmission for EGR valve control
		193	Exhaust emission control device electrovalve
49	Heater fan motor three-position switch	194	Button switch on driver's seatbelt
50	Vehicular hazard warning signal switch with incorporated light	194/1	Button switch on passenger's seatbelt
		194/2	Gear-engaged signal button switch
51	Eight-indication instrument cluster	194/3	Strip switch in driver's seat cushion
54	Engine water temperature gauge	194/4	Strip switch in passenger's seat cushion
57	Fuel gauge	195	Interlock bypass switch
61	Fuel reserve indicator (red)		

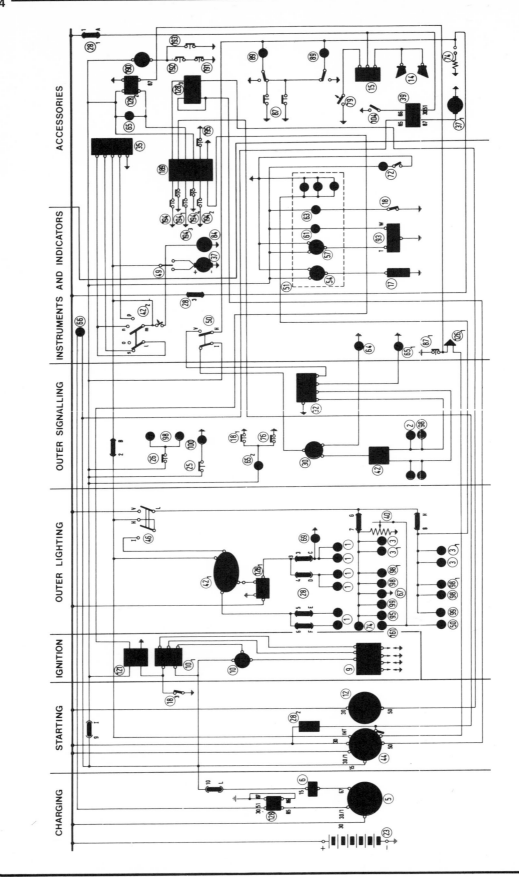

Fig.13.60. Basic wiring diagram — North American Special TC saloon version

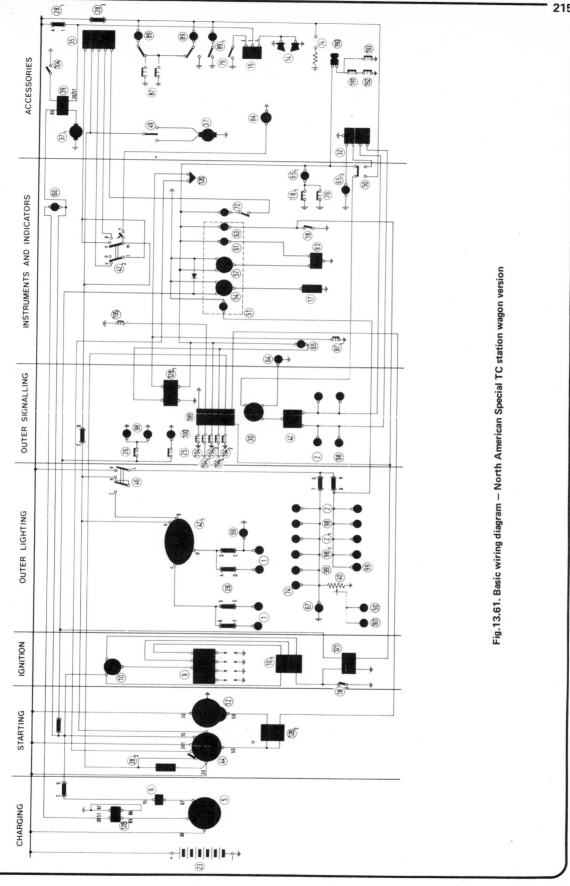

Fig.13.61. Basic wiring diagram – North American Special TC station wagon version

Key for Fig. 13.61

1	High/low beam headlights
2	Front parking and turn signal lamps
2/1	Front side marker lamps
5	Alternator
6	Voltage regulator
9	Ignition distributor
10	Ignition coil
10/1	Ignition mode selection relay
12	Starter motor
14	Horns
15	Horn relay
17	Engine water temperature gauge sending unit
18	Low oil pressure indicator sending unit
18/1	Brake system effectiveness indicator switch
18/3	Thermostatic switch for ignition mode selection relay
23	Battery
25	Back-up lamp switch
26	Stoplight switch
28	8-amp fuses
28/1	16-amp fuse
28/2	3-amp in-line fuse
28/3	16-amp in-line fuse
30	Turn signal flasher
32	Vehicular hazard warning signal flasher
35	Windshield wiper motor
37	Two-speed heater fan motor
37/1	Engine fan motor
39	Relay for motor '37/1'
40	Ideogram lighting potentiometer
42	Turn signal indicator switch
42/1	High/low beams change-over switch
42/2	Wiper/washer three-position switch
44	Steering lock ignition switch
46	Lighting switch (controls also headlights and instrument cluster light)
49	Heater fan motor three-position switch
50	Vehicular hazard warning signal switch with incorporated light
51	Eight-indication instrument cluster
54	Engine water temperature guage
57	Fuel gauge

61	Fuel reserve indicator (red)
63	Low oil pressure indicator (red)
64	Turn signal indicator (flashes green)
65	Fasten belts indicator (red)
65/1	Brake system effectiveness indicator (red)
65/2	Vehicular hazard warning indicator (flashes red)
66	Battery charge indicator (red)
67	Parking and tail lights indicator (green)
69	High beams indicator (blue)
72	Glove compartment light with switch
74	Cigar lighter with housing indicator
76	Handbrake ON switch
79	Horn button
84	Washer pump motor
87	Courtesy light jamb switches
87/1	Remove key indicator jamb switch (driver's door)
89	Front courtesy lights
89/1	Rear interior lamp with switch
93	Fuel gauge sending unit
98	Tail, turn signal, and stoplights unit
98/1	Rear side marker lamps
99	License plate lamps
100	Back-up lamp
104	Thermostatic switch (on radiator) for motor '37/1'
121	Ignition mode selection relay control switch
126	Fasten belts and remove key buzzer
128	Battery charge relay
128/1	Relay for buzzer '126'
128/2	Starter relay
161	Light source, optical fibre illumination
189	Interlock system electronic control unit
190	Exhaust gas recirculation valve
191	Button switch on clutch
192	Button switch on transmission
193	Emission control device electrovalve button switch
194	Button switch on driver's seatbelt
194/1	Button switch on passenger's seatbelt
194/2	Gear-engaged signal button switch
194/3	Strip switch in driver's seat cushion
194/4	Strip switch in passenger's seat cushion
195	Interlock bypass switch

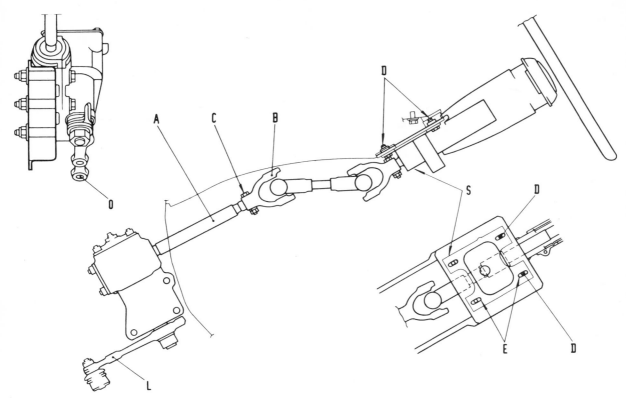

Fig.13.55. Installation and alignment of the three-section type steering gear

A Steering column
B Universal joint
C Pinch bolt

D Bracket mounting screws
E Bracket elongated holes

L Drop arm
O Drop arm eye centre

S Steering column upper
   bracket

12 Suspension and steering

Steering gear — installation and alignment

1 A revised procedure is now recommended for the installation of the three section steering column fitted to later models. Jack up the front of the vehicle.

2 Refer to Fig.13.55 and bolt the steering box to the body-frame, ensuring that the drop arm is set centrally (centre of eye 'O', approximately 1.67 in (42.5 mm) from bodyframe mounting surface).

3 Position the steering wheel so that its two spokes are perfectly horizontal.

4 Connect the joint (B) of the centre section to the splined shaft (A). Insert the pinch bolt (C) but only tighten it finger-tight. Push the joint (B) as far towards the steering box as it will go.

5 Secure the steering column bracket (S) to the facia panel but only finger-tight at this stage.

6 Press on the steering wheel to ensure that the column will not move in the downward direction. If it does, pull the mounting bracket backwards on its elongated holes enough to take up this end play.

7 Turn the steering wheel from lock-to-lock in order to settle the column bracket and then fully tighten the column bracket screws and the pinch bolt (C).

Fig.13.56. Location of air vents (Saloon)

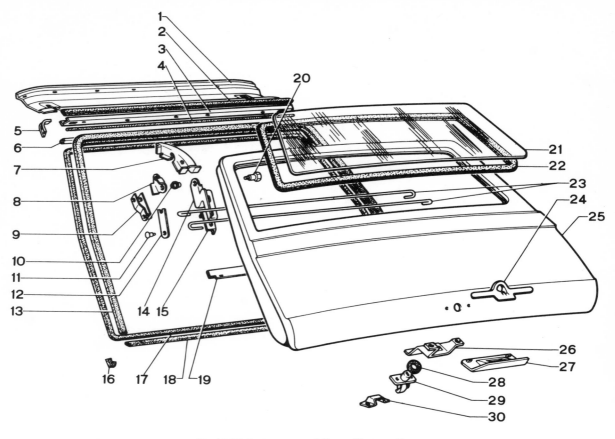

Fig.13.57. Components of Estate Wagon tailgate

1 Cover panel	9 Link	17 Weatherstrip	24 Door pull
2 Rubber strip	10 Bush	18 Rubber seal	25 Tailgate
3 Retainer	11 Link pin	19 Embellishment	26 Tailgate lock rein-
4 Rubber seal	12 Hinge link	20 Hinge pivot	forcement plate
5 Retainer	13 Weatherstrip	21 Backlight	27 Escutcheon
6 Rubber seal	14 Hinge	22 Glass rubber surround	28 Rubber grommet
7 Hinge plate	15 Hinge reinforcement	23 Counterbalancing torsion	29 Tailgate lock
8 Bracket	16 Shim	bars	30 Striker plate

13 Bodywork and underframe

General description

1 Apart from detail changes in the design of small components such as door interior handles and window regulator handles the most important modifications are the addition of air vents at the rear of the body as an essential part of the through-flow ventilation system and in the case of the estate wagon, the addition of a semi-permanent roof rack as a standard fitting.

Estate wagon tailgate — removal and installation

2 With an assistant supporting the tailgate in the fully open position, unscrew and remove the nuts which secure the hinge plates to the tailgate. Before removing them it is a good idea to

mark the position of the hinges to assist in re-alignment when refitting.

3 The counterbalance action of the tailgate is arranged by torsion bars and if they have weakened and will no longer fully open the tailgate then they should be renewed.

4 Detach the cover panel from the rear of the vehicle interior head lining and remove the hinge links by withdrawing the swivel pins.

5 Withdraw the torsion bars using a lever if necessary to counteract their torque.

6 Remove the hinge pivots and withdraw the hinges.

7 Installation is a reversal of removal. The tailgate should be adjusted for alignment within the bodyframe by loosening the hinge nuts and moving them within the range of their elongated bolt holes.

Use of English

*As this book has been written in England, it uses the appropriate English component names, phrases, and spelling. Some of these differ from those used in America. Normally, these cause no difficulty, but to make sure, a glossary **is printed** below. In ordering spare parts remember the parts list will probably use these words:*

English	American	English	American
Aerial	Antenna	Layshaft (of gearbox)	Countershaft
Accelerator	Gas pedal	Leading shoe (of brake)	Primary shoe
Alternator	Generator (AC)	Locks	Latches
Anti-roll bar	Stabiliser or sway bar	Motorway	Freeway, turnpike etc
Battery	Energizer	Number plate	License plate
Bodywork	Sheet metal	Paraffin	Kerosene
Bonnet (engine cover)	Hood	Petrol	Gasoline
Boot lid	Trunk lid	Petrol tank	Gas tank
Boot (luggage compartment)	Trunk	'Pinking'	'Pinging'
Bottom gear	1st gear	Propeller shaft	Driveshaft
Bulkhead	Firewall	Quarter light	Quarter window
Cam follower or tappet	Valve lifter or tappet	Retread	Recap
Carburettor	Carburetor	Reverse	Back-up
Catch	Latch	Rocker cover	Valve cover
Choke/venturi	Barrel	Roof rack	Car-top carrier
Circlip	Snap-ring	Saloon	Sedan
Clearance	Lash	Seized	Frozen
Crownwheel	Ring gear (of differential)	Side indicator lights	Side marker lights
Disc (brake)	Rotor/disk	Side light	Parking light
Drop arm	Pitman arm	Silencer	Muffler
Drop head coupe	Convertible	Spanner	Wrench
Dynamo	Generator (DC)	Sill panel (beneath doors)	Rocker panel
Earth (electrical)	Ground	Split cotter (for valve spring cap)	Lock (for valve spring retainer)
Engineer's blue	Prussian blue	Split pin	Cotter pin
Estate car	Station wagon	Steering arm	Spindle arm
Exhaust manifold	Header	Sump	Oil pan
Fast back (Coupe)	Hard top	Tab washer	Tang; lock
Fault finding/diagnosis	Trouble shooting	Tailgate	Liftgate
Float chamber	Float bowl	Tappet	Valve lifter
Free-play	Lash	Thrust bearing	Throw-out bearing
Freewheel	Coast	Top gear	High
Gudgeon pin	Piston pin or wrist pin	Trackrod (of steering)	Tie-rod (or connecting rod)
Gearchange	Shift	Trailing shoe (of brake)	Secondary shoe
Gearbox	Transmission	Transmission	Whole drive line
Halfshaft	Axleshaft	Tyre	Tire
Handbrake	Parking brake	Van	Panel wagon/van
Hood	Soft top	Vice	Vise
Hot spot	Heat riser	Wheel nut	Lug nut
Indicator	Turn signal	Windscreen	Windshield
Interior light	Dome lamp	Wing/mudguard	Fender

Miscellaneous points

An 'oil seal' is fitted to components lubricated by grease!

A 'damper' is a 'shock absorber', it damps out bouncing, and absorbs shocks of bump impact. Both names are correct, and both are used haphazardly.

Note that British drum brakes are different from the Bendix type that is common in America, so different descriptive names result. The shoe end furthest from the hydraulic wheel cylinder is on a pivot; interconnection between the shoes as on Bendix brakes is most uncommon. Therefore the phrase 'Primary' or 'Secondary' shoe does not apply. A shoe is said to be 'Leading' or 'Trailing'. A 'Leading' shoe is one on which a point on the drum, as it rotates forward, reaches the shoe at the end worked by the hydraulic cylinder before the anchor end. The opposite is a 'Trailing' shoe, and this one has no self servo from the wrapping effect of the rotating drum.

Index

Printed by
Haynes Publishing Group
Sparkford Yeovil Somerset
England